Socialism and the Great War

The Collapse of the Second International

Socialism and the Great War

The Collapse of the Second International

By GEORGES HAUPT

OXFORD
AT THE CLARENDON PRESS
1972

Oxford University Press, Ely House, London W. 1

GLASGOW   NEW YORK   TORONTO   MELBOURNE   WELLINGTON
CAPE TOWN   IBADAN   NAIROBI   DAR ES SALAAM   LUSAKA   ADDIS ABABA
DELHI   BOMBAY   CALCUTTA   MADRAS   KARACHI   LAHORE   DACCA
KUALA LUMPUR   SINGAPORE   HONG KONG   TOKYO

PRINTED IN GREAT BRITAIN
AT THE UNIVERSITY PRESS, OXFORD
BY VIVIAN RIDLER
PRINTER TO THE UNIVERSITY

Preface

THE English edition of this work is not a simple translation but in some ways a new book. The first publication appeared in French in 1965: it was a lengthy introduction to unpublished documents relating to the 'Congress that Never Was'. Two years later there appeared a German version in which the original text was recast into a monograph followed by a number of documents. This text, reshaped and enlarged by the addition of several new chapters, forms the basis of the present book.

The reader may wonder what need there was for this succession of metamorphoses. The answer is found less in the author's method of work than in the nature of the subject.

In 1964 when I decided to add some important documents to a dossier that continues to pose problems to the historian, and to arouse controversy, it seemed that the subject was at last relegated to the realm of history and could be treated with detachment. This proved a vain hope. The question of war and peace remains a burning issue and the International's failure in August 1914 continues to be seen as a topical object-lesson. The old myths are being buried only to be replaced by learned mystifications.

But it was not the topical nature of the subject nor the desire to sit in judgement on history that led me to take up again a book that I had put out of my mind. My motives were—I must confess—more prosaic. As Visiting Professor at the University of Wisconsin, Madison, I was confronted with questions, problems, and also criticism from future historians attending my seminars on social history. As a result I felt compelled to renew my research and have consequently expanded the arguments and strengthened the conclusions.

My task was greatly eased by the late secretary of the International, Camille Huysmans. Ten years ago, in the course of my research, I was privileged to become acquainted with this remarkable personality who was a historian by training and inclination. It was he who invited me to assist him in his work on the ISB archives. Mrs. Ida Huysmans continues to show the same trust in me.

But these are not the only people who have helped me. I wish to express my thanks to Marion Jackson for her help in the early stages of the translation. I have benefited from the assistance, criticism, and patience of many colleagues and friends: Madeleine Rebérioux, Claudie Weill, Agnès Wurmbach-Blänsdorf, Professor James Joll, William Fishman and Bruce Vandervort. The number of those who attended my seminars at Madison is too great for me to mention them individually, but I must thank those who entrusted them to me, my friends Professors Harvey Goldberg and George Mosse.

Contents

Abbreviations

Archives Monatte	Jean Maitron and Colette Chambelland, *Syndicalisme révolutionnaire et communisme. Les archives de Pierre Monatte* (Paris, Maspero, 1968).
AZ	*Arbeiter Zeitung.*
Drachkovitch	Milorad M. Drachkovitch, *Les Socialismes français et allemand et le problème de la guerre, 1870–1914* (Geneva, Droz, 1953).
Grünberg	Carl Grünberg, *Die Internationale und der Weltkrieg, Materiallen* (Leipzig, Verlag von C. L. Hirschfeld, 1916).
ISB	International Socialist Bureau.
IISG	International Institute of Social History, Amsterdam.
Kautsky	Karl Kautsky, *Sozialisten und Krieg. Ein Beitrag zur Ideengeschichte des Sozialismus von den Hussiten bis zum Völkerbund* (Prague, Orbis Verlag, 1937).
Lénine, *Œuvres*	V. I. Lénine [Lenin], *Œuvres* (Paris, Éditions sociales, 1958–71).
Longuet	Jean Longuet, *Le Mouvement socialiste international* (Coll. 'Encyclopédie socialiste, syndicale et coopérative de l'Internationale ouvrière, ed. Compère Morel', Paris, A. Quillet, 1913).
LZ	*Leipziger Volkszeitung.*
NZ	*Neue Zeit.*
Œuvres de Jaurès	*Œuvres de Jean Jaurès*, ed. M. Bonnafous (Paris, Rieder, 1931–9), 9 vols.
Schorske	Carl E. Schorske, *German Social Democracy 1905–1917. The Development of the Great Schism* (Harvard Univ. Press, 1955).
SFIO	Section française de l'Internationale ouvrière.
SPD	Sozialdemokratische Partei Deutschlands.
Victor Adler Briefwechsel	Victor Adler, *Briefwechsel mit August Bebel und Karl Kautsky* (Vienna, Verlag der Wiener Volksbuchhandlung, 1954).
Walling	W. E. Walling, *The Socialists and the War, a Documentary Statement* (New York, Henry Holt, 1915).

Introduction

In the confused and restless years preceding World War I, the Socialist International was considered the most important antimilitarist political force in the world: the International did not merely declare 'war on war', but believed itself capable of mobilizing an army of five million organized workers in the active struggle for peace. Drawing up a balance-sheet of the previous three years' activity, the secretary of the International, Camille Huysmans, wrote in 1912:

We can once again say: only socialism has worked for peace in the Balkans. It did the same during the Moroccan conflict and during the Italo-Turkish War. It has proved the sole factor for peace in the capitalist world. Tomorrow, should any conflagration unfortunately prove impossible to localize, it [socialism] will find itself in the same position.[1]

Contemporary public opinion did not doubt this good intention. As witness to this fact, the International was put forward for the Nobel Peace Prize in 1913, and its candidature was favourably held over until 1914.[2] Indeed, in an age of numerous pacifist organizations, none could compare in either size of audience or scope of activity with the International, which regarded itself as 'the most energetic and decisive factor for universal peace'.[3]

In the summer of 1914 the subject of peace was of universal concern. The Twenty-first Universal Peace Congress was scheduled to meet in Vienna from 15 to 19 September; the Austrian Emperor had agreed to receive a delegation from this congress, and his Foreign Minister, Count Berchtold, had

[1] *Le Peuple* (29 Oct. 1912), 1.
[2] See 'Les rapports du B. S. I.', in G. Haupt, *Le Congrès manqué* (Paris, Maspero, 1965), 281–3.
[3] Longuet, 72.

announced plans for a reception in honour of its members.[4] But this noble patronage notwithstanding, another congress, the Tenth International Socialist Congress, also due to meet in Vienna in August, promised to be the most significant political and pacifist event of the year. The press gave it full coverage and the security services of all the capitals of Europe were preparing files on the participants. Like the French *Sûreté générale* they really believed that 'the debates [of the International Socialist Congress in Vienna] would be of extreme importance and [that] its decisions could have considerable impact'.[5] Why? Because numerous delegations, from five continents, intended to discuss a variety of immediate social, economic, and political questions, aiming above all at a general re-examination of international socialist policy. The Socialist International was expected to outline its main objectives for the next three years and to decide on suitable measures to be jointly undertaken to avert a general war.[6]

Vital to Congress—and of great concern to the various official architects of European national destinies—was the question of a general strike against war. In Vienna, it was hoped, the Socialist International would finally pronounce unequivocally either for or against a simultaneous and internationally organized strike of workers.

But the carefully prepared Tenth Congress never met. It became a casualty of the situation, of the sudden outbreak of war in August 1914. As the world order collapsed, the 25-year old structure of the International underwent its own internal disintegration; rhetorical internationalism was not equal to this test. The anti-militarist resolutions voted at previous International congresses remained a dead letter. On 4 August 1914, the social democrats in the Reichstag voted for war credits;

[4] See *Invitation au XXIᵉ Congrès universel de la paix* (pamphlet in the archives of the International Socialist Bureau, Antwerp, 4 pp.).

[5] Archives nationales, Paris. F7, 13069. Report M967 U; quoted in Annie Kriegel, *Aux origines du communisme français* (Paris–The Hague, Mouton, 1964, vol. i), 44, n. 1.

[6] See Édouard Vaillant, 'Die Internationale und der Friede', in *Festschrift des X. internationalen Socialistenkongresses, Wien 1914. Sondernummer des Vorwärts*, 12.

Emile Vandervelde, the president of the International, joined the Belgian Government; and the *Union sacrée* triumphed in France.

After August 1914 people spoke of 'the betrayal of social democracy' and of the 'failure of the International'. The impotence of the European Socialist movement was recognized everywhere, be it with bitterness or satisfaction, and the subject of 'The International and the War' evoked enough bitter controversy to fill an entire library with books, pamphlets, brochures, and articles. The various groups within the Socialist movement, which quickly formed after the events of August 1914 and clashed violently with one another, all interpreted the events in diverse ways.

Among the 'Internationalists', who were in the minority, it was Lenin who drew the most categorical conclusions. To him 'the failure of the Second International is the failure of opportunism . . . which, in recent years, has in practice dominated the International. The opportunists have long prepared the International's failure by scorning the socialist revolution in order to replace it with bourgeois reformism . . .' In Lenin's view, the majority of the International's representatives, German as well as French and Belgian, had betrayed socialism— a betrayal 'which meant the ideological and political collapse of the latter [the organization]'.[7] Lenin's view of the immediate past was in the last resort determined by the visions and ideals which he projected into the future.

The German radical Left also repudiated the opportunism and reformism characteristic of the International's leadership, and sought to analyse the behaviour of the masses. For Rosa Luxemburg, August 1914 signified the end of an illusion: the socialists, according to her main argument, had overestimated the influence of internationalist ideas on the working masses. For her the war brought out the force and tenacity of nationalism, a phenomenon hitherto neglected by the International and most of all by herself.

[7] Lénine, *Œuvres*, vol. xxi, 10 and 26.

Both the accusations and analyses of the internationalists were dismissed by the left of the Centre, which remained faithful to the old International, and by the majority of social democratic leaders in both belligerent camps. The most popular argument which they used to excuse themselves ran briefly as follows: the Socialists were suddenly confronted with a situation from which there was no way out and they were forced to choose between Internationalism and the Nation.

But although they started from identical premises, the spokesmen of the German, French, and Belgian parties came to totally different conclusions and laid the blame for the betrayal at the door of one or the other of the parties to the war. Everyone was looking for a scapegoat. The Germans blamed Russia and emphasized the defensive character of their war whilst the French and Belgian socialists unanimously condemned German aggression.[8]

But the vast polemic occasioned by the crisis in European socialism, having obscured the prospects of a sober analysis of events, is not the principal subject of this study; it is sufficient to note, and important to remember, that the controversy has projected itself on to contemporary historical research. There are still numerous historians who base their work on the insights of 1914–18, or who see events only through the eyes of the debate's protagonists, without always troubling or being in a position to submit the historical record to either careful scrutiny or critical analysis.

Considerable progress has certainly been made in recent years in the study of 'the International and the war'. But the major historical question still remains: why and how did European socialism reach the position it was in on 4 August 1914?

---

[8] Rakovsky, for example, said in 1915: 'Before the war the socialists of every country regarded it as their strict duty to lay the blame, *however small*, at the door of *their own government, their own ruling classes*. Now in the war the roles are reversed: the French socialists stress the part played by the German government; the German socialists hold Russia and her allies responsible' (Charles Dumas and Christian Racovski [Rakovsky], *Les socialistes et la guerre: discussion entre socialistes français et socialistes roumains* (Bucharest, Cercul de Editură socialistă, 1915), 18 ff.).

The most important research attempts a critical analysis
of the doctrinal developments and the theoretical contradictions
of socialism on the subject of war and peace.[9] Another line of
research focuses on the national parties and in particular on the
dominant force in the International, the German Social Democratic Party.[10] Because of this research we are now familiar
with the process by which German Social Democracy became
socially and politically integrated into the Wilhelmian Empire,
and with the increasingly apparent contradictions between
theoretical formulations which remained radical, in the mode
of Marxist orthodoxy, and their interpretations which were
both reformist and nationalist.[11]

The attitudes and actions of the European socialist leadership
in July 1914 need fuller explanation. Numerous studies on the
subject have produced ingenious observations and interpretations. Yet the tendency to over-explain the evidence remains a
major fault. Instead of studying and analysing the facts object-
ively in a precise historical framework, historians are inclined to
explain events and attitudes in terms of what happened after
4 August, to attribute to the actors—the leading personalities of
the International—the role of traitors and to accuse them of
being insufficiently clear-sighted in the darkness of July 1914.
Similarly, studies of the history of European social democracy

[9] See primarily Milorad M. Drachkovitch's major contribution, *Les Socialismes
français et allemand et le problème de la guerre, 1870–1914*. The controversy which
led to the confrontation between the Third International and the Social Democrats
between the two world wars gave rise to much literature on the position adopted
by the Second International regarding the question of war and peace. G. Zinoviev's
collection of essays, *Der Krieg und die Krise des Sozialismus* (Vienna, Verlag für
Literatur und Politik, 1924, 668 pp.), gives the Bolshevik point of view. See also
Karl Kautsky's basic contribution, *Sozialisten und Krieg. Ein Beitrag zur Ideengeschichte
des Sozialismus von den Hussiten bis zum Völkerbund.*

[10] A critical analysis of these investigations is found in H. Haag's report, 'La
social-démocratie allemande et la Première Guerre Mondiale', in *Comité international
des sciences historiques. XIe Congrès international des sciences historiques. Stockholm, 1960.
Rapports V: Histoire contemporaine* (Uppsala, 1960), 61–96.

[11] See e.g. Schorske; H.-U. Wehler's *Sozialdemokratie und Nationalstaat. Die
deutsche Sozialdemokratie und die Nationalitätenfrage in Deutschland von Karl Marx bis zum
Ausbruch des I. Weltkriegs* (Würzburg, 1962, 300 pp.) gives an account of the SPD's
shift from support for internationalism to full recognition of the German 'national
state'.

on the eve of World War I frequently contain isolated facts and fragmentary truths designed to highlight the deliberate betrayal or the 'frightful duplicity of the opportunists'. But, in truth, is such proof still necessary? Has the time not come to banish the ghosts of outworn polemic in order to say what actually happened? Should not the perspective of research be expanded, and the gaps which exist in our knowledge of both facts and deep-seated political motives be closed?

Many points remain to be cleared up. Very little is known, for example, of the internal circumstances of the International between the famous congress which met at Basle in November 1912 and the crisis of August 1914. Even as the conflicts in international socialism developed during the war, the accusation of betrayal was based on the gap which there appeared to be between the stand taken by the leaders of the European social democratic parties in August 1914 and their theoretical positions and tactics as laid down in the Basle manifesto. This manifesto was rightly regarded as the basic document for socialists. But one important fact was neglected: from 1913 onwards the validity of this manifesto's assessments and analyses was undermined within the International. The International Socialist Congress scheduled to meet at Vienna was to have discussed this fundamental revision and to have reshaped international socialist policy accordingly. This fact has escaped historians of the International as well; not one of them thought to look through the documents of this abortive congress for which preparations began as early as 1912 and which in 1913 and 1914 occupied a central position in the activities of the International Socialist Bureau (ISB).

In an attempt to close the gaps in the documentation available to the historian the present book analyses the texts which existed in print on the eve of the 1914–18 war but which were never circulated. This source material contains no 'sensational' revelations; it merely consists of documents which offer, to those interested in the tragic end of an epoch of socialism, first-hand evidence which is certainly more reliable than the manifestos and newspaper articles hastily put together by the various socialist parties at the end of July 1914.[12]

Access to the archives of the International Socialist Bureau has enabled the present author to take a fresh look at the whole question, to go beyond the traditional approach and to examine the actions of the International. These unprinted sources have permitted him to correct inexactitudes and errors, and to put an end to persistent delusions and insinuations. As a result we have a better insight into the psychological climate, the political motives and mistakes, and into the underlying theories which explain the disarray of the socialist leaders when war broke out and their helplessness in the face of reality.

[12] The best collections of these documents (manifestos and proclamations by the socialist parties and the Second International) remain those of Carl Grünberg and W. E. Walling.

PART I

The Resolutions

1   Towards an International Socialist Policy

'Do you know what the proletariat is? Masses of men who collectively love peace and abhor war.' Jaurès's rhetorical question on the evening of 29 July 1914 in Brussels[1] and his characteristic reply reflect an attitude of mind cultivated by the International for half a century. International socialism defined itself as the 'party of peace'. Socialism and anti-militarism, socialism and internationalism were synonymous conceptions which constituted the central theme of all social democratic propaganda. As Édouard Vaillant pointed out in his speech to the International Socialist Congress in Paris in 1889, 'peace is an indispensable condition for the emancipation of the proletariat'. But until the beginning of the twentieth century the International in a peaceful Europe confined itself to making declarations of principle and stressing that capitalism contained within itself the threat of a conflagration. The acid test for the International and for internationalism was the Franco-Prussian war, and in this context the socialists never tired of recalling the courageous attitude of Bebel and the German social democratic deputies.

At every congress of the First International after 1867, and then at all sessions of the new International, set up in Paris in 1889, resolutions were adopted sharply condemning militarism, denouncing modern war as the vehicle for the aggrandizement of competing capitalist states, and expressing the social democrats' determination to do everything to resist a war in which the workers would be the inevitable victims.[2] These

[1] Speech to the international anti-war rally at the Cirque Royal in Brussels, *Le Peuple* (30 July 1914), 1.
[2] Resolutions which were collected and published on several occasions; for instance, in Grünberg, 5–25. In all the writings dealing with the history of the Second International, the question of militarism and war, as debated at the

resolutions, drawn up after bitter controversy between the various socialist schools of thought, embodied the creed of the average socialist, that the interests of capital make for war and the interests of labour make for peace. In this view, wars are bound to continue as long as the capitalist system prevails, and will only cease with the establishment of a socialist society. The prognosis was gloomy: the socialists asserted that armed conflicts would become more frequent and violent as the capitalist system of production approached its zenith. The only force capable of resisting this development, because its own vital interests were at stake, was the organized proletariat. From this followed the basic postulate on which socialist anti-war policy was based. Internationalism and class consciousness were the safeguards against all attempts to use the proletariat of one country to exterminate that of another. To counteract the militarism inherent in capitalist society, and with the aim of establishing a system to safeguard world peace, the congresses of the International worked out a series of proposals: to abolish secret diplomacy, to replace professional armies by militias, to promote general disarmament, and, finally, at the Congress of London in 1896, an idea dear to the French socialists, to set up an international tribunal. As for practical forms of resistance the duties of a socialist could be summed up in these words: 'Vote against war credits, protest against militarism, demand disarmament.' The idea of a general strike, keenly defended by the Dutch delegates at the International Congress of Brussels in 1891, was rejected for reasons of principle as an anarchist deviation.

For fourteen years, from 1893 to 1907, the International Congresses appeared to be satisfied that a general strike was not an available preventive of war, but that the best that socialists could do was to adopt the other remedy of continuing to refuse to vote a single soldier or a single penny for military purposes, until they were in control of parliaments and could bring about universal disarmament.[3]

congresses, plays a large part. Several surveys of this question have recently been published; see e.g. G. Haupt's bibliography, in *Programm und Wirklichkeit. Die internationale Sozialdemokratie 1914* (Neuwied, Luchterhand, 1970), 230–48.

[3] Walling, 47.

It was in these words that an American socialist, one of the first historians of the Second International, W. E. Walling, correctly summed up the state of mind that prevailed in the socialist parties.

At the beginning of the twentieth century war and militarism ceased to be purely theoretical problems, and the threat made itself felt more and more acutely. The Fashoda crisis, the war between Spain and the United States, the intervention in China at the time of the Boxer Rising, the Boer War, the Franco-German conflict in the Middle East and in North Africa, the Russo-Japanese war, and the Russo-Austrian dispute in the Balkans made the defence of peace a disturbingly topical problem. Vaillant and Jaurès drew the attention of the socialist world to the threat; they demanded that the International should think about the future of a Europe faced with a universal clash and look for a socialist solution to the question, which presented itself in a new form, and which determined every perspective of the proletariat's struggle. Jaurès started from the postulate that the basic prerequisite for the development of socialism was peace ('today everyone who works for peace is a socialist republican because in a peaceful Europe, which has laid down its arms, democracy and the proletariat will have miraculous expansionist powers'[4]) and demanded the definition of an international policy of socialism with the struggle for peace as its goal. It seemed imperative to him that the socialist parties be dependent on each other in an international framework and agree on co-ordinated action. In his opinion the time to proclaim general principles had passed. The generalities of the resolutions adopted at international congresses no longer sufficed.

In December 1902, on the eve of the second meeting of the ISB convened to settle the agenda for the international Congress in Amsterdam, Jaurès gave his views on the topics which he wanted the International to examine in depth. If disarmament and international arbitration were put on the agenda it was, he emphasized,

[4] *Œuvres de Jaurès*, vol. ii, 148.

not a question of renewed semi-fatalistic condemnation of war, and acceptance of it as a necessary consequence of capitalism. What needs to be investigated are the causes of dispute in every country and the origins of the chauvinistic trends which every national section of the Socialist Movement must watch and repress. What exactly is the Pan-German movement? What are the feelings of the Italian, Austrian, and German socialists towards the Triple Alliance?

Do French and German socialists see any possibility of a peaceful settlement of the Alsace-Lorraine question? What effort must each nation make to cultivate among its own people a spirit of peace, and what are the evil trends which it must seek to repress? What can be done to achieve general disarmament? How can the arbitration tribunals be given sufficient standing? These are the questions which need thorough investigation.[5]

It was this determination to formulate clear and direct answers that characterized Jaurès's anti-war campaign, especially after the Congress of Amsterdam when he returned to the issue with a much greater sense of immediacy. Jaurès's efforts tended to be directed wholly towards translating into political terms problems raised in doctrinal form. He introduced into the International a new element, that of the socialist leader who thought and acted like a statesman. At meetings of the International he keenly advocated a policy of 'action': to make socialists exert themselves as much as possible 'to prevent conflicts and to fight war'. At first, his proposals were received with suspicion; the orthodox Marxists, German and Russian, distrusted this 'corrupter of the party'. Kautsky, who remained the unquestioned arbiter of ideological differences in the Second International, for a long period openly questioned Jaurès's socialist convictions. He expressed his grievances in categorical terms in a letter to Adler, dated 28 January 1903:

Jaurès breaks people of the habit of thinking clearly. He is a rhetorical genius but that is precisely why he thinks that he can do anything with words. He carries this national French vice to extremes ... For the rest his talents are those of a parliamentary stringpuller.[6]

5 Jean Jaurès, 'Le Congrès international', *La Petite République* (27 Dec. 1902), 1.
6 *Victor Adler Briefwechsel*, 410–11. In 1904 Plekhanov, in his turn, complained to Vandervelde about Jaurès; see ISB archives.

The elaboration and practical application of an international socialist policy met with several major obstacles. The first resulted directly from the institutional structure of the Second International: as a federation of autonomous parties it left its members complete freedom in political and tactical questions. Each party had its own programme, its own aims, and, according to Vaillant, 'the only issue [at the international congress] must be to discover how, given the conditions prevailing in the various countries, they can best co-ordinate their activities'.[7] All the parties clung jealously to the principle of autonomy. The question of what was part of the general principles and what could only be settled by the national parties remained undecided.

These difficulties became apparent as soon as it became necessary to put the resolutions into practice and to supervise their working. In actual fact, it took twenty years of groping before the new International became an institution with statutes and rules. Until 1900 it consisted only of periodic congresses, which called themselves 'International Workers' Parliaments' or 'Future International Socialist Parliaments'. Their resolutions were of considerable importance and had many repercussions, but there was no organization to ensure continued international action or any co-ordination in the activities of the affiliated parties. It was only after the Paris Congress of 1900 that the International was given the first semblance of a permanent institution, by the establishment of the International Socialist Bureau with an executive committee and secretariat with headquarters in Brussels.[8] One of the main duties of the Bureau was 'to initiate and organize co-ordinated protest movements and anti-militarist agitation in all countries on all occasions of international importance'.

This beginning of an 'institutionalization' which was followed in 1904 by the establishment of an Interparliamentary Socialist

---

[7] Édouard Vaillant, 'Le Congrès international', *La Petite République* (28 June 1896), 1.

[8] See G. Haupt, *La Deuxième Internationale 1889–1914: étude critique des sources* (Paris–The Hague, Mouton, 1964), 23–33.

Commission is not, however, inconsistent with the International's initial refusal to give itself a centralized structure. The principle of the autonomy of the affiliated parties and organizations did not undergo any fundamental change as a result. The International remained a federation which allowed representatives of all shades of socialism to belong to a single body. 'The new International', Friedrich Adler said in July 1914, 'is not an independent organization, it has no sphere of activity which can be separated from that of its sections.'[9]

In practice, the foundation of the ISB was an attempt at co-ordination, necessitated by the spread of the movement throughout the world. The congresses alone could no longer cope with the tasks which the International had shouldered. Yet the ISB, with its authority ill defined, remained for many years no more than a 'letter-box' for the socialist world.

It was not until 1905, after the appointment of Camille Huysmans as secretary, that the ISB was given its final status. The efforts to strengthen the Bureau's position led to the resolutions of the Stuttgart Congress of 1907, which provided the ISB with statutes and rules of procedure and authorized the Bureau to preserve the continuity of the International's work between congresses, thus making it more effective. As the threat of war loomed larger, more and more voices were heard expressing the view that the Bureau's powers and sphere of influence should be extended. Consequently, the Bureau was authorized to co-ordinate socialist efforts for the maintenance of peace. The resolution adopted at the extraordinary Congress in Basle (1912) spelt out these tasks still further by emphasizing that

the International shall redouble its efforts to prevent war, that it shall voice its protest ever more emphatically, and make its propaganda ever more forceful and all-embracing. The Congress therefore charges the International Socialist Bureau to watch events with the greatest attention and, *whatever happens, maintain* and strengthen *the links* between the proletarian parties of all the countries involved.

[9] Friedrich Adler, 'Die Organisation der neuen Internationale', in *Festschrift des X, internationalen Socialistenkongress. Wien 1914*, 13.

The confusion over the ISB's terms of reference remained. This led to a great variety of interpretations of the Bureau's tasks, aptly defined by Vaillant at the SFIO Congress in Paris in 1910: 'The International Socialist Bureau is primarily a linking, not a leading organ.'

In spite of obstacles and opposition the Bureau's standing in the international movement grew steadily. The increasing importance of the Bureau's sessions, and the opportunities provided by the International gatherings—such as the conferences of the Inter-Parliamentary Socialist Commissions, of socialist women, and of socialist journalists—enriched the life of the International without, however, fundamentally altering the structure established in 1889, and without detracting from the role of the congresses. They remained the most representative events in the International's history as an institution.

The 'sovereign congress' was alone responsible for decisions concerning the whole of the International. This paragraph of the statutes was observed to the letter in all circumstances. Not even in the critical days at the end of July 1914 did the ISB think to ignore it.

The lack of a cohesive organization and the absence of an institutional structure in fact reflected a situation and an attitude which was deeply rooted. The period of the Second International was a period of rapid numerical and political growth of the socialist movement in the principal European countries, a period in which modern forms of organization were generally adopted by the political mass parties. But the theories of international dimensions were replaced by nationally restricted political ideas. The second big obstacle to the preparation of a joint international policy was caused chiefly by differences between the SPD Executive and the most important French socialist group on the question of war and peace. The semi-fatalistic attitude and inactive pacifism of the Germans hindered the French party's optimistic call for action.[10]

[10] For further details, see Drachkovitch; and J. Joll, *The Second International* (London, Weidenfeld & Nicolson, 1955), 108 ff.

Between 1900 and 1907 the chief preoccupation of some leading French socialists—particularly Jaurès and Vaillant, who were motivated by a deeply humanistic and historically based philosophy—was that the German social democrats should take the threat of war into serious consideration and that the International should regard it as one of its most important problems. But the differences between the two parties concealed another important phenomenon: the struggle of French socialism for the leadership of the International in the face of German social democratic preponderance, in other words a struggle to gain acceptance for another conception of socialism, for another form of action by the workers. In a passionate indictment at the International Congress of Amsterdam Jaurès clearly voiced his fears to an astonished but enthralled audience:

What at present most weighs on Europe and the world, . . . is the political impotence of German social democracy . . . You no more have the means of revolutionary action, the power which a revolutionary tradition of the proletariat would give you, than you have parliamentary power. Even if you had a majority in the Reichstag your country would be the only one where you, where socialism, would not be the master even with a majority. Because your parliament is only a semi-parliament.[11]

The different standpoints on the general problem of peace became particularly apparent during the Morocco crisis of 1905–6. The temporizing policy of the SPD Executive—strongly criticized by anti-militarists like Karl Liebknecht and Rosa Luxemburg, who belonged to the left wing of the party—was strikingly at variance with the tense and anxious demeanour of the French socialists. In his campaign in the press and the Chamber of Deputies Jaurès emphasized that the arms race would lead to a general European war. Although he had no illusions about the proletariat's ability to preserve peace effectively in the immediate future, he regarded it as the Inter-

---

[11] See *Sixième Congrès socialiste international tenu à Amsterdam du 14 au 20 août 1904. Compte rendu analytique*, published by the ISB secretariat (Brussels–Ghent, Volksdrukkerij, 1904), p. 37. Quoted also in J. Joll, op. cit. 102–3.

national's duty to prepare the proletariat for this role. In 1905, in the midst of the Morocco crisis, he wrote:

We know that in view of these retrograde manœuvres, in view of the systematic unleashing of barbarism, the international proletariat cannot be sure that its desire for justice and peace will prevail; we are therefore prepared for difficult times. But we also know that the working class is slowly and painfully developing its strength . . . that the Workers' International is quickening its step, that it is redoubling its efforts, its propaganda and its organizational work.[12]

Because they wanted to speed up the International's decision, Vaillant and Jaurès in September 1905 jointly proposed to the ISB that the socialist parties of all countries should examine 'the general measures to be taken: (1) in the first instance by the parties of the countries concerned and (2) simultaneously by the international socialist party as a whole, to forestall and avoid war by means of joint international socialist and working class action'. The International must be mobilized 'as soon as secret or public moves give rise to fear of a conflict between governments and make war possible or probable'.[13]

This proposal was discussed at the ISB meeting on 6 March 1906 and adopted. But only the next international congress could take a generally effective decision. Some months later the French socialists registered a new success. At the ISB meeting on 10 November 1906 the question of 'militarism and international conflicts' was put on the agenda of the international congress convened for August 1907 at Stuttgart.[14]

As the appointed date of the congress approached, the differences of opinion between the German social democrats and the French socialists became more apparent. The congresses of the French Socialist Party (SFIO) at Limoges and Nancy

---

[12] *Œuvres de Jaurès*, vol. iii, 228.

[13] See *Bureau socialiste international. Comptes rendus des réunions, manifestes, circulaires*, G. Haupt, ed. (Paris–The Hague, Mouton, 1969, vol. i), 175 and 181–4.

[14] Cf. ibid. 286. Vaillant thought that his proposal which had been adopted by the ISB offered a final solution. At the ISB meeting of 9 June 1907, he was opposed to putting the question on the agenda of the Stuttgart congress. Jaurès disagreed because to him it was very important that the whole International should examine the problem and come to a decision.

considered ways and means of banishing the threat of war and adopted resolutions which presented the German social democrats with *faits accomplis*.[15] The Belgian socialists, followed by the Independent Labour Party of Great Britain, expressed themselves in favour of the French initiative. At its annual conference in 1907 the ILP asked the ISB and the International to pursue an active international policy in order to be prepared if war should become an immediate threat.[16] Thus the ball was set rolling, and the International was very willing to follow up the ILP's suggestion as international tension was growing at an alarming rate. All that was therefore required of the SPD was to ratify the texts adopted by the SFIO or else submit another resolution. The Germans chose the latter.

The international congress at Stuttgart was the culminating point of the life of the Second International. Its work in the political and the theoretical sphere was focused on the problem of militarism and war. Although long and lively discussions took place, both in committee and in the plenaries, the question was not exhausted nor was agreement reached on guide-lines for socialist action or on what attitude to take in the case of war.

The work in Stuttgart gave rise to further violent controversy between the German and French socialists when Gustave Hervé distinguished himself by his passion. But the debates revealed another fact, the importance of which did not escape people at the time. Behind the quibbles over words lay not only differences between particular schools of thought, but marked trends symptomatic of a deep ideological and political split within international socialism.

The Franco-German controversy became apparent only when it came to the assessment of the international situation and the measures to be recommended. It was not concerned with socialist ideology but with the action to be taken. The

---

[15] See Drachkovitch, 323–30; and Richard Hostetter, 'La questione della guerra nel partito socialista francese. Dibattiti interni e internazionali (1906–1910)', *Rivista storica del socialismo*, 13–14 (1962), 489–530.

[16] See Independent Labour Party, *Report of the Fifteenth Annual Conference* (London, 1907), 63 ff.

disagreement between the radical left and the majority of the International revealed profound differences in historical vision and choice of strategy. Whereas the majority wanted, above all, to work out a generally acceptable policy which might help to prevent a European clash, the Left was concerned with the revolution that could result from a capitalist war.

The debates of the commission, whose task it was to prepare a joint resolution, clearly reflected the many different points of view. Four drafts were submitted, the most important being that of Bebel on the one hand, and that of Vaillant and Jaurès on the other.[17] The latter who were concerned with the ways and means of waging 'war on war', proposed a general strike. This suggestion produced a violent reaction from the German delegates, who were utterly opposed to a general strike, because they regarded it as irreconcilable with socialist tactics. As agreement was impossible, a subcommittee was set up to prepare a compromise.

The hostility with which Jaurès and Vaillant's proposal was received enabled Rosa Luxemburg, Lenin, and Martov to push through their own amendment in the subcommittee:[18]

Should war nevertheless break out, they [the Socialists] shall take measures to bring about its early termination and strive with all their power to use the economic and political crisis, created by the war, to arouse the masses politically and to hasten the overthrow of capitalist class rule.

Even now the question remains. When the delegates adopted the resolution into which this left-wing amendment had been incorporated, were they aware of its significance? It seems that the majority of delegates at the congress attached little

[17] See *Septième Congrès socialiste international tenu à Stuttgart du 16 au 24 août 1907. Compte rendu analytique*, published by the ISB secretariat (Brussels, Vve Désiré Brismée, pr., 1908), 109–14. The four drafts of the resolution are found in G. D. H. Cole, *A History of Socialist Thought* (London, Macmillan, 1956, vol. iii, Pt. I: 'The Second International'), 62–71.

[18] For the details, see Olga Hess Gankin and H. H. Fisher, *The Bolsheviks and the World War. The Origin of the Third International* (Stanford U.P., 1940), 55–65; and N. I. Krutikova, *Iz istorii bor'by Lenina protiv oportunizma na meždunarodnoj arene, Štuttgarskij kongress* (Moscow, Gospolitizdat, 1955), 108–30.

importance to the motion because it concerned a hypothetical future and because they thought that for the moment it
committed them to nothing. For them impending revolution
was an effective argument with which to intimidate the
bourgeoisie, not a strategic goal. Moreover, the radically
worded resolution in no way reflected the tenor of the discussions or the attitude of most delegates. Above all it ignored the
objections and arguments of those who differentiated between
defensive wars and imperialist wars, and who declared themselves in favour of national defence and also of the class
struggle. As it was impossible to reach agreement on this
question, which was regarded as purely theoretical and as
being of no importance to the day-to-day socialist struggle,
'the Congress expected this conflict to be resolved only with
the victory of the working class in the principal European
countries'.[19]

W. E. Walling has rightly remarked that this resolution,
'the most important document in socialist history', is 'consciously designed to cover up some of the socialist differences
connected with the war . . . It is a very carefully constructed
compromise, however, and a correct reflection of the *consensus*
of socialist opinion'.[20]

Instead of serving as a basis for socialist anti-war action, this
blunt conceptual instrument perpetuated the existing split
within the International. Paradoxically, in 1907 such a compromise satisfied everybody; each protagonist could regard the
Stuttgart resolution as his victory.[21] For Lenin it meant
the victory of the revolutionary Marxists over reformism. For
the SPD Executive it was a success *vis-à-vis* the extremists of
'the Hervé variety', while Jaurès saw it as 'a decisive victory of
French socialism's international policy'.

Certainly Stuttgart was a turning-point. The authority and
importance of German social democracy within the Inter-

---

[19] Max Beer, *Histoire générale du socialisme et des luttes sociales*, vol. v: *L'époque
contemporaine* (Paris, Les Revues, 1931), 146.
[20] Walling, 25.   [21] Kautsky, 338.

national had suffered a distinct blow, while French socialism registered a perceptible gain in prestige.

Thereafter the relationship between the protagonists became stabilized. And yet the differences between the International's two 'great powers' remained. They became acutely apparent during the ever more frequent diplomatic crises which preceded the First World War. After the Stuttgart congress the antagonism between the representatives of the Left and those of the Centre and the Right grew considerably more marked, and the question of the strategy in the fight against war was hotly debated. Although the controversy affected neither the general direction in which the International was moving nor its activities, it became difficult after Stuttgart to relegate the debates on socialism's international policy to the sphere of pure theory. The crisis in the Balkans which followed Austria's annexation of Bosnia-Herzegovina heightened existing fears. The socialist press stressed the threat. In January 1909 Kautsky revealed his anxiety: 'For weeks Europe has faced the threat of a world war. People hope that the danger will be banished but it continues to reappear in ever more acute form.'[22]

In the course of the same year and in spite of opposition from the SPD Executive, he published his most important work, *Der Weg zur Macht*, in which he noted that the contradictions in capitalism were continuously on the increase and predicted a period of war and revolution.[23]

The problem of the war became the subject of much propaganda literature. The press and the socialist publicists merely repeated the classical themes and the arguments of Marx and kept assuring their readers that the proletariat was determined to defend the peace. Socialist circles, even in Germany, became increasingly aware that it was not enough to draw attention to the threat of war and to assert socialist determination to resist, but that action was needed without waiting 'for war to knock

[22] K. Kautsky, 'Österreich und Serbien', xxvii. 2 (Jan. 1909), 860.
[23] K. Kautsky, *The Road to Power*, trans. A. Simons (Chicago, 1909); for an analysis of this work, see Schorske, 111.

at the door because then it will be too late' (as Franz Mehring observed).[24]

The reaction of the ISB was quick to come. At a meeting in October 1908 the Bureau examined the international situation. A resolution proposed by the French was adopted. It referred to the constant threat of war, and asked all socialist parties (1) to redouble their 'vigilance, activities, and efforts' and (2) with the help of the ISB secretariat 'to search for means and practical measures which, applied in a national or international framework, can, depending on the situation and the circumstances, best prevent war and preserve peace'.[25] Although there was determination and readiness to act, this was obstructed by passive and declamatory pacifism. The warnings of the British delegate, Bruce Glasier, at the meeting 'that such obscure and meaningless resolutions can have no influence on politics' fell on deaf ears. But in fact the ISB could not act otherwise, and it replied to his strictures with references to practical difficulties of organization. These generalizations covered up the weaknesses of socialism's international policy: precise definitions depended on conflicting tactical considerations. As it was, the socialists confined themselves to reiterating that 'the proletariat is the only effective force that can safeguard international peace', while looking at concrete political problems from a limited national point of view. Kautsky said that the parties affiliated to the International 'agreed only on the negative rejection of war' and disagreed totally on 'the positive elaboration of a detailed programme of overall foreign policy'.

To get out of the quandary, there was need to clarify and elaborate the socialist theory on war, the contradictions and weaknesses of which struck even some contemporary socialist theorists. The majority of the International regarded war as an apocalyptic threat inherent in capitalism, a threat which

---

[24] Franz Mehring, 'Die Balkankrise', *NZ* xvii. 1 (Nov. 1908), 73–6.

[25] *Le Bureau socialiste international. Compte rendu officiel.* (*A*) *La deuxième réunion des journalistes socialistes* (*10 octobre 1908*). (*B*) *La dixième séance du Bureau socialiste international* (*11 octobre 1908*). (*C*) *La troisième conférence interparlementaire* (*12 octobre 1908*) (Ghent, Volksdrukkerij, 1909), 47 ff.

increased as the tension between the imperialist powers grew. War was therefore condemned without any definition of its various forms. The term 'imperialist war' was confined to a colonial war or a war of conquest. The social democrats used the terms 'war of aggression' and 'war of defence' without defining them sufficiently for this theory to be applied to political action at a given moment. Although a clarification was demanded, the leading socialists contemptuously rejected it when it was given. In 1907, for example, after the International Congress in Stuttgart, the SPD annual party congress at Essen raised the question of how to decide the parties' tactics in the event of war. Would the decision depend on whether their own government took the offensive or was on the defensive, whether it was the attacker or whether it was defending the fatherland? Bebel, the revered leader of the SPD, elucidated the question in his characteristic way: 'It would be sad if nowadays social democrats could not in every case determine with certainty whether a war is aggressive or defensive.'[26]

Searching for a better theoretical understanding, some young socialist militants, like the Dutchman Van Ravestejn rejected all attempts at simplification. Starting with a thorough analysis of Jaurès's *Histoire socialiste* he stressed the difficulty of defending offensive or defensive war.[27] Taking the Franco-Prussian War of 1870 as one of his examples he came to the conclusion that: 'While social class and national interests persist it will probably always be impossible to make a clear distinction between aggressive and defensive war. War, every war, must be opposed with all possible means.' Kautsky's intervention was very similar. At the party congress at Essen and in many articles written between 1907 and 1909 he categorically rejected as outdated the theory of aggressive and defensive war. In an article

---

[26] *Protokoll über die Verhandlungen des Parteitages der SPD abgehalten zu Essen vom 15. bis 21. August 1907* (Berlin, 1907), 255. On the debates in Essen, where a most 'patriotic' speech delivered by Noske in the Reichstag was vividly criticized, see Fritz Klein, ed., *Deutschland im ersten Weltkrieg* (Berlin, Akademie Verlag, 2nd edn. rev., 1970, vol. i), 174–6.

[27] See W. Van Ravestejn, 'Angriffskrieg oder Verteidigungskrieg? Jaurès über den Ursprung des deutsch-französischen Krieges', *NZ* xxvi. 1 (Dec. 1907), 388–9.

published a short time before the Essen congress he went even further: 'In the given political situation it is impossible to think of a war in which proletarian or democratic interests could be defended or attacked . . . The only threat of war today arises from overseas world policy which the proletariat must resolutely reject from the outset.'

Yet this radical conception, which Kautsky modified and abandoned shortly afterwards, did not go as far as the ideas that prevailed when the Second International was set up. As Lafargue said in a letter to Guesde on 12 July 1881: 'The foreign policy of the worker's party: Peace at any price, to permit the workers' parties of the various countries to be organized and to await events. The only war which this party intends to wage is class war, war against the capitalists, in France no less than in Prussia.'[28] After the turn of the century, only an extremist minority continued to preach ideas such as these, for example, Gustave Hervé in *La Guerre sociale*.

The debates in Essen revealed the confusion that prevailed even in the ranks of the party that was in theory the best armed: the SPD. It becomes clear that it was not only for rhetorical reasons that the preambles to the resolutions were verbose and misused words that had lost much of their impact, thereby giving the anti-militarist campaigns of the socialist press a certain didactic pomposity. Nor can the socialist parties' lack of clearly defined positions when faced with acute diplomatic crises serve as the sole explanation for their doctrinal hesitations.

The International was anxious not to become involved in a discussion which it regarded as purely academic and avoided a definition of the socialist position in the event of a European war. Its energies were concentrated on preparing a preventive strategy. To check the possibility of war, to prevent the threat from becoming a reality, to bring everything into play so as to confine and extinguish any conflagration, such was the policy of the International—a policy which was applied at once during the crisis in Bosnia-Herzegovina. The first task therefore was to

[28] See *Francuzskij Ežegodnik 1962* (Moscow, 1963), 477.

define jointly the steps to be taken so that preventive tactics could be successfully resorted to, making the slogan of 'war on war' a reality. It was hoped that these aims would be achieved at the International Socialist Congress which met in Copenhagen in 1910, and the agenda of which again included the 'question of militarism and disarmament'. The preparations for the congress took place without incident. The SPD steering committee offered no opposition although the German delegates showed great interest and took a very active part in the work. Yet the basic difference in the attitude of the French and the German socialists once again emerged in the heated discussion on the motion submitted by the Independent Labour Party M.P. Keir Hardie and Édouard Vaillant which read as follows:

Among all the means to be used in order to prevent and hinder war, the congress considers as particularly efficacious a general strike, especially in the industries that supply war with its implements (arms and ammunition, transport, etc.), as well as agitation and popular action in their most active forms.

This amendment was too revolutionary even for the representatives of the German Left, like Georg Ledebour, the Commission's *rapporteur*. It created such a stir and was so energetically opposed by the German delegates that it became necessary to adopt a compromise proposed by Vandervelde to the effect that the resolution should be referred back to the ISB for further study and put on the agenda of the next international congress.[29]

The resolution adopted expressed the point of view of the majority of the German delegates. It confined itself to noting that the arms race was speeding up, and limited the means of action to purely parliamentary ones, the refusal to vote for war credits, the demand for an international arbitration Court whose decisions were binding, the restriction of armaments, and autonomy for all nations. Consistent with that delegation of duty, the only things agreed upon at the congress

[29] See *Huitième Congrès socialiste international tenu à Copenhague du 28 août au 3 septembre 1910. Compte rendu analytique*, published by the ISB secretariat (Ghent, Volksdrukkerij, 1911), 311–13 and *passim*.

were almost identical with the programmes of non-socialist peace movements. One of the objectives was 'to make use of such support as could be found among the bourgeoisie for these proposals'.

The Congress in Copenhagen thus failed once again to come to grips with the central problem. The ISB still had the responsibility for co-ordinating socialist efforts in the event of war. But without any clearly defined action agreed upon by the national sections, such responsibility was largely meaningless.

The only definite decision was that whenever a conflict between two or more countries appeared to assume threatening proportions, and when there was likely to be a delay in the replies from the national parties, the secretary of the ISB should urgently, at the request of at least one of the sections involved, call a meeting of the Bureau.

The Copenhagen decisions produced a strong reaction among the left wing of the German socialists which had been powerless at the meeting and which went over to the offensive in its party during the 'discussion on disarmament' which it subsequently initiated.[30] Copenhagen precipitated the split which had existed since Stuttgart and for which the Moroccan crisis was the final catalyst. The Left saw the Eighth International Congress as a backward step after the previous congress, a disquieting move towards bourgeois pacifism. But the majority of the International used a different accounting system. They entered the Copenhagen deliberations on the credit side and showed a surplus on the balance sheet.

In their view the two international congresses had, in spite of strong opposition, managed to agree on certain principles for an international socialist policy. But it was left to the next international congress to decide what means should be used to overcome the differences between the various national parties and what measures should be taken against the threat of war.

---

[30] See W. Wittwer, *Streit um die Schicksalsfragen. Die deutsche Sozialdemokratie zu Krieg und Vaterlandsverteidigung, 1907–1914* (Berlin, 1964), 66–8; and Ursula Ratz, 'Karl Kautsky und die Abrüstungskontroverse in der deutschen Sozialdemokratie 1911–1912', *International Review of Social History*, xii. 2 (1966), 197–226.

At the conclusion of its labours the Copenhagen Congress decided on the time and place of the next international session: Vienna, 1913.

The *leitmotiv* of the Copenhagen Congress, as also of all the resolutions adopted by the ISB after Stuttgart, was the need to co-ordinate as far as possible the efforts of the various national parties and to strengthen and intensify the anti-militaristic movement.

But the major problem remained: How was this task to be performed? By pacifism or by a general fight against imperialism? These alternatives were henceforth to play leading parts in the formulation of socialist international policy.

2   Franco-German Differences in the ISB: the Morocco Crisis

THE deterioration of the international situation after 1911 presented a challenge to the socialist world. It was between 1911 and 1913, the years of the Morocco crisis, the Italian attack on Tripolitania, and above all the Balkan Wars, that the concepts of imperialism and the analyses of the situation crystallized. The repercussions were strongly felt in July 1914. There is no doubt that the German social democrats and the French socialists continued to interpret the general situation and the trend of international politics in different ways and that this divergence of opinion influenced international politics during these years. This partly explains why the necessary unanimity was lacking when it came to the definition of political guide-lines and particularly to the search for ways and means of preventing war. But in the long run the differences over the questions of theory which emerged from the analysis and interpretation of the nature of imperialism were of greater significance than the disagreements over the evaluation of the political situation.

In the feverish search for answers to questions about the immediate consequences of the diplomatic tensions and about the possibility of localizing conflicts, issues of theory were relegated to the background. There was little investigation into the deeper causes of the development of late capitalist society towards imperialism, which the International held responsible for the worsening of the situation. But the attitude of the socialist headquarters during these crises—even more than the debates at the international congresses—revealed that the Achilles' heel of the International was above all its incompetence in matters of theory, a failing aggravated further by the organization's methods of work and the inadequacy of its institutions. When it had to draw up a long-term programme of international policy, it was unable to get beyond formulations so general as to make them useless as practical guide-lines. When faced with a choice between a far-sighted but vague formulation and one that was of immediate relevance but too extreme, it always chose the former.

Yet the divergence of views over the political situation which in 1911 and 1912 preoccupied the ISB and the plenaries was no longer confined to purely abstract discussion. At the end of every debate important decisions needed to be taken: whether to mobilize the masses, whether to go out into the streets, whether to fight in parliament. It is precisely at those times that the national sections showed themselves in their true colours. The diplomatic crises led to profound disagreements between the socialist parties of the countries directly concerned; each party sought to minimize its own country's responsibility and, while justifying its own inactivity, to persuade the others to act. The distrust between the various brother-parties, barely contained at the international congresses, became obvious as soon as there was a crisis.

The Bosnia-Herzegovina affair in 1908 was the occasion of a violent clash between the Austrian and Serbian socialists. The small Serbian party accused the leadership of the Austrian party, and Victor Adler in particular, of judging the crisis not from an international point of view but from that of Austria, thereby playing the game of the Vienna government. The ISB took care to confine these differences to a pamphlet war.[1] Nor was the majority of militant socialists affected by the differences between the German socialists and a group of British comrades over the naval competition between Britain and Germany, which reached its climax in 1908–10 with the building of a new warship, the famous *Dreadnought*, even though this event caused a great

---

[1] See below, Ch. 3.

stir. The attitude of a numerically small but influential group
of British socialists, with Hyndman at its head, was revealing as
regards nationalistic tendencies. While the Labour Party and
the ILP were categorically opposed to rearmament, the leader
of the Social Democratic Federation and Blatchford, an influential journalist, denounced the German threat in the *Clarion*'s
columns—the most popular socialist publication in pre-1914
Britain—and advocated a better navy.[2] At the international
congress at Copenhagen Hyndman's supporters violently
attacked Germany's policy as aiming at world domination,
while defending the armaments policy of their own country—
in particular the increase in the navy estimates.

This was the time when Hyndman's secret distrust of German
social democracy turned into open enmity. Whereas in 1905
during the first Morocco crisis he had confined himself to
criticism of the SPD's political short-sightedness and inactivity,[3]
in 1908 he openly questioned the German socialists' willingness
and ability to act in case of war.[4] In 1911 he went further still.
At the Conference in Coventry he accused the German social
democrats of sabotaging the International's whole anti-war
campaign. He alleged too that on three occasions he had asked
the ISB to bring together the delegates of France, Britain, and
Germany to examine the threat of war and possible preventive
measures and that each time the Germans had refused to
attend such a meeting. Deeply offended by these accusations
Kautsky immediately asked the secretary of the ISB to investigate Hyndman's assertions so that they could be shown to be
defamatory.[5] But the incident was papered over; it was
attributed to the eccentricity of Hyndman who had been a

[2] On Blatchford, see Bernard Semmel, *Imperialism and Social Reform, English
Social–Imperial Thought, 1895–1914* (Cambridge, Mass., Harvard U.P., 1960), 222–
33.
[3] Hyndman to Huysmans, 7 June 1905, ISB archives. This letter was sent by
the ISB in the form of a circular of 21 June 1905 to the secretariats of the affiliated
parties. Cf. G. Haupt, ed., *Bureau socialiste international*, vol. 1, 145–6.
[4] Cf. Kautsky, 389; H. M. Hyndman, *Further Reminiscences* (London, 1912), 397;
Julius Braunthal, *History of the International*, vol. i: *1864 to 1914*, trans. M. Collins
and H. Mitchell (London, Nelson, 1966).
[5] Kautsky to Huysmans, 15 May 1911, ISB archives.

restive element as long ago as the Boer War.[6] In 1908 Keir Hardie had assured 'our German Socialist and Trade Union Comrades that Hyndman and Blatchford speak for themselves alone and that their attitude in this question would be repudiated with practical unanimity by the Socialist and Trade Union movement . . .'[7]

However, neither Keir Hardie's repeated assertions nor Huysmans's dexterity lessened the tension. In fact, the renewed flare-up of the Morocco crisis in 1911 sparked off the 'Hyndman affair' at the same time as it revived a conflict which was more difficult to resolve. Once again the increase in international tension resulted in antagonism between the SPD party executive and the French delegates at the ISB. Their disagreement was centred on three main points:

1. the interpretation and evaluation of the international situation;
2. the International's role and opportunities as a power and as a genuine peace factor;
3. the means for dealing with the threat.

These differences had become marked as early as 1905, in the course of the first Morocco crisis, when the French delegates had for the first time seen the spectre of a European war. They decided to act themselves and also to make the International act. Bebel, however, recommended caution. In June 1905 he opposed a proposal by Hyndman asking for the immediate convocation of an ISB conference on the Morocco conflict, and in the process defined his party's attitude which was to remain the same until 1914: 'It is our impression that people in England are rather nervous and see the situation as more serious than it is. If we convene a meeting whenever there is a minor

[6] On Hyndman's nationalism, see F. Bealey, 'Les travaillistes et la guerre des Boers', *Le Mouvement social*, 45 (1963), 46 ff.; Ch. Tsuzuki, *H. M. Hyndman and British Socialism* (Oxford U.P., 1961), 200 ff.

[7] *Labour Leader* (14 Aug. 1908), 521. The *Neue Zeit* gave much space to this dispute. Cf. Theodor Rothstein, 'Die SPD, Hyndman und die Rüstungsfrage', *NZ* xxix. 2, no. 32 (1911), 179–86; and Harry Quelch's reply, 'Die Sozialdemokratische Partei, Hyndman und die Rüstungsfrage', ibid., no. 34, 270–3.

diplomatic crisis, and immediately pass resolutions, we shall become discredited in no time.'[8]

This attitude was diametrically opposed to that of the French, who were well-disposed towards Hyndman's initiative, as revealed in a letter from Vaillant to Huysmans which dates from this period. 'It seems to me that one cannot search enough for ways and means of mobilizing the socialist parties and the international proletariat so as to prevent the war which the governments are plotting.'[9] These two points of view reveal a paradoxical situation: the German socialists, pessimistic as regards the possibility of preventing war, displayed optimism and calm in every serious diplomatic crisis; the French, on the other hand, confident that the International could stop a general clash, became anxious and active whenever the international situation deteriorated.

However—and this must be stressed—it took some time before the majority of the French socialist party became convinced that war was a real and immediate threat and might result from the Franco-German differences over colonies or from the Austro-Russian rivalry in the Balkans. Only after the congress at Brest in March 1913, and after the introduction of three-year conscription did a real exchange of views take place between senior party members. Jaurès, Vaillant, and Jean Longuet, acutely aware of the situation, were for a long time alone in holding their views. The party, though having confidence in them, did not take the issue they raised seriously. However, they were granted great freedom of action in the realm of foreign policy which was one of Jaurès's constant preoccupations. Assisted by de Pressensé, whose connections gained during his long career in the Foreign Ministry and as a foreign editor of *Le Temps* made him a skilled and thoughtful adviser, the French socialist leader made a thorough study of world affairs. He was the SFIO spokesman in the Chamber of

---

[8] Bebel to the ISB, 25 June 1905. The letter was transmitted to the affiliated parties in a circular of 28 June 1905; cf. G. Haupt, *Bureau socialiste international*, vol. i, 154–6.

[9] Vaillant to Huysmans, 22 June 1905, ISB archives.

Deputies, the severe and admonishing critic of foreign policy, the one who 'sifted out' the international commitments of France. Because they understood the long-term dangers in diplomatic conflicts, Jaurès and Vaillant were convinced that socialists could play an active role in the settlement of international conflicts by striving to mediate and to moderate. The Frenchmen were not motivated by theoretical considerations, but rather by a realistic appreciation of the facts, reached rationally by Jaurès, instinctively by Vaillant.

The German socialists felt considerable suspicion towards the pragmatism of their French comrades and went so far as to maintain contrary opinions in their prognoses and analyses. Indeed, Jaurès's efforts to achieve a Franco-German *rapprochement*, together with his campaign concerning the Moroccan venture, gave rise to Kautsky's accusation that Jaurès hatched 'perfidious designs towards socialism'. But neither his vision of peace nor his conception of the constructive role of socialists in the solution of major international conflicts could win over his audience, even less could it gain the confidence of the German socialist leadership.

The SPD did not concern itself much with problems of foreign policy. Its attitude towards these questions was lacking in unanimity, insufficiently thought out, and often dictated almost exclusively by the circumstances.[10]

Beyond distrust and scepticism, the SPD felt real reluctance to step into the field of foreign policy—a slippery ground, reserved for the dominant classes—where involvement might well lead to repression.[11] In practice the socialist group in the Reichstag did not oppose the expansionist efforts of the German Government and in some instances even supported them.

[10] Max Victor, 'Die Stellung der deutschen Sozialdemokratie zu den Fragen der auswärtigen Politik (1869–1914)', *Archiv für Sozialwissenschaft und Sozialpolitik,* lx. 1 (1928), 154 ff.

[11] In September 1908, when Kautsky was appointed as the German delegate to the Anglo-German demonstrations against the naval armaments, Bebel, who disagreed with the whole venture, advised caution, expressing thus his fear that Kautsky might be expelled from Germany.

Over the Morocco question in particular the attitude of the SPD party executive was open to various interpretations. Revealing in this respect was the *exposé* which Molkenbuhr gave at the ISB session in October 1908. He described the behaviour of the German Government in the Morocco crisis as a poisoning manœuvre and said that the threat was fictitious and superficial. His reasoning in support of this claim represented a remarkable simplification of the facts.[12] How should one see this attitude? As incompetence? As political short-sightedness? Or as a manifestation of nationalistic trends which found expression in the theory of 'Germany's right to a presence in Africa' as advanced by the right wing of the party? Max Victor, who has made a close study of the SPD's foreign policy, inclines towards this last explanation. He says that 'there was less and less opposition to the government's colonial policy in the years before the war'. In 1911 the Party insisted on the preservation of Morocco's sovereignty, if only because a French Morocco barred the Straits of Gibraltar to Germany and thus possible access to her colonies. Over the question of the Congo compensation 'the criticism of the German socialists was limited almost completely to the paltriness of what has been achieved'.[13]

Bernstein wrote in *Vorwärts*: 'The SPD cannot be satisfied with a solution which gives France a free hand in Morocco in exchange for a small piece of Congo', while Bebel defended German colonialism in the Reichstag by claiming that a 'compensation in the Cameroons would have had more chance'.[14] The French socialists who took the same view on colonial policy were not worried by these statements.

The second aspect of these Franco-German differences was the two parties' view of the International as a peace factor. The representatives of the great social democratic party of

[12] *Compte rendu officiel de la dixième séance du Bureau socialiste international (11 octobre 1908)* (Ghent, Volksdrukkerij, 1909), 2.

[13] M. Victor, art. cit., 173.

[14] See Abraham Ascher, 'Imperialists within Social Democracy prior to 1914', *Journal of Central European Affairs*, xx (Jan. 1961), 397–422; Irène Petit, 'La social-démocratie allemande et la question coloniale (1884–1914)', *Le Mouvement social*, 45 (1963), 109.

Germany, which had become a substantial force in domestic politics and which formed a strong opposition in parliament, did not really take the International into consideration.

The SPD delegates doubted the usefulness of making the ISB into an instrument for the reliable co-ordination of the anti-war struggle, and objected to all attempts to extend the Bureau's sphere of influence. Conscious of being 'the great power of the International', the SPD pursued a barely disguised policy of tutelage in its dealings with the brother-parties of other countries and also with the ISB.

The Germans and Austrians were most sceptical concerning the International's ability to find an answer to the changing aspects of diplomatic affairs whose solution depended on the moves and decisions of the governments involved. They regarded co-ordinated international socialist action as impossible to achieve, or even as dangerous. This frame of mind goes some way towards explaining the reluctance of the SPD leaders to appeal to the ISB in diplomatic conflicts, and their refusal to consider the requirements formulated by the delegates of the other parties. Molkenbuhr, in his diary, showed his disapproval after the October 1908 meeting and accused the ISB of not confining itself to 'workers' policy' and of being involved 'in major questions of foreign policy', with the result that it produced nothing but 'pompous statements'.[15]

A remark in a letter which Victor Adler wrote to Bebel on 7 August 1911, at the height of the Morocco crisis, provides a further illustration of this attitude. He says on the question of a possible session in Brussels to discuss the Morocco crisis:

All in all I am instinctively inclined to view the Int. S. Bureau's activity in the diplomatic field with some misgivings. One always feels that one is talking about things of which one is ignorant and exerting an influence which one has not got. If we, as the Bureau, can do no more than any mass meeting can do, namely protest, then we had better leave that to the masses themselves.[16]

---

[15] Molkenbuhr's diary, entry of 14 Oct. 1908, Hermann Molkenbuhr Nachlaß (Bibliothek u. Archiv des Parteivorstands der SPD, Bonn).
[16] *Victor Adler Briefwechsel*, 538.

Diametrically opposed to this attitude was the confidence of
the leading French socialists, Jaurès and Vaillant in particular.
In the years between 1907 and 1914 Jaurès became convinced
that the international organization of socialism had finally
emerged from chaos and become a real force. After the Congress of Stuttgart he said confidently: 'Until now the International has groped its way using its time and effort to organize
itself; now that it is organized it can and must act.' Was this
assessment of the growing powers of the International as a
factor for peace an optimistic exaggeration or 'socialist bragging'?
In the course of his controversy with the antagonistic press
Jaurès himself raised this question, and his answer was unequivocal. His constant references to the International, reflecting
his faith in its influence and its powers, were not mere
rhetoric.

According to Jaurès, socialism, in spite of its weaknesses and
its vacillations, was finally bound to come; it was deeply rooted
and had a definite aim. In the future socialism would have an
international policy and there would be an international institution capable of implementing it: the ISB.[17] The activities of
the French members of the ISB prove the point. Édouard
Vaillant stood out as one of the most active delegates: to any
sign of a threat of war he reacted with remarkable speed.[18]
Whenever there was a conflict, whenever there was any diplomatic tension, he informed the ISB of his fears and sought to
warn the socialist world. His proposals, his constant calls for
action, his prognoses met with incomprehension and even
hostility on the part of the Austrians. During the annexation
crisis Victor Adler commented angrily that 'you can see from
the *Arbeiter-Zeitung* that we Austrians are doing our duty in the

[17] See G. Haupt, 'Jaurès et l'Internationale', *Actes du colloque Jaurès et la Nation*
(Toulouse, published by the Faculté des Lettres et Sciences humaines de Toulouse,
1965), 38 ff.
[18] Here as elsewhere use is made of the extensive unpublished correspondence
between Vaillant and the ISB Secretariat. On Vaillant and the International, see
also Maurice Dommanget's biography, *Édouard Vaillant, un grand socialiste* (Paris, La
Table Ronde, 1956), 220–48.

Balkan affair'.[19] As for the executive committee of the German party, it dismissed the French moves as hasty or mistaken. For example, during the Casablanca crisis of November 1908, Vaillant advocated a joint Franco-German demonstration on Prussian soil after the fashion of the Anglo-German campaign against naval armaments which took place in London in the presence of German socialist delegates in September of the same year. In the name of the executive committee Hermann Müller opposed this suggestion on the grounds that such a demonstration would not have the desired impact. In his opinion it was less important to copy the Anglo-German exchange of delegates there and then than to see to what extent such an exercise could usefully become a precedent.[20] Müller's reply did not display the scepticism that had previously characterized the executive committee's attitude towards pacifist action; his tone and reasoning already reflected the new trend that was developing among the leaders of the SPD, who shed their reserve and thereafter admitted the necessity of becoming involved in the pacifist struggle.

In this connection, the German historian Ursula Ratz has observed that 'one of the motivating elements [of SPD policy] was the feeling of sharing in the responsibility for the development and future existence of bourgeois society', intensified by 'a fear that out of the apocalypse of war might come a false revolution'. From 1908 onwards, the SPD executive committee's pacifist moves did not lead to any 'political reorientation', 'they were rather a sign of resignation and of a feeling that the constantly growing threat of war must be faced'.[21] The party's actions were based on a defensive strategy whose purpose was to wear down capitalism, and which had to be confined to pacifist terms so as not to frighten the bourgeoisie,[22] because the interests of the proletariat and those sections of the

[19] Letter of Victor Adler, 22 Dec. 1908, ISB archives.
[20] Hermann Müller to Camille Huysmans, Berlin, 12 Nov. 1908, ISB archives.
[21] See U. Ratz, art. cit. 221.
[22] See Hans-Christoph Schröder, in *Archiv für Sozialgeschichte* (1966–7, vols. vi–vii), 618.

middle classes that were menaced by the arms race coincided temporarily and thus made co-operation possible. So, the Germans advocated the classic forms of opposition that could provide a basis for joint action by bringing large sections of the middle classes and the lower middle classes on to the side of organized labour.

Because of the view advanced by Kautsky that the influence of public opinion could play a vital role in making war unpopular and in preventing the development of a war psychosis,[23] prominence was given to propaganda. The party's propaganda themes were so many variations on the official view of the executive committee that: 'It will be too late to resist once war has broken out. *What is vital is to avoid a spirit of belligerence spreading among the masses.* Because modern war can hardly happen without the agreement of the masses and if it does happen the rulers have everything to fear from its deadly consequences.'[24] The proper field of anti-war activity therefore was the press and Parliament. Kautsky found a happy mean between the traditional themes and the new pacifist ideas in a magic formula: disarmament connected with an eventual agreement between the great powers; henceforth the SPD vouchsafed him real chances of success. The slogans about socialism being synonymous with peace and capitalism synonymous with war remained part of the propaganda arsenal. But whereas the Radicals offered the alternative of imperialism or socialism, the executive committee offered the alternative of disarmament or world war: a choice upon which Kautsky set the seal of Marxist orthodoxy. As he saw it, the only way of avoiding an eventual conflagration was to set up a United States of Europe, a 'gathering of states with a European civilization in a union that will pursue a common commercial policy, possess a parliament, a government and an army'.[25]

[23] See e.g. K. Kautsky, 'Der zweite Parteitag in Jena', *NZ* xxix. 2 (Sept. 1911), 873.

[24] *Die Internationale für den Frieden. Als Materialien gedruckt* (Berlin, 1911) (Bibliothek und Archiv des Parteivorstands der SPD, Bonn).

[25] U. Ratz, art. cit. 202–4.

Such a vision was not new to the French socialists. But the tactics to be used in order to reach this goal were thought out by the two countries in fundamentally different ways. Apparently the resolution adopted in Copenhagen codified the common credo that 'organized socialist labour was the sole guarantor of universal peace'. The French interpreted this phrase as demanding action: the masses must be mobilized and the methods of militant labour used to combat the threat of war. To the SPD executive committee the sentence affirmed a principle that did not correspond to reality.

'The inevitable efforts of the proletariat to prevent war', Pannekoek said, 'have so far been remarkable above all for their inevitable absence.' It was in this ironical tone that Kautsky replied to the representatives of his party's left wing, who denounced the illusions of the pacifist approach as forming part of the strategy of integration and advocated an offensive anti-imperialist strategy.

The purpose of the anti-imperialist struggle is not to slow down the growth of imperialism but to mobilize the masses against it . . . to mobilize the organised might of the masses that will conquer capitalism.[26]

The disarmament issue was the point of departure for a bitter controversy conducted with great passion before a small audience by the leftist minorities. Pannekoek himself summed up the facts as follows:

For . . . the *Neue Zeit* [run by Kautsky], the doctrine of Marx means *passive waiting* and that all revolutionary *activity* is nothing but unscientific anarchism.
. . . While the old Radicals continually repeated the phrase 'The governments do not dare to begin war for fear of the proletariat, for war means social revolution', the revolutionary Left emphasizes the fact that the proletariat cannot prevent war by standing firm but only by energetic, active aggression.
For this purpose as soon as danger of war appears and nationalistic demonstrations in favour of war begin to be made, the working

[26] K. Kautsky, 'Die neue Taktik', *NZ* xxx. 2 (1912), 663. Quoted in Serge Bricianer, *Pannekoek et les conseils ouvriers* (Paris, EDI, 1969), 118.

men must fill the streets in their masses and chase away the ring leaders. If the danger becomes more threatening, the demonstrations must become more energetic.' Sooner or later there will be an open, bitter struggle.[27]

This discussion which was sparked off by the Morocco crisis of 1911 did not, however, go beyond the frontiers of Germany nor beyond the framework of a doctrinal debate. On the other hand, the conflict between the German and French socialists became more bitter after the Agadir crisis. Though it was still 'behind the scenes', it had obvious consequences: as a result the ISB was unable to fulfil its role as co-ordinator of the anti-war campaign and in these moments of tension proved incapable of effective action. Let us briefly recapitulate the development of the differences within the ISB.

Because of the rising tension caused by the diplomatic conflict between the Spanish and the French governments over Morocco, the CAP (*Commission Administrative Permanente de la SFIO*) met on 20 June 1911 to examine 'the effects which French and Spanish intervention might have on the two countries'. Anxious to be prepared for any eventuality and 'wishing, in accordance with the directives of the International Congresses, to take all measures that might help to prevent any conflict', the CAP decided to get in touch with the secretariat of the Socialist Party of Spain so that they might jointly take the necessary steps. In the event of a further deterioration of the situation the CAP suggested, for example, a conference of the delegates of the two countries to the ISB and of their party secretaries.[28] It was the famous 'leap of the *Panther* to Agadir' that made the French socialist leaders aware of the threat. Jaurès set out his country's dilemma in *L'Humanité* on 2 July:

Either we join in the partition of Morocco with all the powers who feel so inclined, with Spain, Germany and others, and thereby

[27] A. Pannekoek, 'The Great European War and Socialism', *International Socialist Review* (Oct. 1914), 201–2.
[28] Letter from the *Conseil national* of the SFIO to the secretary of the Socialist Party of Spain, 25 June 1911 (copy in the ISB archives); and Vaillant to Huysmans, 23 June 1911 (ibid.).

create a permanent threat to Germany and to peace, or we abandon *publicly* without *arrière-pensée* our present criminal and short-sighted policy and really return to the Algeciras agreement which we were the first to violate.

The French socialists decided in favour of the second alternative, and two days later Vaillant and Jaurès questioned the Government about the situation in Morocco. The secretary of the ISB, Camille Huysmans, was another to appreciate that 'Germany's sudden decision to send a gunboat to Morocco further increased the tension between the states concerned'.[29] He promptly advised the ISB Executive Committee to call the representatives of the countries involved to a meeting in Paris. But Vandervelde was of the opinion that there was no 'great urgency' about any such initiative.[30] The SFIO did not share this view. On 4 July the CAP urgently requested the ISB to call together the delegates of the socialist parties of Germany, France, Spain, and Great Britain to decide upon the attitude to be adopted in so serious a situation. Two days later the ISB secretariat invited the delegates of all the socialist parties to comment on this request.[31] Their views differed. The German delegate, Molkenbuhr, opposed the French initiative on the grounds that the Morocco crisis did not justify bringing delegates together. In his reply, giving his personal opinion, he said that he saw no particular danger signals in the international situation; the Morocco issue was merely a diversionary manœuvre on the part of the German Government, a means 'by which those who govern us wish to divert general attention from the domestic situation and create the right mood for the Reichstag elections'. He said that the German Government would go no further in the Morocco question 'for fear of harming the interests of the great capitalists who have sound judgement and will say "stop"

[29] Telegram of 1 July 1911 from Huysmans to Émile Vandervelde at Château Mariemont, ISB archives.
[30] Vandervelde's telegraphic reply, ibid.
[31] All the replies were reproduced in a circular of the ISB Executive Committee of 14 July 1911 (5 duplicated pages). The document was published in full in the appendix to the *Protokoll über die Verhandlungen des Parteitages der SPD, abgehalten in Jena vom 10. bis 16. September 1911* (Berlin, 1911), 471–3.

before it is too late'.[32] Molkenbuhr's view, which the German
party made its own, was put into words by Bebel: 'The turn
which the Morocco affair has taken lately does not seem to me
to make an ISB meeting advisable for the time being.' Therefore
the ISB should 'wait before convening a meeting and keep its
powder dry'.[33] Bebel's attitude was decisive and the ISB secretariat abandoned the idea of a meeting. All these exchanges
necessarily remained confidential. For the world at large, and
even for the militants as a whole, the ISB Executive Committee's
display of determination disguised its temporizing attitude.

In *Vorwärts* on 7 July, Jaurès demanded energetic action on
the part of the European proletariat.[34] A few days later
L'Humanité published a CAP resolution to the effect that the
SFIO was ready to implement the resolution of the last International Congress. The SPD party executive replied in *Vorwärts* that the German party greatly appreciated its French
comrades' initiative: 'Morocco is worth the bones of neither
the French nor the German workers!' The German party
leadership adopted no definite line. It allowed events to happen
and had difficulty in deciding where it stood. Its attitude
changed with the changing situation. The vacillating German
behaviour, which had a confusing effect within the international
framework, was in fact consonant with a 'national logic'.
Behind the apparent calm there was often complete helplessness
in the face of events. The SPD's anxiety only started when
Germany was affected.[35]

---

[32] For the text of this letter, cf. *Protokoll über die Verhandlungen des Parteitages der SPD, abgehalten in Jena vom 10. bis 16. September 1911* (Berlin, 1911), 472. See also Schorske, 198–200.

[33] Letter from Zürich, 12 July 1912, *Protokoll (Jena)*, 473.

[34] Jaurès's article 'Sang-froid et danger' was published by both *Vorwärts* and *L'Humanité*.

[35] One must also take into account the SPD wait-and-see policy: 'The Executive Committee of the German Social-Democratic Party considered that the German representatives' participation in the ISB meeting would be inopportune because of the impending Reichstag elections. The Committee believed that an active intervention against the policy in Morocco would make the Party look un-patriotic in the eyes of its constituents' (F. Klein, ed., *Deutschland im ersten Weltkrieg*, vol. i, 188).

An incident which occurred in late July 1911 is revealing in this respect. On 21 July, when the Franco-German negotiations threatened to break down and Britain's attitude was becoming critical, Molkenbuhr called on Bebel who was at Scheveningen in Holland to tell him that the party executive '. . . had heard from an absolutely reliable source in Britain that the British Cabinet was adopting a most unfriendly attitude towards Germany over the Morocco question and considered serious action against Germany'.[36] They agreed that Bebel should inform the ISB accordingly. In a laconic letter he asked Huysmans to 'be on the alert' and to make preparations for a possible plenary session of the Bureau and a great international rally in Brussels. However, Bebel protected his rear by adding that these measures should only be taken 'if the crisis became worse'.[37] Three days later, first the secretary of the Social Democratic Federation and then the secretary of the Labour Party asked for the ISB to be convened. The request met with opposition from Bebel.[38] Why? Because meanwhile 'the situation had again become peaceful' and Bebel was convinced that France would not allow herself to be dragged into a war against Germany for the sake of Britain. The French delegates on the other hand, believed that the situation was once more deteriorating and supported the initiative of the British socialists. The ISB Executive Committee did not know what to do. Finally it was the Austrian delegate who decided. On 28 July Huysmans sent a telegram to Victor Adler: 'Do you not think that in the present circumstances, in spite of the contrary opinion of our German friends, the Bureau must meet? Our decision depends on yours.'[39]

As Victor Adler supported the Germans on the excuse that

[36] Light is shed on the background of this venture in a statement by the German Party Executive at the Jena Party Congress. Cf. *Protokoll (Jena)*, 469.

[37] Bebel to Huysmans, 23 July 1911, ISB archives. Huysmans's letters to Bebel on the Morocco crisis are in the Bebel archives at the Amsterdam IISG Cf. also Bebel to Adler, in *Victor Adler Briefwechsel*, 539 ff. [38] ISB archives.

[39] A copy of this telegram, the original of which is in the Victor Adler Nachlaß (Vienna, Arbeiterkammer), is in the ISB archives. Cf. also Adler to Bebel, 7 Aug. 1911, in *Victor Adler Briefwechsel*, 537.

the 'meeting would come too late or too soon', it was postponed once more.[40] Adler gave his real reason in a letter to Bebel to whom he said that

. . . there must be no meeting if you do not want one; particularly in the present situation this would be undesirable and might give the false impression that it is necessary to force the Germans to act in the name of internationalism. The meeting would anyhow be totally useless. What can be done has been done in full measure by the meetings in Berlin and Paris and it is impossible to see what would be gained if Belgians, Austrians, and other savage peoples say what everybody knows, that they are opposed to war. It would be different if one wanted to or could decide on joint *action*. But there is no cause to do so because every sensible human being knows that the Morocco question could not and would not possibly lead to war.[41]

Bebel was in complete agreement with this viewpoint. He succeeded in persuading Huysmans, who visited him at Scheveningen on 30 July, 'that the Bureau must not waste its powder on sparrows' and that he should abandon the idea of a meeting.[42] However, Bebel agreed to send SPD representatives to a Franco-German gathering in Paris. This international rally in protest against the Morocco threat, organized by the CGT (*Confédération Générale du Travail*), took place on 4 August 1911. The German delegation consisted of Molkenbuhr, Ledebour, and trade union leaders.[43]

The indecisiveness of the SPD, its slowness to react, was strongly criticized by the Left who thought that the party executive had proved incapable of grappling with its task in the anti-imperialist struggle. On 24 July 1911 Rosa Luxemburg published in the *Leipziger Volkszeitung* the exchange of letters between Molkenbuhr and Huysmans and severely condemned the party executive's temporizing tactics.[44] The party executive

---

[40] Telegram from Victor Adler to Huysmans, ISB archives.
[41] Adler to Bebel, letter quoted above, n. 39.
[42] Huysmans to Renaudel, 2 Aug. 1911, ISB archives.
[43] Cf. *La Bataille syndicaliste* (5 Aug. 1911).
[44] Cf. Rosa Luxemburg, 'Um Marokko. Unser Marokko-Flugblatt', in *Ausgewählte Reden und Schriften* (Berlin, 1951, vol. ii), 377 ff.; Drachkovitch, 279–81; Schorske, 200–4; R. Hostetter, art. cit. (Pt. II, *Rivista storica del socialismo*, 20 (1963), 437–40).

behaved very clumsily in the ensuing discussion and the silence of Molkenbuhr, who did not dare to reply, was taken by the public as a confession of guilt. Bebel, indignant at Rosa Luxemburg's criticism ('Luxemburg has behaved most disgracefully on this occasion,' he wrote to Adler), despaired at the stupidity of the party executive and was particularly critical of Molkenbuhr whom he described as a 'slow coach'. On 26 August he wrote to Kautsky:

Regrettably the party executive, and Molkenbuhr in particular, have proved completely inadequate in this controversy. I am in a horrible situation; I share in the responsibility and am condemned to silence even though I myself would dearly like to turn against the executive. If things continue like this in the new era I shall resign my office.[45]

But he did not carry out his threat, and at the party congress at Jena in September 1911, at which the discussion on the SPD's behaviour in the Morocco crisis was continued, he expressed himself in complete agreement with the party executive's policy in order to keep up the pretence of unity. The Left submitted two resolutions criticizing the behaviour of the party leadership. In their outbursts Ledebour and Clara Zetkin insinuated that by refusing to act in July the German party had disappointed the International. The party executive, seriously hurt by this criticism, reacted violently. After launching an attack on Rosa Luxemburg's 'indiscretion', Bebel went all out to defend his party's behaviour and said indignantly: 'If there is a nation [national section]—I am saying this without wishing to offend anyone—that has always done its damnedest as regards the International, it is the German party.'[46] After a prolonged struggle the SPD executive emerged victorious from the party congress in Jena and continued to pursue its policy of caution. Nevertheless street demonstrations were organized, particularly as dissatisfaction with its stand spread beyond the

[45] Kautsky archives, D III. No. 184. IISG, Amsterdam.
[46] *Protokoll (Jena)*, 216. In his speech Bebel gave his variant of the suggestion which he put to the ISB.

left wing of the party. *Vorwärts* went beyond the cautious
instructions of the party executive and Hilferding demanded
new methods of anti-militarist training, more preparation of
the proletariat, and more effective international campaigns.[47]

In spite of the strengthening of the anti-war movement
which resulted in the impressive demonstrations in Treptow
Park, Berlin,[48] dissatisfaction still prevailed in French socialist
circles.

How are we to explain the equivocal attitude of the SPD
executive? This question preoccupied the SFIO which was
leading an energetic campaign against French foreign policy
and whose reiterated proposals that the ISB should promote
the international class struggle fell upon unreceptive ears on the
German side. There was profound dissatisfaction in their ranks
with the German party; all the more so because the French
Right did not fail to interpret the attitude of the SPD to its
advantage and to exploit it in its polemics. In the Chamber of
Deputies, Lebel quoted a speech which Bebel had made in the
Reichstag and accused him of nationalism and hostility towards
France. These accusations aroused great excitement and the
socialist deputies found it difficult to defend themselves.[49] At

[47] Cf. Rudolf Hilferding, 'Der Parteitag und die auswärtige Politik', *NZ* xxix. 2,
no. 51 (1911), 800.

[48] The slogans of the demonstrations symbolized the respective national parties:
in September and October 1911 French demonstrators demanded insurrection and
a general strike as a means of preventing an armed conflict between the great
powers, while in Treptow Park in Berlin the demonstrators merely asked that every
political and economic expedient should be used to preserve peace and that the
German electorate should make a recommendation to that effect to its candidates
at the next Reichstag elections. Cf. Jacques Rouge, 'L'agitation contre la guerre',
La Revue socialiste (Oct. 1911), 356–60; R. Hostetter, art. cit. (Pt. II), 437. Nevertheless, while the French Party could hardly mobilize 3,000–4,000 workmen to
demonstrate, in Berlin, by the end of August and the beginning of September,
there were characteristic mass demonstrations. According to the police, there
were 50,000–60,000 demonstrators; according to *Vorwärts*, 200,000. Cf. Jemnitz,
66. Only at the end of September did the SFIO and the Fédération de la
Seine CGT agree on joint action: on the 24th, they organized a mass demonstration at the Aéro-Parc in Paris. '. . . Like their German brothers, they told their
government that they want peace', commented the leading article in *L'Humanité*
(25 Sept. 1911).

[49] Bebel's *démenti* was published in *Cri du Peuple* (11 Nov. 1911). The French
Right also seized upon the speech Bebel had delivered at the Jena Congress to

the opening of the Jena SPD congress, the ISB—which had been paralysed for the two previous months, as a result of the differences between the French and German delegates, to the point of being reduced to passing on the mail—succeeded both in preventing a public clash between its two main sections and in getting the International out of its quandary.

From outside socialist circles, an unforeseen initiative raised the tension to its climax, thus necessitating urgent action. So, without any preparation the ISB was involved in the maze of secret diplomacy.

A Belgian Cabinet Minister on 11 September 1911 gave Vandervelde a piece of information emanating from the Belgian ambassador in Berlin concerning the German Government's uneasiness at a campaign of aggression which was being waged by some French politico-financial circles close to *Le Temps* and which risked aggravating the situation.[50]

The same Belgian minister, whose identity Vandervelde did not reveal, returned anxious from a visit to Paris, with the impression that France 'while recognizing the principle of the open door intends to lay claims on all profitable rail, mining and similar concessions, etc.', a factor which was likely to lead to a miscarriage of any negotiations with the German Government. He thought that 'if the negotiations fail or if relations are broken off the situation will really become dangerous and there will have to be an all out anti-war effort'.[51]

The ISB Executive, bewildered, had to act speedily. What mattered first was to inform the parties concerned and to contrast the SPD's 'patriotism' with the SFIO's 'anti-patriotism'. The French socialists—in a difficult position—found themselves constrained to defend Bebel. Cf. *L'Humanité* (16 and 20 Sept. 1911).

[50] Vandervelde to Dubreuilh, 12 Sept. 1911; telegraphic answer by Dubreuilh, ISB archives.

[51] Letter (copy) by Vandervelde which reached Huysmans on 16 Sept. (morning); Vandervelde specifies: 'As for the conversation between K. W. and C[aillaux], diplomatic secrecy is strictly kept.' It was only one day later that the correspondent of Vandervelde was disclosed as a Belgian minister of the Civil Cabinet. (Cf. confidential letter from Huysmans to Bebel, 17 Sept. 1911, ISB archives.)

investigate whether the German Government, which in fact knew of the Belgian minister's indiscretions,[52] was, or was not, misusing the ISB for its own ends. In a private letter to Dubreuilh, the SFIO secretary, concerning recent interfering elements, Vandervelde asked that the CAP should convene urgently so that it could be given a confidential communication and join 'in the search for means to ensure the implementation of the resolutions of Stuttgart and Copenhagen'.[53] The telegraphic answer was a warm approval on this decision.

The CAP convened on 14 September in the presence of Camille Huysmans who gave them a report of the news collected from diplomatic sources.

On the other hand, Albert Thomas went and met Caillaux who confirmed Vandervelde's assertions.

'Our comrade, Deputy Albert Thomas (Paris) has had an interview with the French Prime Minister who has advised him confidentially that the majority of the French Cabinet would stand firm in case of conflict, whereas he, Caillaux, and the minister of War, Messimy, wanted peace: An attitude which the press—under the inspiration of the Ministry of Foreign Affairs—had familiarized the public with for a long time.

Thus the news from Paris confirmed the news from Berlin.[54]

The fear of a strengthening of the hard line within the French government was stressed.[55] It was too heavy a responsibility for the national council of the SFIO to face this alone: the socialists' participation in secret diplomacy could be considered as a serious infringement of the very principles which condemned such diplomacy. So, after a proper examination, there began a debate on the heart of the matter: the CAP, alarmed, stuck to its stand, convinced as it was that the crisis had never been so serious and that, since 1870, war had never come so close. The resolution to which Huysmans acquiesced advocated firmly that the ISB should convene

---

[52] Same letter from Huysmans to Bebel (ISB archives).
[53] Vandervelde to Dubreuilh, 12 Sept. 1911 (ibid.).
[54] Huysmans to Bebel, 17 Sept. 1912 (ibid.).
[55] Letter by Vandervelde which reached Huysmans on 16 Sept. (ibid.).

immediately and that an international anti-war protest should be issued. The SFIO for its part, in a radically worded manifesto, undertook to fight a possible conflagration with all means, even insurrection. 'The unanimous answer of the working classes of all countries to the crime of the governments must be a revolutionary rising so as to preserve international peace.'[56]

At the same time, before leaving for France, Huysmans dealt with the SPD. As early as 12 September, he had sent the following telegram to Bebel at the party congress in Jena: 'Have reasons to think situation deteriorating. Do you agree that meeting of Bureau or of French British German delegates advisable. If yes suggest Saturday 16 [September].'[57] But this telegram never reached its destination: it was kept back by the Jena post office authorities.[58]

When he received no answer, Huysmans dispatched an identical message to Vandersmissen, the Belgian delegate at the Jena Congress.[59] Neither Bebel nor Adler nor the Executive Committee could grasp the motives for this agitation,[60] especially as on 14 September Vandervelde, in a letter to Bebel, insisted on the need to alert the French socialists, but said at the same time that 'since Monday the apprehensions which caused our telegram have been partly dispelled:'[61] according to him, this meant that the ISB meeting was no longer a matter of emergency.

On 17 September, Huysmans sent an explanatory letter to the leader of the German party; in an attempt to humour him he said:

[56] For the texts which were adopted at the meeting, cf. *L'Humanité* (14 and 15 Sept. 1911).

[57] ISB archives.

[58] Ibid. See also the report of the Jena Congress. Bebel protested vehemently in the Reichstag against such scandalous proceedings. It is likely that the German Government cleared itself in the eyes of the ISB by putting the blame on some underling.

[59] ISB archives.

[60] 'Bebel has not received anything. We do not understand why situation worsened. Expecting news.' The telegram was signed by Adler, Bebel, Vandersmissen, and Bracke (ibid.).

[61] Vandervelde to Bebel, 14 Sept. 1911 (in Jena), ibid.

The centre of gravity of the problem lies more in France than in Germany, and this is why it is our duty to exert our influence upon the French socialists. It is for this reason that I went to Paris where I said that I would write to you personally. As a result, the Party has decided to organize 20 or 30 meetings in the great cities, to placard a proclamation, and the National Council has raised formally the issue of an immediate convening of the Bureau, which, according to the resolution passed at the Copenhagen Congress, we cannot refuse.[62]

The proposal to call a meeting was reluctantly accepted by the SPD Executive leaders;[63] they could not reject the suggestion because the Copenhagen resolution gave the affiliated parties the right to convene the Bureau whenever they considered it necessary. Bebel on his part replied immediately to Huysmans's letter: 'At last I see clearly and am able to understand why you insist on calling a meeting. And now, I have changed my mind. I shall come to the meeting . . .'[64]

The ISB convened in plenary sessions on 23 and 24 September in Zürich. The central theme on the agenda was the Moroccan crisis which gave rise to yet another Franco-German confrontation: Bebel sought to reconfirm the Copenhagen resolution, whereas the motion submitted by Vaillant provoked an animated discussion on the expediency of the general strike[65]—

[62] Huysmans to Bebel, 17 Sept. 1911; the letter also reached Victor Adler (cf. copy in Victor Adler Nachlaß) and Ramsay MacDonald on 18 Sept., ISB archives. In a letter to Bebel of 18 Sept., Huysmans added: 'France wants the Bureau to be convened. According to the regulations it is impossible to refuse. Personally, I cannot discuss it. As someone said in Jena, I am paid to apply the resolutions.' (ISB archives.)

[63] On 18 Sept., Hermann Müller wrote in the name of the SPD executive that they would stand by the conclusions Vandervelde had expressed in his letter of 14 Sept. and according to which convening the Bureau was no longer a case of emergency (ISB archives).

[64] Bebel to Huysmans, 19 Sept. 1911, ibid.

[65] Vaillant had produced the following motion: 'The ISB wishes to remind each national section and especially those of the countries which are directly concerned today—Germany, England, Spain, France—of the resolutions against war which have been passed at their national congresses and at the international congresses of Stuttgart and Copenhagen.

It [the ISB] relies upon them [the sections], upon individual as well as joint action, to prevent and to avert war; and in case war cannot be avoided, to paralyse all military activities on each side of the borders.' (ISB archives, records on Morocco.)

a discussion which rapidly led to a 'mental overhaul' of the International's preparedness for action.[66] It ended once more with a compromise which was to invite the socialist parties to intensify their protest movement against the colonial partitions that were then taking place. The ISB stated that every effort must be made 'to strengthen the anti-war movement'.[67]

One point remains obscure. Why was the meeting, in contrast to the ten previous ones, held *in camera*?

The 'indiscretion' said to have been committed by Rosa Luxemburg was used as a pretext to keep the debates private. But this excuse is inadequate. Plekhanov's notes of that session suggest that the SPD Executive's complaint about Luxemburg's 'disloyalty' was only briefly discussed. The likely explanation is that while some of the International's leaders saw the outcome of the Zürich meeting as a victory, others had no praise for a dangerous deviation which implied the use of secret diplomacy. Several facts corroborate this hypothesis. From the notes taken by Plekhanov, it appears that the urgency of the meeting was motivated by the necessity of passing on to the delegates the files on the diplomatic dealings with the ISB during the month of September. That the debates

---

[66] The discussion on the Vaillant draft—the second part of which was quickly deleted so that all would agree on the decision—revealed that it was impossible to find an effective definition of collective action. Between the pessimists and the optimists there were so many rifts. The former, and Bebel among them, could only agree to a declaration of impotence. Adler was less categorical: 'When Bebel mentions our impotence, he merely states a fact: our incapacity to go beyond pure agitation.' As for Molkenbuhr, he was rather doubtful about the possibility of taking action after the declaration of war, and Quelch agreed with him: 'When war is declared, it will be too late to take any measures but there is much to do before it comes to this point.' This was also the attitude of Troelstra who, objecting to the defeatist way in which his first intervention had been interpreted, came to the conclusion that: 'We can do something already. See, for instance, the diplomat's dealings ministers and Vandervelde.' (Cf. Plekhanov's notes at the ISB meeting, Arkhiv Doma Plekhanova, Leningrad.) Rosa Luxemburg and Vaillant were in the ranks of those who were willing to believe in the efficiency of the International even after a declaration of war. Thus Vaillant believed that an eventual rising in France might spread. But amidst an assembly which did not dare to assume for itself more than limited powers, both stood apart.

[67] See the brief report of the meeting and the text of the resolution in the *Periodical Bulletin of the ISB* iii. 8 (1912), 127–9.

were held *in camera* may have favoured a frank exchange of ideas and views which under any other circumstance would not have been possible.[68] On the other hand, in spite of these precautions, a new indiscretion was committed at the end of October concerning the contacts established by the ISB in mid September which formed the subject of the meeting. The socialist leader Troelstra said in the Dutch Lower House during the debate on the Dutch military law, that 'various members of governments have managed to find the address of the International Socialist Bureau in their anxiety to avert the threat of war'. One government had appealed to an intermediary, another had addressed itself directly to the ISB, asking it to join in the diplomatic bargaining intended to iron out the Morocco conflict.[69] Persistent rumours mentioned France and Germany. The German Government hastened to issue a *démenti*. The Brussels *Le Peuple*, regarded as the semi-official organ of the ISB, discreetly confirmed Troelstra's assertions.[70] The revolutionary syndicalists in France denounced the International's involvement in secret diplomacy as scandal-mongering.[71] But the secrecy of the discussions of the Zürich meeting was never betrayed and the Bureau issued no official communiqué to confirm or deny the rumours which originated in the Dutch Parliament and were spread by *Het Volk* and the *Frankfurter Zeitung*.

On 4 November France and Germany concluded their agreement on Morocco.[72] For the moment the crisis proved less

---

[68] Cf. Arkhiv Doma Plekhanova, Leningrad.

[69] See *Vorwärts* (22 Oct. 1911).

[70] See the critical comment in *LZ*, no. 255, 5 (3 Nov. 1911), 1.

[71] Charles Rupert, 'La force qui maintient la paix', *La Bataille syndicaliste* (26-7 and 30 Oct. 1911). Rupert claimed that he knew from well-informed sources that 'some members of the Government' had called for the Socialist International's help to preserve peace, and that the members of the ISB had had a decisive influence on the French Cabinet's attitude.
For a cryptic hint of the International's involvement in the Moroccan negotiations, see 'La voix de l'Internationale', *La Guerre sociale* (26 June 1912).

[72] During the parliamentary debates from the Moroccan treaty in December 1911, the SFIO deputies emphasized the positive aspect of the agreement. They saw it as a justification of their faith in international arbitration. See Carlo Pinzani's detailed analysis, in *Jurés, l'Internazionale e la guerra* (Bari, La Terza, 1970), 221-6.

threatening to the balance of power in Europe than the French socialists had believed. This explains why in the last resort the solution of the Morocco crisis considerably increased the prestige of the German socialists. Their prognoses had come true, whereas in the eyes of many of the leaders of the International the French delegates to the ISB had once more proved their lack of sang-froid. And yet the Italian colonial war in Tripolitania which followed the Morocco crisis in the autumn of 1911 was a typical instance of imperialist trends and antagonisms. All this was not really understood by the International.

3　The Wasps' Nest in the Balkans

AFTER three months of indecision and hesitation the clumsy and complicated mechanism of the International was put into motion by the resolution which the Bureau adopted in Zürich. The workers' anti-war protest movement had begun too late to be effective during the Morocco crisis, but it was in time to oppose Italy's sudden aggression in Tripolitania.[1] The ISB knew of the intentions of the Italian government forty-eight hours before the event. It was Vandervelde who divulged that while the ISB in Zürich 'was in the final stages of its deliberations, a telegram from a reliable source had informed him that the Italian government had decided to send an ultimatum to Turkey and to start war immediately afterwards'.[2] This news drove the Bureau to adopt a resolution stating that it was 'necessary and urgent [for the Bureau] to take charge of the direction of our anti-war movement'.

How was this to be done and by what means? Although this question remained open, the ISB Executive Committee believed that it had been given a mandate to take the steps demanded by the situation. It therefore did not hesitate to describe the Italian aggression as 'an act of brigandage . . . fraught with danger and new conflicts' and to suggest a plan of action. On

---

[1] The CGT, for example, on 1 Oct. 1911 urgently convened in Paris a national conference of its organizations. 'Faced with the possibility that war might break out at any moment and in view of the terrible consequences that a Turko-Italian war might have for Europe', the conference adopted a resolution declaring that: 'The decisions of the trades union congresses on the behaviour of the working class in case of war shall be implemented as soon as war is declared.' The importance of this resolution lies in the fact that the response to any declaration of war was to be a 'revolutionary general strike'.

[2] Cf. Émile Vandervelde, 'La guerre italo-turque et l'Internationale', *La Revue socialiste* (1911), 484. (Speech delivered in Paris, 5 Nov. 1911.)

7 October the draft of a confidential circular was sent to the delegates to the Bureau.[3] This document contained a clear and coherent statement of the position adopted by the ISB. Starting from the assumption that it was the duty of the International to 'prevent conflicts or to bring about their early termination, to the extent that the forces at the disposal of the proletariat allowed', and that the International's decisions could be interpreted in one way only, it called for the implementation of the provisions of the resolution of Copenhagen. Two major and immediate objectives were thus defined: (1) to make every effort to bring armed conflict to an end, or at least to ensure that it remained localized and did not spread to the Balkans; (2) 'to oppose all schemes, whatever their nature or origin, designed to profit from the expedition against Tripoli by pursuing a policy that could lead to a clash in the Balkans'.

The document said unequivocally that the exceptional situation demanded a modification of that part of the resolution that emphasized the action of the parties of the countries involved in the conflict. In the opinion of the Executive Committee the ISB's mandate had been confirmed and it was authorized to intervene directly, particularly if,

. . . as in Turkey, the working class of the countries immediately involved is too weak to be really active or if, as in Italy, it has been content with action that has proved inadequate and, what is worse still, if people have been found in the ranks of the proletariat who support Signor Giolitti's policy.

How should the ISB proceed? It could mobilize the socialists of all countries by calling upon the workers' parties of the great powers, Austria, Germany, France, and Great Britain, to organize an energetic protest movement with press campaigns, manifestos, and questions in parliament. It could also help the socialists of the countries directly concerned, particularly the Italians, to discharge their obligations, as defined in the resolutions of the International; finally it could support the Balkan socialists in their efforts to stop their governments from

---

[3] ISB archives. The circular was sent to all affiliated parties on 12 Oct. 1911.

exploiting the situation and attacking Turkey, so as to put an end to an uncertain *status quo*, even if by their action they threatened to push Europe into the abyss.

This plan of campaign was finally adopted. Put to the test, the International's effectiveness in action showed satisfactory results as well as considerable defects.

Let us first look at the credit side, at the great protest movement among the socialists of central and western Europe.

At the beginning of October 1911, the ISB Executive Committee suggested that international rallies should be organized to protest against the Balkan aggression, and so as 'to give these demonstrations as much publicity as possible', it advised the socialist parties to hold them simultaneously.[4] The suggestion met with the approval of many delegates, although most of them did not share the Executive Committee's view about the extreme seriousness of the situation.[5] Bebel said openly that he was of a different opinion. On 13 October he expressed in a letter the SPD Executive's point of view

. . . At present the Tripolitanian question is of no interest. We are still completely preoccupied by the Morocco affair. Given the pathetic behaviour of Turkey it seems that the question will very soon be settled. At the moment there are no danger signs suggesting major complications in the Balkans.[6]

Immediately before the Reichstag elections the SPD had no desire to participate recklessly in a campaign that criticized the foreign policy of its government which, as a member of the Triple Alliance, was on the side of Italy.

Bebel's reply was at the same time an expression of the profound dislike of Turkey that was widespread among socialists. No sympathy was felt for the victim of the Italian attack. Instead, we find the traditional hostility towards the

---

[4] ISB archives.

[5] The ISB secretariat's confidential circular no. 10 contains the most important of the replies (ISB archives).

[6] The original of this letter appears not to be in the ISB archives. The records of the secretariat's correspondence, preserved by Camille Huysmans, contain extensive extracts in French from this letter, from which the quotation is taken.

'sick man of Europe', the Ottoman Empire, and complete distrust of the Young Turks against whom, as Vandervelde put it,[7] 'the International had the most legitimate grievances'.

The Young Turk revolution in July 1908 had certainly been applauded by Europe's socialists who saw it as an important step forward. It had aroused in them the hope that, thanks to the efforts of its reformers, backward Turkey would become an important factor in the struggle for peace and for the preservation of the *status quo* in the Balkans. 'I have fought and shall continue to fight for the consolidation of the new regime in Turkey,' wrote Rakovsky, one of the most respected socialist leaders in the Balkans, in 1909.[8] The International shared this opinion. On 11 October 1908, the ISB voted for a resolution welcoming the fall of Abdul Hamid's regime because the various peoples of the Ottoman Empire would now be able to determine their own destinies and introduce 'modern liberties', thereby giving the more recent workers' movement a chance to develop. However, the Bureau's support waned when the revolution of the Young Turks changed direction. The reprisals against the nationalities and the young socialist movement—and this in spite of the fact that the movement supported the regime[9]— made the International see that there was reason for concern. 'The Young Turks often surpass even the old regime of Abdul Hamid in criminal brutality', said a report on the situation in Turkey submitted by the socialist parties of Serbia and Bulgaria to the Copenhagen Congress.[10]

The representatives of the various socialist groups in Turkey, who gathered in Salonica in January 1911, demanded 'the support of the International in the struggle of the Ottoman proletariat against reaction'[11] and the ISB secretariat responded to this appeal. The persecutions of socialists in Turkey raised

---

[7] Vandervelde, art. cit. 486.
[8] Cf. G. Haupt and Madeleine Rebérioux, 'Le socialisme et la question coloniale avant 1914: l'attitude de l'Internationale', *Le Mouvement social* 45 (1963), 28 ff.
[9] Cf. G. Haupt, 'Les débuts du mouvement socialiste en Turquie', ibid. 127–8.
[10] Cf. ibid. That is, the Bulgarian leftist socialist party.
[11] ISB archives.

violent protests in the European workers' press which severely criticized the regime of the Young Turks. Jaurès alone supported them. Although alarmed by the developments in Turkey he thought that caution should be exercised in judging the new regime.[12] In his opinion the situation was primarily the result of the fatal policy of the European powers '. . . who motivated by base competitive instincts were unwilling to push through successful reforms in Turkey and who also lacked the necessary intellectual authority to give the country good advice'.

According to Jaurès, it was the duty of European socialism to support the Young Turks' regime because it would be a misfortune for civilization 'if the world of Islam in the form of a new Turkey could not be made to share in the development and progress of modern Europe'. Jaurès admitted that the anti-socialist policy of the Young Turks was disastrous, but maintained that the International must not lose sight of the more important and more general problem of peace. Indeed the consolidation of the new regime in Turkey meant the stabilization of the situation in the East. One thing had been certain for Jaurès since 1908: the East in general and the Balkans in particular had become the focal point of the European powers' struggle for spheres of influence, the centre of constant conflicts that could degenerate into a European war.

I have dealt with Jaurès's attitude in some detail because his views, which were for a long time rejected by the socialists as a whole and even attacked by the Balkan socialists, had a strong influence on the ISB Executive Committee in October 1911. In the face of an aggression that was fraught with consequences for the precarious Balkan equilibrium, Jaurès's view prevailed. The International agreed that its own attitude towards Turkey must be motivated not merely by ethical considerations but by political ones, with the aim of preserving the peace. The Executive Committee set out to persuade the affiliated parties to accept this line and to create a movement

---

[12] For the details, see G. Haupt, 'Jaurès et l'Internationale', in *Actes du colloque Jaurès et la Nation* (Toulouse, 1965), 47–50.

of support for the victim, Turkey. Its language, the arguments in its circulars, showed that there were difficulties to overcome:

We are not among those who have drawn a veil over the mistakes of the government of the Young Turks. The working class in particular has reason to complain of the laws preventing the formation of coalitions, and at Copenhagen all reports emanating from Turkish organizations pointed to the dangerous consequences of this anti-working-class policy.

Nevertheless, the International was anxious 'to prevent conflicts and to terminate them',[13] and therefore to forget for the moment its quarrel with the Young Turks.

This point of view won the day, thanks to the unexpectedly moderate attitude of the Workers' Socialist Federation of Salonica and to the efforts of the leaders of the Young Turks to achieve a reconciliation. As early as October 1911 the executive of the Workers' Socialist Federation of Salonica informed the ISB secretariat that its organization would not attempt to make difficulties for the Turkish government, that it would eschew all hostile demonstrations which might lead to upheavals and 'give Italy a justification for her aggression'; it would wait for the conflict to end 'before drawing up a balance sheet of gains and losses' and before taking the leaders of the Young Turks 'seriously to task'.[14] On the other hand, the president of the Turkish Chamber of Deputies, Ahmed Riza, on 16 October addressed a letter to the president of the International, Vandervelde, appealing to European socialism for assistance.[15] This appeal, which was published by the socialist press, achieved the desired result. The ISB adopted the Executive Committee's proposal of 3 November to call upon 'the workers' organizations

[13] Cf. the circular of 12 Oct. 1911 quoted above (p. 57, n. 3). In the speech he made in Paris on 5 Nov., Vandervelde declared: 'The workers' International has very legitimate grievances against the government of the Young Turks . . . We are not going to forget them and consequently, had we not been faced with such a vile process we should not have given the government of the Young Turks tokens of our sympathy' (Vandervelde, art. cit. 486).

[14] Saul Nahum to Camille Huysmans, 3 Oct. 1911, ISB archives.

[15] The text of the letter was sent on 2 Nov. 1911 as circular no. 12 by the ISB secretariat to all ISB delegates.

of the cities of Europe' to organize 'rallies or demonstrations' to coincide with the 'pilgrimages' of Turkish parliamentarians to these cities.[16]

But above all, the overwhelming majority of delegates to the ISB agreed on the wording of the manifesto[17] which called for international anti-war demonstrations and which reconciled the points of view of Jaurès and of the Balkan socialists. Basically this document saw the Italian attack as a criminal venture

. . . that will prove disastrous, perhaps more disastrous for the victor than for the victim, that threatens to unleash the scourge of a world war and to open up an abyss between Europe and the new Islamic world and that is bound in the last resort to provide the powers with an excuse to make the existing military burdens more oppressive than ever.

At the same time the International expressed the wish

. . . that the Turkish Government by drawing the obvious lesson from the events shall try to redress existing ethnic differences and take note of working class complaints—thereby making an effective contribution towards a *rapprochement* between the Balkan nations until such time as their closer union into a federative organization can take place.

The International's slogan (condemnation of the aggressor and support of the victim, Turkey) and its recommendations to condemn not only Italy's policy but all imperialist policy were by and large accepted by the executives of the socialist parties and the broad mass of organized labour. The big demonstrations that took place on 5 November 1911—the day on which the Italians announced the annexation of Tripoli—in all European capitals in the presence of delegates from the ISB, assumed such dimensions[18] that they gave rise to optimism and to faith in the power of international socialism. In the opinion of its leading personalities the International had passed

[16] Confidential circular by the ISB secretariat of 3 Nov. 1911, ISB archives.

[17] This manifesto was reprinted by the socialist press the world over.

[18] The reports on the international demonstrations of 5 November prepared by the secretaries of the affiliated parties for the ISB, are revealing in this context. (ISB archives, unclassified documents).

the test and proved its ability to oppose war. European socialism put all its energies into this peace offensive and continued
with every means at its disposal to promote the growing pacifist
movement among the workers. The peace offensive was the
central theme of the SPD election campaign late in 1911 and
early in 1912, and the propaganda material[19] distributed
among party members emphasized the need to tell the electorate that:

The anti-war protest is not a platonic peace demonstration, not
merely an expression of sympathy for the victims of the madness of
our rulers. *It is our own affairs, the most urgent affairs of the German
proletariat that are at stake.* All foreign entanglements, however distant
the country, all colonial acquisitions, even if seemingly peaceful, are
today a threat to the peace of Europe, and, for the German people in
particular, they constitute a threat which the growing conflict between British and German capitalism makes ever more dangerous.

The elections of January 1912 ended with a victory for
the SPD which presented itself as the party of peace. But despite
this success within the International the situation did not im-
prove. Its campaign against the Turko-Italian war failed
because of the lack of action by the sections of the countries
directly concerned, above all the Italian and partly also the
Balkan sections. For the former the resolutions of the International remained for a long time a dead letter; in the eyes of
the latter they ridiculed the Bureau's authority.

At the ISB session in Zürich the Italian delegate, Pompeo
Ciotti, had in the name of his party pledged his word to take
action against any militaristic moves by his government.[20]
When in the night of 26/27 September the Italian Government
addressed an ultimatum to Turkey, and forty-eight hours later
declared war, the ISB had no doubt that the socialists of the
peninsula would do their duty. The Italian section was considered one of the International's most important; the socialist
party seemed to have taken a firm foothold in Italy and the

[19] *Die Internationale für den Frieden*, 13. (My italics.)
[20] Vaillant to Huysmans, 3 Nov. 1911, ISB archives.

ideas of its theorists, such as Labriola, had made their mark. In 1905 and particularly in the spring of 1911 the Italian socialist party (ISP) had proved its internationalist attitude and, when the tension between the two countries had reached its peak, its determination to preserve peace by initiating, together with the socialists of Austria-Hungary, a campaign to oppose higher military expenditure and the threat of war.[21] This campaign was not intended merely as a piece of propaganda, limited to a statement of principles, but, as Victor Adler said, allowed 'the parties of the two states that are facing each other in arms, Austria-Hungary and Italy, to discuss concrete points of disagreement and to adopt a concrete political stand on them'.[22] As the crisis subsided the socialist summit meeting planned for Easter 1911 in Rome was postponed. This move, of which the ISB was informed, led the socialist world to think that the Italians were vigilant and determined to act if there was a crisis.

Hence the disappointment at the end of September 1911 when the executive of the ISP, having tried to call a general strike,[23] allowed itself to be bribed by liberal reforms and Giolitti's promise to introduce universal suffrage, and retreated. Under the pressure of growing nationalism its reformist right wing, headed by Bissolati and Bonomi, publicly supported the government's policy and joined the supporters of the Tripolitanian war.[24] This volte-face caused tremendous excitement

[21] Cf. *AZ* (4 Feb. 1911), 3; and the documents preserved in the ISB archives.

[22] Victor Adler to the Executive Committee of the ISB, 13 Mar. 1911, five typewritten pages, ISB archives. For the joint action envisaged by the Austrian and Italian socialist parties, see also Renato Monteleone, 'Iniziative e convegni socialisti italo-austriaci per la pace nel decennio prebellico', *Rivista storica del socialismo* x. 32 (1969), 1–43.

[23] At the ISB meeting on 23/24 Sept., the Italian delegate, Ciotti, declared: 'We have finally decided to have recourse to a general strike. To-morrow there will be meetings taking place all over Italy. Only two deputies in the parliamentary socialist group favour the venture in Tripolitania' (Plekhanov's notes, Arkhiv Doma Plekhanova, Leningrad).

[24] Details are found in Gaetano Arfe's study, 'Les socialistes italiens et la question coloniale', *Le Mouvement social* 45 (1963), 82–5; on the frame of mind then prevailing in Italy, see Ronald S. Cunsolo, 'Libya, Italian Nationalism and the Revolt against Giolitti', *Journal of Modern History* xxxvii. 2 (1965), 171–85.

in both the Italian workers' movement and the International. The delegate of the Workers' Socialist Federation of Salonica immediately informed the ISB secretariat of the 'confusion created by the pitiful failure of the socialist party' and drew its attention to the fact 'that it could be dangerous for the International if such non-compliance with jointly adopted resolutions remained uncensored'.[25] The Executive Committee voiced censure without, however, going to the extreme. In the confidential circular of 12 October it told the Italian socialists firmly 'that the proletariat cannot have two views, neither can it pursue two policies. Its anti-war activity must be *unanimous*'.[26] This reprimand had the support of only some delegates, including Vaillant, who asked the Executive Committee to tell the Italians 'that in Italy as elsewhere a socialist who forgets the instructions on the anti-war struggle which he has been given by his party congresses and by the international congresses at Stuttgart and Copenhagen, fails in his international duty'.[27] What effect did this admonition of the secretariat of the International have in Italy? The letters from Camille Huysmans, which contained the criticism of the Bureau and of the other affiliated parties, were discussed at the plenary meeting of the ISP Executive and the complaint was rejected. The party executive stated that 'its conscience was clear and it was convinced that it had made the party do its duty, namely to protest against the Tripoli venture', and it authorized the party secretary, Pompeo Ciotti, to protest to the ISB 'against the unjustified criticism of the Italian socialists by the other nations'.[28] So as not to add further fuel to the fire the Executive Committee pretended to soothe the Italians but did not hide its misgivings. In its public documents the Bureau therefore avoided any denouncement of the failure of the ISP, but

[25] Saul Nahum to Camille Huysmans, 3 Oct. 1911, ISB archives.
[26] Circular of 12 Oct. 1911, ISB archives.
[27] Camille Huysmans to Pompeo Ciotti, 10 Oct. 1911. See G. Haupt, 'L'Internazionale socialista e la conquesta libica', *Movimento operaio e socialista* xiii. 1 (1967), 17–18.
[28] Pompeo Ciotti to Camille Huysmans. Cf. ibid. 20–1.

made few references to the efforts of the Italian comrades. While the Bureau through its secretary continued to exert pressure on the ISP leaders, reminding them of their duty and asking them for an account of their actions against the Italian government press, the Italians reassured the Executive Committee that the ISP Executive lost no opportunity 'of fulfilling its socialist duty in compliance with the joint principles and resolutions of the International Congresses'.[29] In all his replies Pompeo Ciotti manifested a suspicious sensitivity and constantly emphasized that even in extremely difficult moments his party 'never gives way and maintains its reputation'. In December 1911 Ciotti went so far as to claim that '. . . in view of this fact all criticism must cease and all requests for more energetic manifestations—from whatever quarter they emanate —must in justice be described as exaggerated and irrational'. And he added:

Further I must draw your attention to the fact that in a situation similar to but less difficult than ours the socialist comrades of other countries have done very much less than we to stave off the threat of war, to preserve peace and to protect against aggressive colonial policies. It seems unnecessary for me to go into details as you are better acquainted than I am with the history of international socialism.

The ISB secretariat ignored Ciotti's attacks and doubted his explanations.

Instead of opening an investigation, the Bureau put the case of the Italian section in the files. But in the eyes of the International the ISP had become discredited by its attitude during the Turko-Italian war. Hence the initiatives of the Italian party in 1913 and 1914 were, as we shall see, received with suspicion and even contempt. And in spite of the ISB's wish to preserve the unity of socialism at any price, the decision of the Congress of Reggio Emilia in 1912, to expel Bissolati and his friends from the ranks of the ISP, was received with undisguised satisfaction.

[29] See Pompeo Ciotti's letter to Camille Huysmans. Cf. ibid. 22–4.

If in Italy it was the presence of various trends within the same party and the domination of the right wing that paralysed the effective pacifist action desired by the ISB, in the Balkans the same effect was brought about by rivalry and hostility between various factions of the Left. Although in 1911 most Balkan socialist parties could claim to have existed for twenty years, they were numerically weak. In spite of common characteristics of development they were slow to abandon their short-sighted viewpoint and to consider the Balkans as a whole. Christian Rakovsky, an outstanding personality through his activities in the Balkans and in international socialism, played an important part. He was the one who 'shattered the barriers'. After the Congress at Stuttgart, he suggested that the socialist party leaders of south-east Europe should come to an agreement and work out common issues as regards the social and national problems in the Balkan area.[30] It was only under the pressure of international events, after the annexation of Bosnia-Herzegovina, that this proposal, which had Kautsky's support, was implemented.[31]

The theoretical and political conclusions to be drawn from these events had been clearly put at the first conference of Balkan socialist parties, held in Belgrade from 7 to 9 January 1910. The common goal decided upon was the foundation of a democratic federal republic of Balkan countries. With this federation the socialists hoped to solve the burning nationalities question in the Balkans, ensure social reform, and bring about democratic changes. Thus they thought they could clear up the 'wasps' nest in the Balkans', free themselves 'from the tutelage imposed by European diplomacy', and resist the intrigues of the great powers. They expressed their opposition to European capitalism's policy of intervention and conquest and

[30] See the report of the Rumanian Social Democratic Party in the *Periodical Bull. ISB* v. 11 (1914), 76–7; cf. also C. Racovski, *Vers l'entente balkanique* (Mayenne, C. Colin, 1908, 23 pp.).

[31] There are many references to the roles played by Kautsky and Christian Rakovsky in the unpublished correspondence between the two men. (Cf. Kautsky archives, Amsterdam, IISG.)

said that for this there was only one remedy: to free the Balkan peoples from particularism and from the isolation in which they lived. 'We must break down the frontiers that separate these peoples whose cultures are identical, these countries whose economic and political fortunes are closely linked, and thus shake off the yoke of foreign domination which robs nations of the right to determine their own fate.'[32]

The first Belgrade conference had defined the principles which were based on anti-imperialist feeling. It was to be the task of a second assembly to implement these principles and to work out joint tactics. In August 1911 the social democratic party of Rumania suggested a second Balkan Socialist Conference. But the violent fratricidal strife that had raged since 1903 between the two socialist parties of Bulgaria (the leftist 'Narrow Socialist Party' and the reformist 'Broad Socialist Party) wrecked this initiative.

With the Turko-Italian war the threat to the Balkans suddenly became a terrible reality. Concerted action by the Balkan socialists was now no longer a propaganda demand or a theoretical postulate but a tangible and urgent necessity.

When at the beginning of October 1911 the Serbian socialist party issued a renewed call for a conference, the ISB Executive Committee actively supported the initiative. But the 'Narrow Party' remained adamant and stuck to the demand that no representatives of the 'Broad Party' must be allowed to attend the conference. Their insistence wrecked a venture from which the ISB expected great political results. Only a simple preliminary meeting was held in Belgrade on 18 October. Because of the absence of the 'Narrow Party' it could but issue statements about the desirability of and the necessity for joint anti-war action by the Balkan socialists without being able to take a single concrete step. At that moment the ISB intervened directly and its Executive Committee sent an urgent and energetic

[32] A short report on the conference and the resolution was published in the *Periodical Bull. ISB* i. 1 (1910). A good general picture is given in L. S. Stavrianos, *Balkan Federation, a History of the Movement towards Balkan Unity in Modern Times* (Hamden, Connecticut, Archon Books, 1964), 182–90.

telegram to the two Bulgarian parties in an attempt to bring
them to reason and to make them promise to attend the second
conference which was to be held as soon as possible.[33] The
ISB's intervention was unsuccessful. Not only did the 'Narrow
Party' not give way, they even attacked the socialist party
of Serbia.[34] At a critical moment, therefore, the socialists who
were opposed to 'Balkanization', and whose programme included
the creation of a federation of Balkan peoples, themselves
provided a spectacle of discord and hostility.

Another circumstance contributed to maintain utter confusion. As well as differing among themselves, the socialists of
southern Europe disagreed with the socialists of central and
western Europe about the solution of the Balkan problem.

The representatives of the Workers' Socialist Federation of
Salonica vainly asked the International to 'lay down for the proletariat of the world a single guide-line on the eastern question'
and so assist 'the democrats of the Balkan countries in their
struggle against the forces of reaction and against European imperialism'. They were convinced that a decision by the International could 'contribute substantially to the removal of the
differences between the socialist parties of the Balkan countries';
that by doing so 'it could greatly influence the parties and the
political factors' of the explosive European situation, and that
'once they are compelled to take European democratic opinion
into account' these forces must change 'their imperialist and
anti-working class tactics'.[35] But the large sections of the International were for a long time content with general statements.
In 1904 the ISB declared itself in favour of autonomy for the
oppressed minorities of the Ottoman Empire, and at the Copen-

[33] The telegram of 27 Oct. 1911, a copy of which is in the ISB archives, reads:
'Under pressure of joint heavy responsibility Bureau Executive urges that both
affiliated parties participate unconditionally in second Inter-Balkan Conference.'
[34] On the development of socialism in Bulgaria and the struggle between the
'Narrow Party' and the 'Broad Party', see Joseph Rothschild, *The Communist
Party of Bulgaria, 1883–1943* (New York, Columbia U.P., 1959), 32–44 and 210–11;
on the conflict between Bulgarian and Serbian socialists see M. Isusov, 'The Links
between the Workers' Movements in Bulgaria and Serbia at the Beginning of the
Twentieth Century' (in Bulgarian), *Istorčeski Pregled* 3 (1964), 29–32.
[35] Saul Nahum to the ISB Executive Committee, Sept. 1912, ISB archives.

hagen Congress the International expressed the same point of view in a resolution on the situation in Turkey. This resolution returned to the points of the programme prepared by the first Balkan Socialist Conference. But the socialist parties of Germany, France, Austria, and Britain persisted in their unwillingness, or their inability, to understand or to share the point of view of the Balkan socialists. It was the aim of the west Europeans to preserve peace in Europe or—if the worst came to the worst—to confine any conflict to the Balkan countries. They believed that the Balkan question should be considered in a world-wide context and not from the narrowly restricted angle from which, in their opinion, the socialists in Bucharest, Sofia or Belgrade saw it. Starting from this assumption the west Europeans regarded the preservation of the *status quo* in south-east Europe as essential. They assured the Balkan socialists of their sympathy and supported the principle of a Balkan federation, but advised them to adapt themselves to the changing circumstances and to reconcile their ideology with the facts. Such advice could only bewilder the Balkan socialist leaders, whose amazement grew, when after the annexation of Bosnia–Herzegovina they noticed that the concept of 'internationalism' was interpreted differently in Vienna and in Belgrade.[36]

The Balkan socialists, whose strength was not sapped by nationalism and who were doctrinaire socialists, observed that the socialist party of Austria, while disapproving of its government's foreign policy, viewed the situation from the Austrian perspective with the assumption that the monarchy had a cultural mission in the Balkans. The Austrian socialists protested against the annexation of Bosnia–Herzegovina[37] but at the same time violently attacked the Serbian Government and

[36] See Ivan Avakumović, *History of the Communist Party of Yugoslavia* (Aberdeen, 1964, vol. i), 11 ff.; and mainly Sergije Dimitrijević's well-documented study, 'Učešće Balkanskih socijalista u Drugoj internacionali od njenog stvaranja do međunarodnog socijalističkog kongresa u Kopenhagenu (1889–1910)', in *Prilozi za istoriju socijalizma* (Belgrade, 1966, vol. i), 30–61.

[37] Cf. Enver Redžić, 'Die österreichische Sozialdemokratie und die Frage Bosniens und der Herzegovina', *Österreichische Osthefte*, ix. 5 (1967), 361–78.

accused it of making it difficult for Austria to fulfil its mission. The Serbian socialists turned angrily to the ISB and asked for the dispute to be submitted to all the affiliated parties. The ISB confined itself solely to giving information; it published a memorandum submitted by Tucovič at the October 1908 session,[38] and sent out in the form of circulars without comment the documents presented by the delegates of Serbia together with the sharp reply of the Czech delegate, Nemec, who—under the cover of conciliation—fully supported the point of view of the socialists of Austria-Hungary.[39] Tucovič then placed these differences of opinion before the Copenhagen congress where, in the name of the Austrian Party, Renner made a public apology. There was a public reconciliation in the style beloved of the congresses of the International which relished the spectacle of rhetorical internationalism. But the distrust remained.

In the years 1911 and 1912, with attention focused primarily on the Balkan countries, the socialist journals of the West gave the Serbian, Bulgarian, and Rumanian socialists ample space to explain their attitude. The Marxist theorists of Germany and Austria also devoted themselves to this complex question; Otto Bauer in 1912 published a remarkable study in which he developed his theory of the 'awakening of the nations without history' who in their attempt to achieve autonomy support the proletariat's struggle for emancipation.[40]

While these analyses prepared the way for a dialogue on theory they did nothing to bridge the gap between the western socialists and those of the Balkans in their respective approaches to the basic issue, nor did they change the position of the great European socialist parties. The Germans, and also the French, let themselves be guided by the idea of maintaining the *status quo* in the Balkans. The ethical idealism of Jaurès, to whom the

[38] *Compte rendu officiel de la dixième séance du BSI*, 97–100. D. Tucović was the delegate of the Serbian Socialist Party to the ISB.
[39] These circulars have been indexed by the present author in *La Deuxième Internationale*, 313–14.
[40] Otto Bauer, *Der Balkankrieg und die deutsche Weltpolitik* (Berlin, 1912).

supreme criterion was world peace at any price, was put
severely to the test. For him sympathy for the cause of liberation
of the oppressed nationalities of the Ottoman Empire could not
be allowed to overshadow political considerations of a global
character.

But the difference between the western socialists and those of
the Balkans was not one of tactics. It arose from two fundamentally different views of the nationalities issue, of the national
question, and of the imperialist phenomenon. The Balkan point
of view was put forward bluntly, without attention to style, in a
confidential note which Dušan Popović, the secretary of the
Serbian socialist party, sent to the ISB secretariat on 1 August
1912.[41] He argued that all tension in the Balkans, all 'militancy
on the part of the inhabitants of the Balkans', all manifestations
of nationalism and chauvinism were provoked by European
capitalism. He, too, wanted to maintain the Balkan *status quo*.
But that *status quo* spelt death for the Balkans, because it helped
'the capitalist powers who are the enemies of peace and civil-
isation' and in whose interest it was 'to preserve the existing
conditions in the Balkans, conditions which would be a perpetual source of discontent, disorder, revolution and war'. The
status quo condemned the Balkan peoples to immobility, in fact
it prevented them from pursuing their vital objective, 'to
destroy barbarism in their own region' and to 'prepare a
transformation of the relationship between the inhabitants of
the Balkans'. The *status quo* was thus no guarantee of peace but
on the contrary a permanent source of war. The great western
socialist parties could help to 'confine the Balkan wasps' nest'.
But this could only be done by one method: non-intervention.
It must be the 'duty of international socialism' to make it clear
that 'for Europe the best solution of the Balkan question is to
leave it unresolved. Whoever opposes the colonial policy of the
European capitalist powers, whoever stops them from interfering in the affairs of the Balkan peoples and states, whoever

---

[41] Manuscript note written in French in answer to the secretariat's circular on
the Vaillant–Keir Hardie amendment; ISB archives.

makes Europe into a simple observer of the events that take place on the Balkan stage, whoever does these things will do much to preserve peace in Europe and will successfully prevent a general war.' The point of view of the Serbian socialists—as stated by Dušan Popović—would be ignored until everybody was faced with the *fait accompli*: the Balkan war. Then, the extent of the threat was taken into consideration. And the Austrian socialist party at once issued the slogan: 'the Balkans for the Balkan peoples'.

This difference, which was both theoretical and political, showed up the paradoxes in the International's policy. The socialist leaders were explicit when it came to their diagnosis that the Balkans represented a threat to the equilibrium of the world. But as soon as the crises, the states of alert were over and the conflicts had been solved, the ISB returned to its daily routine; no provisions were made to deal with any possible complications. Instructions were relegated to the arsenal of rhetorical propaganda whose *leitmotiv* was to deplore 'the terrible increase in military expenditure, the burden of war'. It seemed to the ISB that in the case of the Balkans it would be easy to apply the new tactics of localizing conflicts to as limited as possible an arena until 'sane forces from among the leading quarters of the major powers intervene to calm down the militant spirits'—as Vandervelde put it—and to see arbitration as 'the ideal solution which will isolate the wicked imperialists from the community of peaceful states'.

Although in 1912 the socialist press still made pessimistic predictions about the impending end of the era of peace, and about Europe and the world embarking on a period of troubles and antagonisms, most socialist leaders did not share this view. In November 1911, when the Turko-Italian war remained localized, the president of the International, Vandervelde, questioned the possibility of a 'spread of the war'. He expressed the quintessence of his views as follows:

There are in Europe at present too many pacifist forces, starting with the Jewish capitalists who give financial support to many governments, down to the socialists who are determined to prevent the mobilization of the nations, and in the event of defeat to spring at the throat of their rulers.[42]

Called upon to deal with situations resulting from the diplomatic crises, the ISB did not rise above pragmatism and prudent compromise between the various conflicting points of view, which after Stuttgart ceased to change. The International's activity in periods of calm showed that its great fight for peace was in effect perpetual improvisation. Yet the year 1912 was no calmer than previous years. Danger signals appeared in the Balkans; there were revolts in Albania, unrest and pogroms in Macedonia, rising nationalism in Bulgaria. The Balkan socialists continued to draw attention to the explosive situation which threatened the peace of Europe,

since the Balkans, because of their geographical position, represent one of the parts of the globe where the concealed antagonisms of world capitalist interests are revealed tangibly in the rival aspirations of the great powers; one of those parts of the globe where the Gordian knot of capitalist interests is cut by a blow of the sword; one of those parts of the globe over which the thunder and lightning accumulated by European capitalism will break.[43]

The news and the alarming reports from the Balkans met with indifference on the part of the majority of the affiliated parties. The SPD continued to keep cool. Only the French delegates remained steadfast in their appreciation of the situation, manifesting their concern to the ISB and stepping up their calls for action; meanwhile the Executive Committee, acting as an information service, was concerned with another topic—the next international congress.

When at the end of August 1912 the secretary of the ISB consulted members on the exact date of the congress which, in accordance with the resolutions, was due to be held in 1913, the Dutch representatives Van Kol and Troelstra submitted a counter-proposal: as 'there is no urgency to convene an

[42] Vandervelde, art. cit. 492.
[43] D. Popović, note referred to above; ISB archives.

international congress', they proposed its postponement until 1914. They recalled that in 1914 the International would celebrate its fiftieth anniversary, a good reason for giving the congress 'an up-to-date character, suitable for propaganda purposes'. The Dutch proposal was submitted to the representatives of all the affiliated parties.[44] Only a handful of delegates, Lenin among them,[45] failed to reply. A small majority expressed themselves in favour of the Dutch proposal.[46] Those who were in favour of postponing the Congress treated this as a simple question of procedure, and asked no questions, because they knew that it was the German social democratic party that was behind the Dutch proposal. Taking advantage of a lull on the international scene, the SPD executive committee hesitated for time before it was obliged to make a decision about the Vaillant–Keir Hardie amendment.

On the other hand the Dutch proposal met with violent resistance from the French and the British—for different reasons.[47] The British section rejected the postponement of the congress for reasons of principle. It published its protest in October 1912 (after it had learned from the press that at the party congress at Chemnitz the SPD had adopted a resolution in favour of the postponement), and stated that such a procedure 'is unworthy of the traditions of the great German party and contrary to the principles of democracy'.[48]

The French objection was of a political nature. Because of the possible unrest that could result from the consequences of

[44] Circular No. 19 of 7 Sept. 1912, ISB archives. The extensive correspondence with the delegates of the affiliated parties is in the ISB archives.

[45] See G. Haupt, ed., *Correspondance entre Lénine et Camille Huysmans, 1905–1914* (Paris–The Hague, Mouton, 1963), 117.

[46] They were the representatives of the socialist parties of Holland, Germany, Austria, Bohemia, Croatia, Italy, Portugal, Spain, Denmark, Sweden, Norway, Greece, the Argentine, the *Bund*, and of the Armenian socialists.

[47] Among those in favour of keeping to the original date were the Russian social revolutionaries, the socialists of Switzerland, the United States (De Leon), the Bulgarian 'Narrow Socialists', and the Workers' Socialist Federation of Salonica.

[48] The protest signed by Belfort Bax, Hyndman, and Quelch appeared in *Justice*, 9 Oct. 1912.

the Balkan crisis the international congress should meet as arranged. In this spirit Vaillant wrote to Camille Huysmans on 9 September 1912:

In my opinion it is not for us to question the convening of the international congress for 1913 in Vienna; the matter was agreed upon unanimously at the proposal of and after discussion by the ISB at the Congress at Copenhagen. The congresses have more important and vital roles to perform than to mark anniversaries. Never, given the murderous and predatory adventure of colonial capitalism, the growing military preparations, and the threat of war, has it been as necessary and urgent as now for the International to lay down at a congress what active steps it will take for the welfare of the proletariat and the preservation of peace.[49]

The same argument was advanced by the representatives of the Balkan socialist parties who thought that the political situation in Europe had never been as confused, and the threat of a general clash never as frightening, as at that moment. 'In these circumstances it is the International's duty to demonstrate as quickly and as solemnly as possible its desire for peace, and its wishes to hold a Congress.'[50]

Because of the French and British demand for an explanation, the secretary of the ISB, in his reply, was compelled to tell the truth about the postponement of that congress. His letters clearly reflect the uneasiness and the serious differences of view that existed within the International. On 3 October 1912 he wrote to Vaillant:

We cannot assemble in Vienna in the midst of German–Czech hostilities. We hope that the affair will be settled by 1914. In addition there is the disagreement between the Poles, the Russian Social Democrats, the Bulgarians, and others, and the fact that the situation has reached such a pitch of bitterness that the Vienna Congress, coming immediately after the Eucharistic Congress, would be the congress of socialist schism.[51]

[49] ISB archives.
[50] Saul Nahum, delegate of the Workers' Socialist Federation of Salonica, to Camille Huysmans, Paris, 10 Sept, 1912, ISB archives.
[51] ISB archives.

Hyndman received a similar explanation:

The situation in Austria and Bohemia is *quite deplorable*. Our comrades there devour each other. Discord has reached a peak. Feelings are running high and if we assemble in Vienna we shall have a congress of strife which will make the worst possible impression on the world. Not only the Austrians and the Czechs are in this situation; the same is true of Poland, the Ukraine, Russia, and Bulgaria. In any case we must gain time to allow passions to subside.[52]

While the secretariat studied the voluminous correspondence on the date of the next congress, and tried in vain to find ways and means of reaching agreement, the situation in the Balkans took a dramatic turn. The crisis was developing unmistakably into an armed conflict. In a letter to Camille Huysmans of 20 September the Serbian socialist leader D. Lapčević warned the ISB that the general atmosphere in the Balkans was extremely oppressive and that war could break out at any moment. His party therefore considered a second conference of Balkan socialists essential and urgent and asked the ISB's help in cutting the Gordian knot: the point was to persuade the 'Narrow Party' and the 'Broad' Bulgarian Party to sit down together at the same table. In order to cut short the discussion on procedure, he suggested a solution which Huysmans quickly made his own: that the Rumanian delegate, Rakovsky, should be formally invited by the Bureau urgently to convene a conference and to organize it on the Bureau's behalf.[53] Huysmans's reaction—taking an initiative which went beyond his powers—was due to his awareness of the situation. He saw in this conference a possibility of shaking the leaders of the great socialist parties out of their indifference. According to him the objective of this meeting of the Balkan socialist parties was to give urgent information to 'the ISB and the other affiliated parties whose governments can exert an influence on

[52] Personal letter from Huysmans to Hyndman, 4 Oct. 1912, ISB archives.
[53] ISB archives. See also Dragiša Lapčević, *Rat i srpska socijalna demokratija* (Belgrade, 1925), 32 ff.

the situation'.[54] But Rakovsky was not in Bucharest, and by the time the letter reached him in Constantinople, it was impossible for him to embark on the complex negotiations which his mandate presupposed.[55] The performance of the previous year was repeated. Even the threat of an immediate war did nothing to remove the obstacles between the 'Narrow Party' and the 'Broad Party'. If anything it accentuated their antagonism.

At the beginning of October the scale and significance of this storm in the Balkans caused the confident optimism among socialists to give way to uncertainty and even to panic. Bebel prophesied a great catastrophe, a great European war,[56] while Huysmans wondered realistically whether this time the International would be in a position to anticipate events. And on 2 October 1912, the ISB secretary wrote bitterly to Adler:

> For a long time we have tried to make all affiliated parties come to a Balkan conference; but our efforts have met with resistance from the 'Narrow Socialists'. Tired of the struggle, we have asked Rakovsky to convene the conference in the name of the Bureau in a manner that all parties are morally obliged to attend. Unfortunately it seems to me that events are moving faster than our good intentions.[57]

As regards the Balkans Huysmans was right. The war put an end to this initiative because, as Rakovsky reported in mid-October 1912, 'At the moment the activities of the socialists of Serbia, Bulgaria, Greece, and Turkey are completely paralysed. The organizations are depleted. The entire population of mili-

---

[54] ISB archives. In circular no. 24 of 3 Oct. 1912 the Executive Committee informed all affiliated parties of its decision to convene the Second Balkan Socialist Conference under its auspices.

[55] ISB archives. According to Dragiša Lapčević, who spoke in the name of the Serbian Socialist Party, the responsibility for the failure fell upon the ISB whose indecisiveness had motivated it. Thus he wrote to Christian Rakovsky on 25 Sept. 1912: 'As far as this affair is concerned, the ISB's postponements are regrettable, considering that we warned it against the impending threat of war.' (D. Lapčević, op. cit. 40.)

[56] *Victor Adler Briefwechsel*, 550.

[57] The letter is in the Victor Adler Nachlaß (Vienna, Arbeiterkammer).

tary age is at the frontier.'[58] Nevertheless, he succeeded in composing a manifesto addressed 'to all workers of the civilized world' and having it signed by all Balkan socialist parties. The socialist press immediately published this document which greatly impressed public opinion.[59]

As the International grew more aware of the seriousness of the situation, it raised the then traditional question: What could it do to avert the threat of war? The French and British demanded an immediate meeting of the ISB. Again the German party hedged. No sooner had the first threat passed than Bebel recovered his composure and once more advised caution. Again the French socialists took the initiative. They saw their fears confirmed and did not hesitate to act accordingly. Jaurès immediately made a new proposal to the ISB: that the international congress should meet as soon as possible in Vienna to give 'particularly forceful' expression to the international solidarity of the workers. 'Even if the present conflict has been settled, deep-rooted and dangerous seeds of force and war remain.'[60] To him the congress was indispensable because it could help to localize the conflict, and also to force public opinion to face the threat and abandon the illusory hope of finding a solution by diplomatic means.[61]

On 14 October the ISB secretariat convened a plenary meeting for 28 October in Brussels. This summit meeting of Europe's most important socialist leaders was of tremendous

---

[58] Letter of 19 Oct. 1912 by Christian Rakovsky from Bucharest to the editor of the paper *Népszava*, Budapest. The original of the letter, in French (nine type-written pages), is in Amsterdam, IISG.

[59] 'The manifesto of the socialists of Turkey and the Balkan countries' was reproduced many times by the contemporary socialist press. The text is also found in French, English, and German in the *Periodical Bull. ISB* iii. 9 (1912), 4–7.

[60] *Œuvres de Jaurès*, vol. v, 134.

[61] Jaurès wrote, for example, on 12 Oct. 1912: 'The threat must make all honest democrats in Europe think. The working class must organize itself even more effectively and express even more strongly its determination to preserve the peace. International socialism which alone from the start of the Morocco crisis has seen the threat, pointed to it and defined it in detail, must use all its energies and make every effort to save Europe and the whole of humanity from the most terrible catastrophe.' (Ibid. 143.)

importance. The previous day, Jaurès expressed the general requirements and expectations:

It will be very important to give strong and clear voice to the joint ideas and the joint will of the socialists of all Europe. The International Socialist Bureau which meets on the 28th of this month in Brussels will bear a very great responsibility. Even if it is too late to advance the date of the international congress in Vienna, even if there are material difficulties, the Socialist Bureau must organize immediate, impassioned, and effective international action to oppose any possible spread of the war, action that will unite the whole thinking proletariat, and rouse it into making a unanimous protest, an unambiguous demonstration.[62]

This time, Victor Adler, who was always cautious and hopeful, admitted that 'at that moment the secretariat was in the most difficult situation in which it had ever found itself'.[63]

Even so, Bebel, prevented by illness from going to Brussels, advised the German delegates not to be fooled by the French and British, and to keep their sang-froid in a situation which he regarded as chaotic. In his opinion, they could give way only on one point: they could dissociate themselves from the party's decision to postpone the international congress until 1914.[64]

When the ISB met in Brussels the first Balkan War was in full swing. How could the conflict be localized? How could the threat of its spreading be countered? These were the questions on which the discussions of the socialist leaders focused. Adler expressed the view that the International should 'strive for the autonomy of the Slav nations of the Balkans'; it was not enough to protest against the war which was an undeniable fact: 'What matters is to prevent Austrian and Russian intervention.' Vaillant emphasized the action which the International must take; he thought that if there were sufficiently powerful movements in every country 'for governments to fear the pressure of revolutionary agitation', the conflict would not spread. Proceeding from this assumption, Vaillant argued that it was the

[62] *Œuvres de Jaurès*, vol. v, 148.
[63] See the report of the ISB meeting of 18 Oct., in *Le Peuple* (19 Oct. 1912), 1–2.
[64] Bebel to Adler, 15 Oct. 1912, in *Victor Adler Briefwechsel*, 552.

duty of the national sections to produce 'powerful, general agitation . . . so as to make war, if not impossible, at least unlikely'.

Jaurès remained optimistic: 'I believe that basically the governments do not want war . . . they would like the booty of war, and peace.' But he thought that the moment had come to convene an international congress so that governments became aware of 'the proletariat's determination to take action' and to oppose any intervention on the part of the great powers in this dangerous war.

Next the meeting discussed whether the date of the congress should be advanced or whether, as the Dutch delegation proposed, the congress should be postponed until 1914, and an international conference convened solely to determine the proletariat's attitude towards the threat of war. This issue was discussed at great length. When it seemed as if the work of the session would be ruined by questions of method, Vandervelde suggested that the European sections should meet at Christmas at Basle and that the congress should be held on the date originally arranged. In the end Jaurès decided the question. He explained:

To postpone the congress in the present circumstances would be a miserable admission of failure and we would simply be copying official diplomacy which usually acts too late. The Dutch proposal, which was given support at Chemnitz, was made at a time when the war had not yet begun.

His proposal, to convene an extraordinary congress at Basle at Christmas and to postpone the Vienna Congress until 1914, was adopted.[65]

So as to make the Basle congress as impressive and effective as possible, the ISB asked the workers' organizations and the affiliated parties to embark at once on a 'methodical and intensive campaign of agitation' against war and to oppose all 'self-interested intervention' by the European powers in the

[65] See G. Haupt, 'Jaurès à la réunion du BSI des 28 et 29 octobre 1912' *Bulletin de la Société d'études jaurésiennes*, 11 (Oct.–Dec. 1963), 3–9.

Balkan conflict. Although the 'International's anti-war manifesto', drafted by the Bureau at this session, was couched in emotional language, its substance was free from the old rhetoric. It was a serious and precise document that was not concerned with the protection of peace in the abstract.[66] 'The hours ahead will doubtless be hours of trial and responsibility for the socialist party and the proletariat' because 'the Balkan conflict can at any time become a general conflict'. That those to whom the manifesto was addressed understood this language is proved by the fact that in accordance with the ISB's instructions from early November onwards the European proletariat opposed the threat of war 'with its whole organizational might, with mass action'.

The ISB manifesto of 29 October is one of the International's great texts which at that moment became the expression of the workers' hopes and aims. Aided by the time factor, the manifesto stimulated pacifist reaction and active resistance to nationalistic intoxication. The history of these mass demonstrations—which began on 20 October, when in Berlin alone more than 250,000 workers were mobilized—remains to be written.[67] If the historic importance of workers' demonstrations depends on their cohesion of aim, on the unanimity of those who organized them as much as on their success, the demonstrations of October–November 1912 completely meet this criterion. It was a unique moment. Faced with concrete, great, and immediate danger the European socialist parties united in action. Public opinion was mobilized and the workers proved that they were determined to oppose a general clash. These demonstrations gave the International an illusory power that was highlighted by the Congress in Basle.

[66] Published in *Le Peuple*, 304 (30 Oct. 1912), 1; *Vorwärts* (30 Oct. 1912), 2. The text of this resolution which was drafted by Kautsky was agreed upon by a committee composed of Adler, Vaillant, Jaurès, Haase, and Rosa Luxemburg.
[67] The interesting study published by the Soviet historian I. M. Krivoguz in *Voprosy istorii KPSS* 5 (1962), 79–96, is far from exhaustive.

4   Basle: War on War

BECAUSE of the deterioration of the situation at the beginning of November 1912 the date of the extraordinary Congress was advanced at the SPD's request.[1] It was hastily fixed for 24 and 25 November 1912 in Basle. There was need for quick action because the 'frightful spectacle of war' became ever more menacing.

Turkey is defeated. The Sultan's empire is disintegrating. Now the struggle over the booty begins. The Great Powers are divided. There is a danger that the Balkan war will become a world war.

In a leaflet[2] bearing these alarming headlines the socialist party invited the workers of Vienna to take part in a peace demonstration on 10 November.[3]

Neither Victor Adler nor the SPD executive shared the optimism of the aged Bebel who wrote to Vienna on 14 November: 'I hope that everything will be resolved reasonably satisfactorily and that we shall be spared a European war.'[4] And nobody laboured any longer under the illusion 'that the Balkan states might do us the favour of coming to a quick understanding with the Turks, or concluding an armistice and starting peace negotiations'.[5]

On this occasion, faced with a possible explosion of the Balkan powder-magazine, the German socialists were unequivocal in their attitude; with much energy and zeal they began their pacifist operation, or more precisely an intensive psychological anti-militarist campaign. During these tense days the party chairman, Hugo Haase, addressed a letter dated

---

[1] ISB archives, documents of the Basle Congress, i.   [2] Ibid.
[3] On this great peace demonstration, see *AZ* (11 Nov. 1912), 1–3.
[4] *Victor Adler Briefwechsel*, 554.   [5] Bebel to Adler, 16 Nov. 1912, ibid. 555.

15 November to his comrades in his native town of Königsberg
setting out the objectives of the pacifist campaign:

I hope because there are strong peace-promoting forces at work we
shall be spared this terrible disaster. Nevertheless it is our duty to
strengthen these forces continuously. If war is made unpopular, if the
great mass of the people look upon it with loathing and abhorrence
governments will be chary of it; victories, as the Balkan War has
recently shown again, need a mood of exuberance. We are therefore
working unceasingly to prevent the emergence of such a mood . . .
An impressive peace demonstration took place in the Tempelhofer
Park a few weeks ago. I shall never forget the sight of the crowd of
over 200,000 who were gathered there. As they raised their hands to
vote the scene was lit up by the rays of the sun breaking through the
clouds.[6]

To emphasize the importance of this anti-war campaign even
further large-scale mass protests were organized on 17 November in all European capitals by the parties affiliated to the
International, at the request of the SPD.[7] On this occasion
representatives of various socialist parties, Jaurès and Renner
in Berlin, MacDonald, Vandervelde, and Scheidemann in
Paris, spoke up and warned governments that 'they shall not
set Europe ablaze with impunity'. The dramatic wording of
the manifesto[8] which the International sent out in the first days
of November had an immediate effect. Its appeal 'to take action
against war and against the spread of the Balkan conflict'
mobilized the major part of Europe's workers. In Pré-Saint-
Gervais near Paris over 100,000 people demonstrated. 'We are
not powerless', the whole socialist press said again and again,
'because the rulers will not wage war if they realize that the
people do not want war.'

It was in this tense and troubled atmosphere that the preparations for the Extraordinary International Socialist Congress
began. In accordance with the decisions of the ISB a committee
composed of Jaurès, Vaillant, Bebel, Keir Hardie, Adler,

---

[6] Ernst Haase, *Hugo Haase, sein Leben und Wirken. Mit einer Auswahl von Briefen
Reden und Aufsätzen* (Berlin [1929]), 99.

[7] ISB archives, documents of the Basle Congress, i.

[8] Published in *L'Humanité* (7 Nov. 1912).

Rubanovich,[9] and Huysmans, the secretary of the International, gathered before the congress took place to draft the resolution to be submitted to it.[10] The 'sages' of the International were called together primarily to prepare a text that offered a clear and detailed analysis of the situation and of the tasks of international socialism. But at the same time the idea was to prevent differences of opinion from reaching the public. The Basle Congress was meant to be 'a powerful demonstration of the unity of the socialist movement in the anti-war struggle, a harmonious expression of the power of the International'.[11] In other words, the ISB wanted to prevent a recurrence of such disputes as had arisen over the Vaillant–Keir Hardie amendment at the Copenhagen congress. These fears were justified. The opinion of the leading German socialists had not changed in the least, and Vaillant too was determined to stick to his guns. The intention behind Vandervelde's suggestion at Copenhagen, that the question of a general strike should not figure on the agenda until the next congress, had been to achieve a respite. But Vaillant was not prepared to agree to the suggestion.

At the beginning of November 1910 he had sent a letter to Huysmans reminding him of his firm promise at Copenhagen, and demanding that the draft proposal should be sent as soon as possible to every section of the International, to be examined in detail and to be commented on. On that occasion Vaillant had said:

The Vienna Congress of 1913 must examine the issue not only with reference to international law but also with reference to the national solutions that must be the prelude to the international solution of 1913.

The strike of the French railway workers has shown that a solution is feasible at national and at international level and we must now

---

[9] Rubanovich, the delegate of the Russian Social Revolutionary Party, was appointed to this commission with the agreement of Plekhanov—who was at the time ill—and of Lenin, who had settled in Cracow and could not leave at once for Basle. Cf. *Correspondance entre Lénine et Huysmans*, Haupt, ed., 121–5.

[10] Kautsky attended the meetings of this commission as Bebel's interpreter.

[11] Longuet, 71.

examine the question on the assumption that practical action is possible, a fact which hitherto more than one friend of the ISB may have doubted.[12]

Vaillant rejected Huysmans's advice to moderate the text of the proposal and on 13 November 1910 addressed another letter to the ISB, stating categorically:

We have no other proposal to submit to the different nations [i.e. the national sections of the International] to whom the Keir Hardie–Vaillant proposal was referred back at the same time as to the ISB. They must discuss it and, depending on what they decide, they must debate the proposal and their amendments to it at the Vienna Congress in 1913.

But nobody has the right to alter the resolution of the Copenhagen Congress in any way during this process of consultation. Neither Keir Hardie, nor Vaillant, nor the ISB is entitled to change the text or to replace it with any other. It is quite possible and proper that consultation of the individual nations and the ISB may result in the adoption of the proposal, its rejection, or in an amendment. But the subject of the consultation must be this proposal pure and simple.[13]

Huysmans abided by these instructions. In December 1910 he sent a circular containing the text of the Vaillant–Keir Hardie proposal to all affiliated parties and asked them to let the ISB have their comments as soon as possible.[14] But only four parties replied.

Dissatisfied, Vaillant reminded Huysmans on 18 April 1912 that the ISB had been asked to consult the national sections on the proposal, and demanded an account of their replies. Vaillant thought of appealing to the trade unions to exert pressure on the party leaderships.[15] On 18 May he asked the ISB secretariat to consult the trade union organizations directly. He pointed out that the French CGT had already commented and decided to react to any plan for war with a general strike

[12] Vaillant to Huysmans, 1 Nov. 1910, ISB archives; see also Vaillant's interview in *Le Mouvement socialiste* (Oct. 1910), 207 ff.
[13] Vaillant to Huysmans, 13 Nov. 1910, ISB archives.
[14] *Periodical Bull. ISB* iii. 8 (1912), 114.
[15] Vaillant to Huysmans, 18 Apr. 1912, ISB archives.

and insurrection.[16] In the end Vaillant adopted Huysmans's suggestion, that a new circular should be sent to all affiliated parties, reminding them that their answer was wanted and asking them at the same time to consult the headquarters or organizations of their respective countries' trade unions.[17]

Did the special commission, whose duty it was to prepare the text of the resolution and which met in private, re-examine the proposal before the Congress at Basle? It seems so.

The commission examined several drafts and there were lively discussions on the question of a general strike. References to these differences are found in Vaillant's statement to the Congress:

All the members of the commission entrusted with the preparation of the manifesto have expressed the wish to endow the manifesto with the same spirit as is evident in the resolutions of our French national congress.[18] But some of these ideas, which to many of us seem particularly important, could not be explicitly incorporated into the manifesto without danger to, or doubt on the part of, other sections.

[16] Ibid. On 10 May, Huysmans asked Vaillant whether he thought that the ISB ought to ask for consultation with the CGT. 'Would the latter give an answer?' Vaillant suggested that Huysmans should appeal personally to the CGT 'so as not to violate in the least its independence or its autonomy'. Besides, Vaillant added that 'The CGT rightly claims that its opinion and rights should be respected, but it is ready to side with the militant proletariat at any moment, especially against war and militarism' (letter from Nice, 17 May 1912, ISB archives).

[17] ISB archives. The new circular was sent in June 1912 to the secretaries of the affiliated parties. Two months later, Vaillant published in *Le Socialiste* an article entitled 'La grève générale contre la guerre', in which he restated and developed his arguments and finally concluded in a categorical tone: 'What has been up to now nothing but a wish, has become a possibility, and thus the International's duty, an imperative duty' (quoted from M. Dommanget, *Édouard Vaillant*, 505–6).

[18] Vaillant is referring to the extraordinary congress of the SFIO which met in Paris on 21 Nov. 1912 just before the Congress of Basle. The resolution adopted once more emphatically confirms the determination of the French socialists: 'In case of war the International must make use of the entire energy and efforts of the labouring classes and of the Socialist Party to avert war by every means, including parliamentary intervention, open agitation, manifestos, as well as general strike and insurrection . . .' But if, in spite of all these efforts, France does become involved in war, 'the French workers and socialists can honestly claim that the peoples being set against each other have never been more justified in resorting to revolutionary means, such as general strike and insurrection, to avoid this conflict, or to bring it to an end, and to render powerless the ruling classes which have unleashed the war' (*L'Humanité*, 22 Nov. 1912).

But the idea of a general strike and insurrection has not been rejected nor has the determination to use them, as a last resort, against war. Insurrection and strike were the best weapons of the revolution in Russia in 1905: they are being used again today and it is they that are keeping the intrigues and military adventures of Czarism in check. But the language of the International cannot be the language of one national section. The International calls upon all national sections to take action against war, it has confidence in each one of them, convinced that each will do its duty and use its available means and strength and the whole of its energy to make war impossible.[19]

The national section Vaillant referred to was the German section. But as we shall see, the German reservations were not only of a legal nature.[20] Vaillant interpreted the debates in the commission in his own way and mistook his wishes for facts. The episode referred to remains shrouded in mystery. On the day before the congress, during the whole of the evening of 23 November 1912, and the morning of the next day before the ceremonial opening, the ISB met to consider the commission's draft manifesto and to prepare a joint text that could be adopted unanimously without discussion by the 550 delegates present in Basle.[21] We do not have the official report of this meeting. It seems that it was Victor Adler 'the wittiest man of the Second International', as Charles Rappoport called him —and on whom the ISB relied to smooth out the differences— who suggested a compromise solution. In spite of its strong language the manifesto failed to satisfy some delegates, Rosa Luxemburg among them. They asked for a paragraph to be incorporated into the text stating that it was necessary to take

[19] Vaillant's speech has been translated from the French report published in the *Bulletin périodique du BSI* [no English version], iv. 10 (1913), 14 ff.

[20] According to Kamenev, 'The words "general strike and insurrection" were not included in the manifesto adopted by the Basle Congress because of the same considerations which determined the resolutions of the Stuttgart and Copenhagen congresses' (O. Hess Gankin and H. H. Fisher, *The Bolsheviks and the World War*, 87).

[21] Longuet, 74. According to the Bolshevik delegate Kamenev: '. . . a special commission of five members . . . worked hard on the elaboration of the manifesto and also . . . the International Socialist Bureau [which] had devoted several of its meetings to this subject' (ibid.).

radical steps such as an anti-militaristic genera strike to prevent or to end war.[22]

The fact that it was impossible to reach agreement explains why the text submitted to the congress for adoption made no reference to concrete means of preventing war. Jaurès commented that: 'because of the enormous variety of possibilities' the resolution envisaged no particular course of action but at the same time 'did not exclude a single one'. Jaurès's most important idea is undoubtedly found in the second part of the sentence. It was impossible to foresee what means ought to be resorted to in the fight against war because the decision could only be taken on the basis of unpredictable and particular circumstances.[23] On 30 November 1912 Jaurès elaborated his ideas in a commentary on the work of the congress published by the *Dépêche de Toulouse*:

If in spite of all our efforts war should break out tomorrow or the day after, if a criminal and senseless conflict should pit our nations, the workers of all countries who have sent us here [to Basle], against one another, what would we do then? It is really impossible to give a universally valid answer to this momentous question. It is impossible to say in advance: it is by taking such and such an action that the proletarians will make their power felt in the troubled hour of the storm.[24]

[22] On this meeting, we have a short and inaccurate account by Manó Buchinger, the Hungarian delegate to the ISB, quoted in J. Jemnitz's article, 'A II Internacionale Bázeli Kongreszusa', *Történelmi Szemle*, no. 1 (1962), 80. On the other hand it is known that at the ISB meeting of 29 Oct. 1912 Rosa Luxemburg demanded that the manifesto should say 'that the only effective means of preventing a world war is proletarian mass action. This action must be strengthened in form and intensity as the threat of war increases so that in the event of the ultimate calamity it can culminate in decisive revolutionary mass action'. (See the report of the ISB meeting in *LZ*, 31 Oct. 1912.)

It must be noted that at Basle, the Bolshevik delegate, Kamenev, entirely approved of the draft: 'I, who represented the Central Committee of the RSDL Party in the International Socialist Bureau, considered that the reference to the methods of fighting as stated in the manifesto was entirely sufficient' (O. Hess Gankin and H. H. Fisher, op cit. 87).

[23] K. Kautsky advanced the same argument as Jaurès in his article 'Der Baseler Kongreß und die Kriegshetze in Österreich', *NZ* xxxi. i, no. 10 (1912), 338.

[24] *Œuvres de Jaurès*, vol. v, 186 ff. For Lenin's interpretation of this manifesto, see his article 'The Failure of the International (1915)', published in *Œuvres*, vol. xxi 212–15 and 318.

According to Karl Kautsky the Basle resolution—known as the International's Manifesto—was a 'wise and carefully thought out' document, or as Walling says: 'It unquestionably represents the point, as well as limit, reached by the overwhelming majority of Socialists at the outbreak of the present war, as to the general issue it involves.' By leaving unresolved the question of the means to be used, it allowed the representatives of the various factions and the leaders of the national parties complete freedom of interpretation. Whereas congress resolutions were normally limited to a few generalizations, an effort was made on this occasion to state clearly what the proletariat's international policy should be depending on the circumstances. After summarizing the arguments of past congresses and defining the principles of socialist foreign policy, the resolution continued with the categorical statement that the war to come could only be an imperialist one. It stressed that: 'The great nations of Europe are constantly in danger of being set against each other without anyone being able to justify these crimes against humanity and reason with even the slightest pretext of any national interest.' In the second part the document outlined the tasks of the socialist parties of the Balkan peninsula, Austria-Hungary, and Russia. But 'the most important task of the International's action' fell to the working classes of Germany, France, and Great Britain; they were required to do their utmost to bridge the differences between the great powers. At the same time the congress warned the ruling classes that war could only cause 'exasperation and anger among the proletarians of all countries' and unleash a revolution.

Proletarians regard it as a crime to shoot at each other for the profit of capitalists, to further the ambitions of dynasties, or for the sake of secret diplomatic treaties. If the governments, by cutting off every possibility of normal development, drive the proletariat of Europe to desperate steps they must bear the whole responsibility for the consequences of the crisis which they have provoked.

The International for its part promised solemnly to redouble its anti-war efforts by 'ever more energetic propaganda, by ever firmer protests'. The manifesto offered a theoretical and political solution to the question that had preoccupied socialist thinking for years: how to give greater prominence to the struggle for peace. The anti-war movement must be expanded to include, besides the proletariat, the middle classes and all pacifist elements.[25] This was how the Basle Congress, without offering anything new, ended a subtle and fruitless discussion in defence of the policy advocated by Kautsky, a policy which the Belgian socialists had pursued for years and which the ISB Executive Committee tried to carry out in collaboration with the Inter-Parliamentary Union. The congress thereby rejected the theories of the Extreme Left (Radek, Pannekoek, and Lensch) who said that the nature of capitalism was such that war could not be prevented. They therefore denied that it was possible or necessary to involve the middle classes in the fight against militarism and regarded the International's general disarmament policy as utopian and anti-revolutionary.

In the history of socialism the extraordinary Congress of Basle remains 'the most powerful and impressive anti-war demonstration' organized by the socialists before 1914. The numerous delegates' reports are filled with exultation and enthusiasm:

In the deliberations, in the words, and in the thoughts of the International convened in Basle [wrote Jaurès] there was a poignant emotion and a form of tragic seriousness. Indeed none of us will ever forget those days, as Bebel said . . . It was evident there that for all those who cared about peace and civilization the International of the socialist proletariat is a great moral force, the last refuge and the last hope.[26]

A letter Alexandra Kollontai wrote to T. L. Ščepkina-Kupernik gives evidence of the same exultation:

One felt the need to frighten Europe, to threaten it with the 'red spectre', revolution, in case the governments should risk a war.

[25] Kautsky advanced the idea of a broad anti-war front in his article 'Der Krieg und die Internationale', *NZ* xxxi. i. 14 (1912), 474. This idea was taken up during the congress by Haase and Adler.
[26] *Œuvres de Jaurès*, vol. v, 187.

And standing on the table which served as a platform I did threaten
Europe . . . It was tremendous, you know, the protest of the peoples
against war, and Jaurès's marvellous voice, and the wonderful and
hoary head of my beloved Keir Hardie, and the great organ, and
the revolutionary songs, the meetings . . . I am still dizzy with all I
have lived through . . .[27]

The reverberations of the congress were considerable, not
only in the ranks of international socialism but also among
wider sections of public opinion in Europe and in government circles. The Basle Congress was a reassuring moment
in the severe crisis which Europe experienced in November
1912.

Nevertheless, the great display of unity and radicalism of
the international socialist movement which the congress was
meant to be depended on clever staging before the awesome
backcloth of a European war which seemed imminent in those
days. As soon as the tension raised by the Congress eased
the basic lack of unity became apparent. The report of the
Basle Congress which was intended for the general public
showed that the trend and the radical terminology of the
speeches made on that occasion had disturbed a substantial
section of German social democracy. Clara Zetkin pointed out
to Camille Huysmans in December 1912 that the editors of the
German report of the Congress had 'for opportunistic reasons'
weakened the text by making a number of cuts where delegates'
speeches had been too radical for them.[28]

Today the historian sees this fact as symptomatic, but at the
time the leaders of the International did not ascribe to it any
political meaning. In the serious international situation of
December 1912 these 'small deviations' seemed not to detract
from the great fighting spirit displayed by all sections of the
International. In the months following the congress the socialist

[27] Quoted from G. D. Petrov, 'A. Kollontai nakanune i v gody pervoj mirovoj
voiny (1908–1916 gg.)', *Novaja i novejšaja istorija*, no. 1 (1969), 76.
[28] G. Haupt, *La Deuxième Internationale*, 37, ft. 3.

parties, supported by the trade unions, were ready to carry out the Basle resolutions to the letter. In December 1912 great anti-war demonstrations by the workers took place everywhere in Europe. The Austrian socialist party, which was the one most concerned, concentrated its energies on opposition to the diplomatic manœuvres of the government of the monarchy.

Although the ISB persisted in its view and although the pacifist enthusiasm of the working masses continued to grow, no decision had really been taken. Were the leaders of the International aware of this? In their public utterances the main spokesmen of socialism—with the exception of Jaurès, who made no secret of his fears—expressed great confidence in the outcome of the international crisis. But the unpublished documents have revealed another side of the picture: the precarious position of the International's leaders who were determined not to let themselves be dictated to by events, but who were paralysed by the course of these very events, the significance and extent of which threatened to escape them. The doctrine had been laid down at Basle, but its application depended upon whether the real impact of the threat could be foreseen. In fact the socialist leaders were poorly informed about the fluctuations of the conflicts between the great powers, and even the socialist deputies did not know what took place in their state chancelleries. This lack of news—the repercussions of which were to be felt so seriously in July 1914—was to the fore in December 1912–January 1913. In the highly confused political situation during this period the ISB, without reliable news by which to judge the situation, faced the dilemma of acting either precipitously or too late. By premature action the International stood to lose its prestige and to jeopardize the future of the whole pacifist struggle, while waiting too long would mean total defeat. The uncertainty and the risk involved explain the manner in which the ISB implemented the Basle resolutions during the First Balkan War.

Early in December 1912 the situation seemed again so disastrous and European war so near that Jaurès spoke anxiously of the 'fear that grips all nations'. 'We are not certain whether the nightmare that shakes our conscience and tortures our reason will not soon become a reality.'

The sole object of our anxiety and of our campaign is to ward off the threat of war [Vaillant wrote to the Secretary of the ISB]. If the French government is pacifist and if we make every endeavour to strengthen its attitude [pacifism], we can still not do as we should, and, besides, we regret that it [the French government] remains so inert when one could act more efficiently for peace through drawing closer to Germany which seems to be a pacifist country, and through tightening the bonds of friendship with England. But a government ruled by helpless advocates of pacifism does not want, and does not dare to, take any steps in that direction.

Vaillant believed that, except for Austria's threat, the most important factor for peace was Germany's determination and wish to maintain it.[29]

In their attempts to judge the situation the ISB and the socialist leaders had only two sources on which to rely: press agency dispatches and the information provided by the executives of the socialist parties of the countries concerned. Accurate news from Austria was eagerly awaited because the Austro-Serbian conflict which concealed the Austro-Russian conflict was regarded as the most immediate threat. The news published in the press merely created confusion. Vaillant wrote to Huysmans on 14 December 1912:

Every day the press, depending on the influences to which it is subject, carries reports of the danger threatening from Austria and of Austria's aggressive preparations or of provocative behaviour and speeches by Serbia and we have no means of knowing how much truth there is in these claims.[30]

The French socialists did not know that a large part of the French press was involved in a clever defamation campaign,

---

[29] Vaillant to Huysmans, 13 Dec. 1912 (dated 14 Dec.), ISB archives.
[30] Vaillant to Huysmans, 14 Dec. 1912 (ibid.).

directed or financially assisted by the Russian ambassador in Paris from the beginning of the Balkan crisis.

In December 1912, in the midst of 'so much confusion and so many apparent or real differences'[31] the leaders of the International waited impatiently for 'an estimate of the situation by such a sensible man as Adler who knows or rather, at this moment will certainly know whether the danger is imminent or inevitable, or whether it is definitely receding',[32] though the 10 December issue of the Austrian socialist party organ, *Arbeiter Zeitung*, sounded the first soothing note and declared that the immediate danger of an armed conflict between Austria and Serbia had died down.

The Austrian socialists thereafter tended to consider a Balkan war as a peripheral conflict, 'inevitable [. . .] just and liberating for the Balkan peoples', in Adler's terms, but which lay beyond the influence and sphere of action of European socialism. The International was indeed obliged to espouse the cause of the autonomy of the Balkan and Slavic peoples, but in the circumstances and on a practical level, it had to confine itself to delaying tactics which mainly served to palliate the danger. It was this point of view which prevailed. Even Vaillant resigned himself to limiting the activities of the ISB as suggested by his Viennese counterpart to ensuring that the war would not spread to Russia and Austria.

As a result of the impossibility of translating its pacifism into concrete action, the International was henceforth condemned to follow the events without being able to influence them. As a pressure group, it was practically impotent. It had no other powers left but to offer its good services in the diplomatic sphere, as it had done during the Morocco crisis. Such was the task which devolved upon the Executive Committee. Its secretary, Huysmans, was willing to consider any suggestion which might facilitate negotiations. And there was no lack of

[31] Vaillant to Huysmans, 18 Dec. 1912; Vaillant remarks regretfully: 'At such distance and being so badly informed, we can hardly know what is happening' (ISB archives).

[32] Vaillant to Huysmans, 13 Dec. 1912 (ibid.).

suggestions. In mid-December, the French delegate, Vaillant, proposed to the International Socialist Secretariat two moves. Firstly, that it should take the initiative to convene a joint conference of Austrian and Balkan socialists as soon as circumstances permitted. In the opinion of Vaillant, the immediate threat came from the Austro-Serbian conflict, and therefore anything that could lead to an easing of this tension 'served to promote peace in Europe'. On 14 December, he recalled in support of his suggestion,

> that in the case of every—at least seemingly—limited conflict the International has always been of the opinion that intervention by the socialists of the countries concerned, who have jointly at a conference searched for ways of solving the conflict, was a socialist and practical necessity.

In addition, on 18 December, Vaillant asked Huysmans to investigate the possibility of letting the neutral countries, such as Belgium, Holland, and Denmark, ask for an arbitration tribunal through the International's respective national sections.[33]

Huysmans had reservations regarding the first suggestion because, in the circumstances, calling such a conference might raise a number of difficulties. Nevertheless, he immediately passed on Vaillant's proposal to Adler.[34] As for the second suggestion, it was merely implementing an initiative which Huysmans had already taken in response to a Scandinavian proposal. In his reply to Vaillant he referred to his own efforts:

> Referring to the resolutions of the Scandinavian group, which is composed of all parties and whose aim it is to unite the neutrals so that they might submit to the great powers a proposal for progressive disarmament, I recall that I have already twice suggested the idea in the Belgian Parliament and on the second occasion the reply of

[33] ISB archives.
[34] On 16 December Huysmans sent Adler Vaillant's letters dated 13 and 14 Dec., with the laconic comment: 'Are you still optimistic?' (Victor Adler Nachlaß, Vienna, Arbeiterkammer).

the Belgian Government was not entirely negative. I have called upon all the neutrals to continue the work of the Scandinavians so that one of the important states will make a start and put the proposal into practice. As a result the neutrals have held a special meeting to discuss how they can carry out my plan.[35]

The attention of the secretaries of the socialist parliamentary groups affiliated to the International was drawn to this discussion by means of a circular.[36] No further step was taken, since the Austrian socialists regarded the situation as less serious and less hopeless than did their French counterparts.

When Adler received the copy of Vaillant's letter he immediately telegraphed to Brussels: 'Calm down, the situation is less threatening than ever.'[37] On the same day, 19 December, in a long letter to the ISB he surveyed the general situation in Europe.[38] He accused the Executive Committee and the delegates of the French section of judging the facts from reports in a tendentious press. He well understood, he wrote, the existing disquiet 'since you and our Paris friends are under the influence of *Le Temps* and *Le Matin*, which both present Austria as even more stupid and provocative than she really is'.[39] Nevertheless

[35] ISB archives. A year later the secretary of the International wrote in his report on his activities for the year 1912–13: 'While the Balkan war was in full swing—a war which for the Workers' International was an incentive to continue and to strengthen its anti-militaristic activities begun during the Morocco conflict and the Turko-Italian war—we directed, at the request of our Swedish comrades, who were supported by the Danish group, the attention of the socialist parliamentary groups, which are members of the Inter-Parliamentary Union, to a disarmament campaign of the Swiss Inter-Parliamentary group on the issue of implementing the decision taken at the Geneva Conference (September 1912), to call upon the national inter-parliamentary groups to use every opportunity, particularly budget debates, to bring the armaments questions before their parliaments. Although the parliamentary groups are profoundly divided on the question of participation in the work of the Inter-Parliamentary Union, we have, in view of the objective, thought it right to agree to the request of our Scandinavian friends.' The full text of the report is published in Haupt, *Le Congrès manqué*, 277–81.

[36] Circular no. 28 for 1912, ISB archives.

[37] ISB archives.

[38] Ibid.

[39] In his letters, Victor Adler expressed his suspicion: according to him, the Parisian press drew its inspiration from the Russian embassy. *Le Temps*, *Le Journal des Débats*, and *L'Écho de Paris* had in fact received important subsidies through a special agent, Davidov. Cf. Caroll Malcolm, *French Public Opinion and Foreign Affairs, 1870–1914* (New York, 1931), 266–74.

he hoped that the trend of the last few days had convinced the French and Belgians that Austria did not want war.

There are certainly signs pointing to extensive preparations the cost of which probably amounts to not less than one billion [crowns]. But this is apparently a bluff designed to frighten the Serbs. Among the latter there had been a considerable reaction which reached its climax during the Basle Congress; since then things have quietened down. It seems that Russia does not want to risk war and it is possible that conditions in Eastern Asia are playing a greater part in this than fear of revolution, even though in Poland, and particularly in Galicia, revolutionary preparations are in progress on a scale hitherto unknown . . . You will realize that because our Poles are very sympathetic towards a future revolution they are less afraid of the war, indeed they almost hope for it because it offers an opportunity for revolution. The pitiful state of the Poles, less in Austria than in Russia, can be gauged from the fact that they are even ready to join forces with Austria. As it seems that a sobering influence is now being exerted also on Serbia, I regard the threat of war as more remote than ever and believe that, unless something completely unexpected occurs, peace is assured.

Adler went on to say that he had strongly supported the idea of a meeting of Austrian and Serbian socialists which Vaillant, who had confidence in the Austrian party, had suggested on several occasions. Still, his answer was a polite and diplomatic dodge, since he considered the Serbian party as temporarily paralysed by the war in the Balkans.

Adler's letter was sent as 'strictly confidential' to Vaillant and Jaurès. It arrived at a time when the socialist leaders, who were anxiously following the work of the London conference, feared a breakdown in negotiations.[40] On 24 December Vaillant wrote to Huysmans:

The catastrophe which we expected in London has fortunately not occurred and the papers report this morning that there was no breakdown and that the conference is meeting. We can hope therefore that Adler's optimistic forecast will come true. It is wonderful that

[40] On the conference which opened in London on 18 Dec. as well as on the diplomatic shifts during the Balkan crisis, cf. Douglas Dakin, 'The Diplomacy of the Great Powers and the Balkan States, 1908–1914', *Balkan Studies* iii. 2 (1962), 356–73; Fritz Fischer, *Der Krieg der Illusionen* (Düsseldorf, 1969), 249 ff.

the spirit of belligerency in Austria should have abated to such an extent and we can only hope that demobilization, which is so desirable and which our friend has not mentioned, will follow soon. If events take a peaceful turn as he [Adler] envisages and as now seems very probable we shall have a chance of being doubly pleased; not only will war have been avoided but the International will reap the fruits of its great effort in the form of increased power and growth.[41]

From late December 1912 onwards Adler spread increasingly reassuring news about the immediate future.[42] The French delegates, however, found it difficult to accept these optimistic predictions: 'It seems unlikely that the Austrian cloud will disperse as quickly as our friends appear to believe.'[43] Vaillant, who was worried about the threat of war, addressed more and more letters to the ISB. Therefore Adler wrote to him direct on 1 February. He reassured Vaillant that he was under the influence of the Paris press, particularly of *Le Matin*

which simply tells lies. I must openly admit that whenever I pick up these papers I myself become nervous and start believing in the threat of war. By warmongering the Austrian Government has committed a fearful crime, the result of which is making itself felt in a serious economic crisis, but it does not want to wage war and will not do so as far as one can see today.

Vaillant's repeated request for a meeting of Austrian and Balkan socialists was neither practical nor necessary. The conflict was no longer between Austria and Serbia but between

[41] ISB archives.

[42] Adler, for instance, wrote to Bebel on 26 Dec. 1912: 'Otherwise things are at last looking a little brighter and for the moment we are at last rid of the fear of war. It is becoming increasingly clear that—as I suspected—our people did not *seriously want war*, that the whole show of armaments was merely intended to intimidate.— But this has cost roughly one billion in cash and has produced an economic depression which is quite terrible. The shortage of money has led to bankruptcy and reduced output on a frightening scale and the diplomatic 'success' can never remotely compensate for what we have lost.—As a party we have done extremely well and instead of the great to-do which threatened immediately after Basle there have been second thoughts and, more important, real Austrian weakness which makes it impossible for the Austrians to be either consistently wicked or consistently good' (*Victor Adler Briefwechsel*, 558).

[43] Vaillant to Huysmans, 5 Jan. 1913, ISB archives; Vaillant to Adler, 25 Jan. 1913, Victor Adler Nachlaß (Vienna, Arbeiterkammer).

Bulgaria and Turkey. From this Adler concluded: 'Because
Russia and Austria do not want war, and this seems absolutely
certain for the time being, we need have no serious fears about
the immediate future.'[44]

The CAP like the Austrian socialists, believed that the
Balkan disagreements would shortly be resolved by peaceful
means. But at the same time the French delegates repeatedly
advised the ISB not to relax its energetic anti-militarist efforts.
On 4 February 1913 Vaillant sent a copy of Adler's letter to
Huysmans through Albert Thomas with the following comment:

We can rely on the discreet vigilance of our Austrian friends who
will do their duty as before in resisting the war if there is a new
threat . . . Given that the most important factor in the struggle for
peace is a pacifist orientation of public opinion, a trend which
thanks to the International's efforts is noticeable even among the
unorganized proletariat, it is important that our propaganda against
war and for peace does not diminish and that the anti-war and anti-
militarist campaign is always placed on the agenda of all demonstrations and rallies for whichever reason they are held, in all
countries, in yours, ours, and everywhere else. Only by these means
can further and perhaps imminent threats be banished.[45]

The profound anxiety which characterized the attitude of the
French socialists during this period did not diminish. They
followed international developments closely day by day.

As the situation seemed once more to be deteriorating, the
CAP at its meeting of 18 February 1913 investigated 'the
dangerous situation created by the ominous increase in military
expenditure in most European countries'.[46] The general
opinion was that 'for this reason and also because of the con-

[44] A copy of this letter is in the ISB archives.
[45] Vaillant to Huysmans, 4 Feb. 1913, ISB archives.
[46] Cf. Louis Dubreuilh to the ISB secretariat, 20 Feb. 1913, and Vaillant to
Huysmans, 20 Feb. 1913, ISB archives; the request for an ISB session was published
by the ISB secretariat in *Le Peuple*, 22 Feb. 1913, 1: 'The French socialists demand a
session of the ISB.' At its meeting of 18 Feb. the CAP voted for a resolution expressing its whole-hearted opposition to any attempt by the government to increase military expenditure and to the 'three year conscription law'. Cf. 'Le parti
socialiste et les syndicats ouvriers contre le militarisme', *Le Mouvement socialiste*
(Mar./Apr. 1913), 237–9.

tinued war in the Balkans international peace [is] perhaps more threatened than ever'.

The CAP therefore asked Jaurès, Guesde, and Vaillant to demand that the ISB should be convened at the earliest possible opportunity to examine two questions:

1. How to continue and to co-ordinate in the present critical situation anti-war activities decided upon by the International at Basle.
2. How to counter the offensive of militaristic imperialism and the new armaments campaign, particularly in Germany and France.[47]

In the opinion of Vaillant who transmitted the CAP's proposal, 'socialist public opinion is waiting impatiently for [the ISB] to be convened because it counts on joint and energetic action by all sections of the International'. The proposal was transmitted immediately to Victor Adler and the SPD executive.[48] This time, it reached them at the right moment. The acceleration of the armaments race in Germany and, on the other hand, the growing feeling of revenge among the French alarmed the SPD executive. A letter from Haase to his son is most revealing in this respect:

Those sections that are susceptible to chauvinism are made absolutely rabid by fear. France is in an awkward situation because being less populated, she finds herself increasingly overshadowed by Germany. Army corps cannot be conjured up, whereas in Germany one can draw on the great reservoir of manpower. But rearmament in our country borders on madness. According to the latest information the military estimates require a nonrecurring expenditure of one billion marks and a recurring annual expenditure of a quarter of a billion marks.[49]

When the SPD executive received Vaillant's letter of 21 February, it met at once. Pronouncing against the CAP's initiative, it nevertheless agreed with its fundamental purpose.

---

[47] Vaillant to Huysmans, 21 Feb. 1913, ISB archives.   [48] ISB archives.
[49] Hugo Haase to Ernst Haase, 2 Mar. 1913, in E. Haase, *Hugo Haase*, 101. Concerning the growth of feelings of revenge in France, see Eugen Weber, *The National Revival in France, 1905–1914* (Berkeley–Los Angeles, UCL UP, 1959), 113.

It submitted to the French a counterproposal identical with the idea publicly suggested by the SFIO representatives in 1912: strengthening mutual relationships and joint action.

Bebel laconically imparted to Adler the results of the debates: 'A week ago, at the SPD executive we rejected Vaillant's proposal; we decided to call on the French to draft an open statement together.'[50]

On 24 February Albert Thomas, the SFIO delegate, arrived in Berlin with the draft of a Franco-German manifesto written by Jaurès. Later he described how for forty-eight hours he fought bitterly to have it adopted. Bebel and Scheidemann had been critical, Haase, Bernstein, and others in favour.[51] After long discussions a final, more restrained, text was agreed upon which retained the original author's most important ideas. On 26 February Albert Thomas returned to Paris with the manifesto. On the day of Thomas's departure from Berlin Hermann Müller informed the ISB Executive Committee of the outcome of these negotiations.

Since last Friday we have been in direct negotiation with the French party leadership. A member of the French socialist parliamentary group [Albert Thomas] was here for several days for an oral exchange of views and has now returned to Paris. We have agreed with our French comrades on joint opposition to the Franco-German armaments demands.[52]

The CAP also received from the Secretary of the ISB a copy of Adler's reply to the former, agreeing with the German point of view. Victor Adler said that in view of 'Germany's military requirements and their echo in France Franco-German collaboration is all that was necessary'. But the authority of the ISB must not be brought into play because

these are things that go through *parliaments*, that must and will be fought in parliament and at rallies *in every country*. All the ISB can

[50] Bebel to Adler, 28 Feb. 1913, in *Victor Adler Briefwechsel*, 562.
[51] B. W. Schaper, *Albert Thomas: trente ans de réformisme social* (Paris, PUF, [1960]), 88.
[52] Cf. Hermann Müller to the ISB, 26 Feb. 1913 (copy of this letter in the ISB archives).

do by way of action is to organize a *protest* and such a manifesto—particularly if signed jointly by the Germans and French—can be issued equally well without convening the ISB. I am afraid that we would have *nothing new to say* if we meet—and what we want to say we can say—*sans déplacement.*[53]

This intervention dispelled the last reservations as clearly shown at the meeting of 28 February, on which Vaillant reported to the Executive Committee in these terms:

Yesterday at the meeting of the CAP Bureau and the socialist group in parliament we declared, as they [the German Executive] did, that there are firm and permanent links between the German and the French Socialist Party for the purpose of joint action against militarist projects and new armaments—joint action that finds expression in the joint manifesto published today—, that such joint action is the best way of proceeding in the present situation and that we agree with our German and Austrian friends that for the moment there is no need for the ISB to meet.[54]

At the beginning of March 1913 both the German and Austrian socialists and the SFIO therefore believed that the Balkan crisis, although continuing to be a source of potential trouble, was approaching a peaceful solution or was at least becoming localized. The International thought that there was no longer a serious threat to peace. The burden created by the International's responsibility in case of an imminent European clash was becoming lighter; it no longer seemed imperative to decide on measures to prevent an early conflict. What seemed important in the long run was to further the beginning of an international *détente*, to work for closer relations between the great powers in order to find new solutions for disputed questions (for example, Alsace-Lorraine); also to insist on arbitration courts and then to agree on general, gradual disarmament. The International was of the opinion that first of all an end had to be put to the reign of 'armed peace', that the arms race, the emergence of militaristic and chauvinistic tendencies in

[53] Cf. Victor Adler to the ISB, 26 Feb. 1913 (typewritten copy of this letter from Monte Carlo in the ISB archives).
[54] Letter by Vaillant of 1 Mar, 1913, ISB archives.

France and Germany must be resisted, thereby contributing to a *rapprochement* between the two countries as a first step towards an alliance of the three western powers (Britain, France, and Germany). This was the new theory which the International advanced in 1913 and to which it clung until July 1914. Joint action by French and German socialists was thus not only the result of the resolutions adopted by the congress in Basle. It marked a turning-point and heralded a new line in international socialist policy.

PART II

The Road to Defeat

5
Turning-point 1913

In 1913 the air seemed clearer than in previous years. The endless conflict in the Balkans in which, as Jaurès put it, 'nerves had been strained to breaking point' was settled. The end of the serious crises through which Europe had passed in 1911 and 1912 produced a wave of optimism in the International; it also provided justification and a point of departure for short-term theories, thereby distorting all long-term analysis of the growth of tension between the great powers.

This reappraisal of the trends of international policy was not merely based on an evaluation of the political situation. It was, as we shall see, the consequence of an approach to imperialism that came to be endorsed by Kautsky, Bebel, Otto Bauer, and others.

With the end of the Balkan crises the theory that a European war was improbable appeared to have found confirmation. Its advocates, among whom there were a growing number of leading socialists, believed that the new economic interests of capitalism would in the very near future lead to a policy of *rapprochement* among the great powers and to general disarmament. As for the more cautious among those leaders, they subscribed to the analysis that Georg Ledebour, one of the centre left theorists of the SPD, had formulated in 1911, that 'there are so many and such powerful anti-war factors at work in the capitalist order of society that capitalism can no longer be regarded as wholly militant in its overall activity'.[1] This theory which finds clear expression in the documents of the International is one of the major and momentous results of the ups and downs of the Balkan crisis; it was the product of an exaggerated faith in the possibility of peace found among pacifists of all trends. Jaurès

[1] *Vorwärts* (8 Apr. 1911).

was aware of the danger inherent in such an attitude; on 13 April
1913 he wrote with a clear-sightedness that contrasted sharply
with the easy optimism of most of the International's leaders:

Europe has been afflicted by so many crises for so many years, it has
been put dangerously to the test so many times without war breaking
out that it has almost ceased to believe in the threat and is watching
the further development of the interminable Balkan conflict with
decreasing attention and reduced disquiet. Yet if one goes to the
heart of the matter the threat has never been greater than now.
Every day that passes shows up ever more cruelly the degree of
Europe's impotence and greatly increases her loss of repute.[2]

But before long the Balkan crisis seemed to have passed its
peak and there appeared to be a definite turn for the better.
The Second Balkan War was accepted very calmly as an after-
effect of the preceding conflict and as a phenomenon of only
regional importance which could no longer seriously threaten
the peace of Europe.[3]

Although Jaurès and the SFIO were affected by the wave of
optimism, the latter did not relax its international activity nor
did its preoccupation with peace diminish. The socialist press
was constantly appealing for vigilance against militarism, but
it did so undramatically and without conveying the feeling that
the threat was still immediate. The ISB maintained the role of
spectator; in doing so it adopted the advice of Adler who was
for ever exhorting it to pursue a policy of caution. The Austrian party leader's international prestige had risen during this
crisis because his analysis of the situation was evidence of his
political insight and remarkable astuteness. He thought that in
the new circumstances the International must try not to lose the
impetus received at Basle; the ISB must not be allowed to
commit itself to careless action that might jeopardize its success.
'I am convinced that we must not weaken the brilliant effect of
Basle by campaigns in which the exertion is in inverse relation

---

[2] *Œuvres de Jaurès*, vol. v, 233.
[3] In this connection the unpublished correspondence between the ISB secretariat and the delegates of the socialist parties of the Balkan countries, Austrian,
and France is conclusive.

to the result,' Adler wrote to the ISB in February 1913.[4] The offensive impulse generated by the Basle congress was weakened and then stifled in the ranks of the socialist movement.

In 1913 the *Neue Zeit* noted the collapse of the anti-militarist movement in Germany. Rosa Luxemburg accused the party leadership of infamous behaviour for not carrying 'the torch of Basle' more widely into the working class.

> According to the letter and the exact meaning of the Manifesto the congress should not have been the end but the beginning of a vast anti-militarist campaign, the signal for using every ounce of energy for this purpose . . . Here in Germany almost nothing has been done after Basle to exploit the results of the international congress.[5]

At the Jena congress in September 1913, Scheidemann admitted that the party leadership had failed to make the efforts required to maintain the offensive impetus, but according to him, this was an impossible task. A certain weariness had taken hold of the whole population, 'the people have been in a turmoil of protest for many months what with the demonstrations against the rising "cost of living", against the Balkan war, the military bill protests, etc'.[6] In fact this change of direction, marked by the end of the anti-militarist offensive, was not the result of tactical considerations. It was the consequence of the International's basic orientation, of its entire strategy.

Although the struggle for peace remained a propaganda topic, it was no longer possible to mobilize the masses for this cause. The settlement of the European crisis was one of the elements responsible for a wave of optimism that was given further impetus by the International's attitude during this difficult period. The conviction continued to grow that European socialism and proletarian internationalism could resist the threat of war and the emergence of chauvinism. It was but a reflection of the socialists' self-satisfaction.

As far as militarism is concerned [the secretary of the International said in the spring of 1914] I note with satisfaction that we have done

---

[4] Victor Adler to Camille Huysmans, 26 Feb. 1913, ISB archives.
[5] Cf. *LZ* (6 June 1913).   [6] *Protokoll* (Jena, 1913), 228–32.

good work . . . We can say that during these past three years the
Socialist International alone has resisted war in all countries—in the
Balkans and in Italy, in Germany, and in Britain. Socialism is and
will continue to be the great force in the service of peace.[7]

Huysmans saw proof of this in the fact that in 1913 the International 'had nearly received the Nobel Peace Prize from the
capitalist class of Scandinavia'. In fact it went to a socialist, the
Belgian senator Henri La Fontaine. The International was convinced that only the prejudice of its political enemies had robbed
it of this award which nevertheless went to honour the efforts
of a socialist. In his report for the year 1913 the secretary of the
ISB announced that 'we have been told by the socialist parliamentary group of Sweden which nominated the ISB for the
Nobel Prize that it will renew its proposal at the next opportunity'. The self-satisfaction which the ISB displayed confirms
that in the eyes of its leading personalities, and of the affiliated
parties, the International had given brilliant proof of its determination to make war on war. Few leading socialists attached
any importance to the breakdown of the leadership of the Italian
section, which over the Libyan war had adopted a nationalistic
attitude. What was pointed out proudly, on the other hand, was
the example of the small socialist parties in the Balkans[8] and
above all the consistent and firm stand and campaign of the
Austrians.

With success the socialists' attitude and also the relationships between the parties changed. The differences of views
which had been so obvious all along seemed to have disappeared.
Thus Jaurès acknowledged the efforts of the German socialists
when he said:

The German socialists are indeed an admirable factor for peace and
civilization. In spite of the weakness of the German parliamentary

[7] Speech delivered by Camille Huysmans at Bradford, 11 Apr. 1914. 'Special
Coming of Age Conference—the 21st Anniversary of the Establishment of the
ILP', ISB archives.

[8] The reports of the socialist parties of the Balkan countries on their activities
during the war were sent by the ISB Executive to the affiliated parties, and the
socialist press of the day frequently published news about the anti-militaristic
struggle of the Bulgarian, Rumanian, and Serbian socialists.

system, in spite of the absolutism and feudalism that still survive in Germany there is no power, however intoxicated with its divine right, that can afford to ignore the clearly expressed determination of four million human beings united in the socialist party and fight for democracy and peace. It is, after all, more difficult to issue the order for war if one knows that the masses have conscientious objections to all use of force.[9]

Jaurès's statement reflects the spirit in which the joint campaign of the two socialist parties, the French and the German, first planned in March 1913, was conducted. The proletariat of the two countries represented not merely an irresistible pressure group, and thus a guarantee for peace, it could also be instrumental in bringing the two countries closer together. 'It is obvious'—Jaurès explained—'that the better the understanding between Germany and France in the sphere of international politics the easier it will be to reduce if not to do away with the historical differences between them.'[10]

The first move in the campaign agreed upon by the two parties was reported by *L'Humanité* on 1 March 1913. It drew the reader's attention to an agreement with the socialists of Germany and Austria: it had been decided to postpone the ISB meeting called for by the CAP, 'as it had been rendered superfluous in the present circumstances by the joint campaign against the militaristic plans of their governments, announced, undertaken and maintained by the German and the French socialists'.[11]

A joint manifesto by the two parties, published in the same issue of the paper,[12] described the links between the two organizations:

[9] *Œuvres de Jaurès*, vol. v, 239.
[10] At the Congress of Brest, Vaillant advanced the same argument: 'A Franco-German *rapprochement* is the only means by which peace can be established throughout the world, once and for all, on a firm and steady basis, and this will bring forth the progress of civilization and of the human institutions for which socialism is fighting and mankind striving.' (*Xe Congrès national tenu à Brest les 23, 24 et 25 mars 1913. Compte rendu sténographique* (Paris, 1913), 244–5.)
[11] See also Vaillant to Huysmans, 1 Mar. 1913, ISB archives.
[12] It was published at the same time in *Vorwärts*, 1 Mar. 1913; quoted in Grünberg, 26–7; see also *Periodical Bull. ISB* v. 11 (1914).

At a time when the governments of Germany and France are preparing to submit new legislation that will further increase their vast military expenditure, the French and German socialists regard it as their duty to close their ranks more firmly than ever before to fight jointly against these mad machinations of the ruling classes.

Into this text, drafted in the spirit of the Basle manifesto, were incorporated all the themes and all the views put forward by the International in that year. The socialists of the two countries regarded themselves as the spokesmen of the German and French people, most of whom also detested war. In order to safeguard peace and to ensure national independence and the progress of democracy, the socialists demanded, in the domestic sphere, the replacement of standing armies by a peoples' militia 'intended only for the defence of the country' and, in the international sphere, the solution of every conflict between countries by means of arbitration.[13]

The manifesto of 1 March 1913 which Haase saw as 'eloquent evidence of the unanimity of the two parties'[14] was received with great interest and gained the general approval of international socialism. The determination of the workers of the two countries to oppose the armaments race seemed the best tool with which to implement the International's foreign policy.

With the establishment of direct contact between the two parties the mediation of the ISB secretariat became, if not superfluous, at any rate more limited. In practice the International had no means of controlling the extent to which the socialist parties of France and Germany fulfilled their obligations. It trusted them and approved of their joint action, described by Jaurès in *L'Humanité* of 2 May 1913:

What makes the present struggle of French and German socialism particularly interesting is . . . that it is concerned with such a

---

[13] On this subject, cf. E.-M. Garber, 'L'arbitrage international devant le mouvement socialiste français (1890–1914)', *La Revue socialiste* 105 (1957), 293–313.
[14] E. Haase, *Hugo Haase*, 105.

wide range of problems. It is a struggle that is huge in scale and precise, passionate and attentive to detail, general and technical. It is concerned with arbitration and with the limitation of armaments; with ensuring peace through international understanding between workers, and through socialist and proletarian action, and also with genuine preparedness to support the willing efforts that all parties and all classes can make, once they have understood the horrors of war and the great evil of armed peace. It is a vigorous and documented denunciation of the scandals of the capitalism of shells, cannons, and machine-guns. It is an attempt to spare the people new military burdens and to ensure that the formidable organs of adventure and aggression develop into a democratic, popular, and purely defensive army. It is concerned with changing the system of taxation so that the wealthy classes, being responsible for the chaos in Europe, are made to shoulder the financial burden of their glory-seeking, reckless, and confused policy. It is in all these spheres that the battle is fought.

Two common aims became clear in the process. In the first place it was necessary to prepare public opinion (among the bourgeoisie as well as the workers)[15] for Franco-German understanding. In France the SFIO conducted an energetic campaign whose main purpose was to draw attention to the pacifist tendencies of the mass of the German workers, to the SPD's anti-war activities, and to the anti-militarist training given by the German party for many years. The electoral triumph of German social democracy in January 1912 which brought it four million votes and 110 seats (out of a total of 397) in the Reichstag, was celebrated by *L'Humanité* with these words: 'The victory of the German socialists is a victory of the proletariat as

[15] The violence of the reaction to the Camille Huysmans incident at the SFIO Congress at Saint-Quentin in April 1911 (cf. *Compte rendu sténographique du Congrès de Saint-Quentin*, 237–44) is indicative of the strength of some of the anti-German feeling in the French party. Because in Belgium Huysmans had expressed himself in favour of handing Ghent over to the Flemish nationalists, he was accused, primarily by Lafargue, but also in less violent terms by de Brouckère and Sembat, of ignoring his obligations as secretary of the ISB. Lafargue even demanded the removal of Huysmans. Light is shed on the background to these attacks by Camille Huysmans's reply of 23 May 1911 to a letter from Louis Dubreuilh requesting an explanation in the name of the SFIO. Huysmans concluded his letter ironically with the sentence: 'As yet I can see neither Anseele nor myself in the pay of Wilhelm II.'

a whole. It is an expression of the universal desire for peace and of the determination to preserve it.' This idea was prevalent in 1913, when many articles appeared in the French socialist press on the internationalism of the German party and thousands of copies of Jean Longuet's pamphlet *Les Socialistes allemands contre la guerre et le militarisme* were distributed. Longuet's central theme was that the internationalism of the SPD 'remains today as strong, as sincere and just as active as it has been from the start'.

The question arises whether in 1913 the majority of the French socialists had fundamentally revised their critical opinion[16] of the German socialists or whether this new approach was simply a propaganda ruse. The evidence is contradictory: it indicates that the mistrust lived on, and also offers proof of complete trust on the part of the majority of French socialists towards the SPD.[17]

One point is certain: in 1913 Charles Andler's evidence of nationalistic and imperialistic trends among German socialists —immediately before the joint Franco-German campaign[18]—

[16] This critical attitude is frequently found in the syndicalist press, for example in Paul Lang, who concludes his lengthy article on the Chemnitz party congress: 'One is forced to ask the question which continues to come to mind: all this is admirable but does it really affect Germany? . . . What in fact is the purpose . . . of these profound discussions, this relentless discipline?' And after recalling the criticism of German social democracy voiced by Jaurès at the Amsterdam Congress, he ends with the words: 'Let us wait and watch the colossus grow' (*Le Mouvement socialiste* xxxii. 245 (Nov. 1912), 261).

[17] Interesting information on this subject is contained in the memoirs of Tseretelli who reports on his conversations with Albert Thomas during the latter's visit to Petrograd in 1917. See A. Tseretelli, *Vospominanija o fevral'skoj revolyutsii* (Paris–The Hague, Mouton, 1963, vol. i), 189 ff.

[18] Referring to various publications by German social democrats Andler drew attention to the existence of a 'neo-Lassallean' trend which led the working classes to feel in sympathy with capitalism, Germany's colonial policy, and an armaments policy which was 'defensive in principle but offensive in an emergency'; he expressed the view that 'if the German Reich is involved in an offensive or a defensive war the German workers cannot desire Germany's defeat.' Andler claimed that recently a substantial number of German socialists had become converted to this form of socialism which was characterized by a lack of scruples. While it continued to safeguard the immediate interests of the workers, this kind of socialism unashamedly betrayed the basic principles of the International. In brief, the new doctrine 'protects the interests of a single proletariat, those of the German proletariat' (Charles Andler, *Le socialisme impérialiste dans l'Allemagne contemporaine.*

had the effect of 'a veritable time-bomb suddenly exploding among the ranks of the Second International'.[19]

Andler's articles—he was a professor at the Sorbonne, known as a socialist and a specialist on German questions—caused a great stir in France and Germany. Jaurès disagreed with him and the SFIO publicly dissociated itself from his views.[20] Was it for political reasons (Andler's arguments were taken up by the opponents of socialism and exploited by the champions of the 'three year conscription law') or for propaganda reasons? (His arguments weakened the campaign for a Franco-German *rapprochement*.) Was the SFIO under the influence of a myth (of international socialist solidarity)? These are questions that cannot be answered without a thorough study of the climate of opinion.[21]

The SFIO's disavowal of Andler certainly did not satisfy the SPD leaders who were stung to the quick. Their indignation is clearly revealed by a letter, dated 2 March 1913, from Haase to his son who happened to be in France:

Andler in his articles completely misunderstands and distorts the views and activities of German social democracy, thereby merely adding grist to the mill of the French chauvinists. If there is one party which has consistently fought militarism and imperialism in the clear realization of what lies at the root of these manifestations, it is German social democracy; and developments are increasingly proving it correct.[22]

Dossier d'une polémique avec Jean Jaurès (1912–1913) (Paris, Bossard, 1918), 261 (1st edn. Paris, 1913, 44 pp., 'L'Action nationale' series).

[19] Alfred Rosmer, *Mouvement ouvrier pendant la guerre* (Paris, 1936, vol. i), 79.

[20] Jaurès accused Andler in March 1913, particularly in *L'Humanité*, of being 'the great purveyor of poison against the socialists' and even of using mutilated or invented texts in his campaign against the German socialists. Lucien Herr, the librarian of the École Normale, a friend of both men, sought to mediate between them. But he was unable to dissuade Andler from leaving the French socialist party and from continuing his campaign. On the dispute see Ernest Tonnelat, *Charles Andler, sa vie et son œuvre* (Paris, Les Belles-Lettres, 1937), 136–50; Harvey Goldberg, *Life of Jean Jaurès* (Madison, 1962), 436 ff.

[21] A great deal of information is contained in Gilbert Zibura, *Die deutsche Frage in der öffentlichen Meinung Frankreichs von 1911–1914* (Berlin, 1955, 'Studien zur europäischen Geschichte, aus dem Friedrich-Meinecke-Institut der Freien Universität Berlin', vol. i); Claude Digeon, *La crise allemande de la pensée française (1870–1914)* (Paris, PUF, 1959). [22] E. Haase, *Hugo Haase*, 101.

Kautsky accused Jaurès and the CAP of being slow to reply to Andler, and without waiting for their comments, published in the *Neue Zeit* a forceful article by Salomon Grumbach refuting Andler's claims.[23] But this article, described by Longuet as a 'devastating answer', could not really clear the atmosphere.

And yet the controversy for which Andler was responsible did not diminish the strength of the Franco-German campaign whose second political aim—opposition to growing armaments —was translated by the socialist party in France into an energetic crusade against the 'three year conscription law'[24] with powerful workers' demonstrations against war and militarism.[25] In Germany the SPD suggested a campaign against the draft laws to raise military expenditure. It must be added that the social democratic group in the Reichstag failed to fulfil its obligations. In June 1913 it approved the increased army estimates by 52 votes against 37. This failure was criticized by the party's left wing ('the moment we give the government the funds to cover military expenditure our whole struggle against militarism becomes a farce'[26]) but not by international socialist opinion, which was satisfied with the explanations of Haase, who tried to prove that the law could in fact help the anti-militarist struggle 'because the special military assessment represents the first step towards a system of taxation corresponding in principle to the demands of social-democracy'.[27]

[23] See Kautsky archives, G8, Amsterdam, IISG.
[24] Cf. *Dixième Congrès national (Brest)*, 243. The Congress authorized the CAP and the socialist group of the Chambre des Députés to initiate a strong and determined campaign in support of Franco-German understanding and the International Courts of Arbitration, and against the 'three year conscription law'.
[25] The election programme of the SFIO of spring 1914 said: 'While the German social democrats could not prevent the latest increase in armaments—no more than we could prevent the 'three year conscription law'—they have forced the imperial government to place the main burden on the privileged by introducing a very high property tax. Thus the bourgeoisie is for the first time feeling the direct consequences of its chauvinistic folly' (*Le Mouvement socialiste* (1914), 233).
[26] Words spoken by Kurt Geyer at the Jena Congress in September 1913.
[27] Those were the terms in which the socialist deputy Hermann Wendel put the matter in *The New Review* of September 1913. The article is reproduced in Walling, 67–81.

The desire for joint Franco-German action certainly never led to a concrete initiative or to any particularly spectacular mass demonstration. The campaign was conceived primarily as a struggle against prevailing opinion and intended to be conducted within the framework of parliamentary activity in which the socialists tried to involve all left-wing and liberal groups. Therefore they were on the look-out for suitable formulas for collaboration acceptable to these deputies.

On 9 April 1913 a number of public figures in Switzerland convened a conference of German and French parliamentarians to protest against increased armaments and to seek a peaceful solution to the points at issue between the two nations, in particular the Alsace-Lorraine question. In socialist circles the invitation was received with great interest and the secretary of the ISB, who was at the same time secretary of the Inter-Parliamentary Socialist Commission, immediately gave this initiative his full support.[28] The only question that remained was in which form, and on which conditions, the French and German socialist parties would participate. Vaillant maintained that 'the socialist party cannot take part in this conference in the same way as the other parties without thereby weakening its own campaign'; hence it must state its own point of view by a declaration of principles.[29] This suggestion was adopted. The declaration, 'worked out and put on paper in direct agreement' by the CAP, the German party executive, and the socialist parliamentary groups of the two countries, was designed to promote co-operation with bourgeois pacifist movements.[30] After recalling the resolutions of Basle and the attitude adopted in the joint manifesto of 1 March 1913, the declaration set out the principles of socialist pacifism and went on to emphasize:

Modern wars with their fearful horror and unspeakable devastation threaten the widest sections of the middle classes. All efforts by

[28] ISB archives, Records of Switzerland.
[29] Vaillant to Huysmans, 14 Apr. 1913, ISB archives.
[30] This statement was read at the opening of the Berne Conference on 11 May 1913.

bourgeois groups and parties directed against the chauvinistic provocation of the nations, against the policy of conquest and the increase in armaments can count on the fullest support of the social
democrats of both countries.

The conference met on 11 May 1913 in Berne;[31] it was
attended by 155 parliamentarians, 34 from Germany and 121
from France. Among the German deputies, 28 (in fact, the
overwhelming majority) were socialists; and among the French,
38; whereas 83 deputies or senators represented the radicals,
the independent socialists, and other groups.

This conference, whose socialist spokesmen were Bebel, Haase,
Karl Liebknecht, Scheidemann, Molkenbuhr, Jaurès, Vaillant,
Albert Thomas, and Sembat, took place in a friendly atmosphere and culminated in a resolution couched in general terms[32]
acceptable to the pacifist bourgeoisie. In the last paragraph of
this document all parliamentarians present at the conference
committed themselves 'to a tireless campaign' aimed at 'clearing
up and preventing misunderstandings and conflicts' between
their countries; and, with this end in view, a plea was made for
the limitation of naval and military expenditure and the settlement of international conflicts by The Hague arbitration
Court.[33] An interparliamentary committee for Franco-German
rapprochement was set up with the aim of continuing and expanding the work of the conference.

[31] On this conference for Franco–German parliamentary understanding, see the
*Stenographisches Protokoll der deutsch-französichen Verständigungskonferenz, abgehalten am
Pfingstsonntag, den 11. Mai 1913 zu Bern*, herausgegeben vom Organisationskomitee
(Berne, Unionsdruckerei, 1913, 46 pp.); Pierre Renaudel, 'La conférence de
Berne et la paix', *La Revue socialiste* (June 1913), 557; Philipp Scheidemann,
Memoiren eines Sozialdemokraten (Dresden, 1928, vol. i), 225–31.

[32] This resolution was also published in the *Periodical Bull. ISB* v. 11 (1914); see
Grünberg, 27 ff.

[33] Compulsory international arbitration for all differences and all conflicts that
might arise between states was one of the basic principles of the pacifist movement.
Cf. Aldred H. Fried, *Handbuch der Friedensbewegung* (Leipzig–Berlin, 1911–13, 2
vols.). At the Berne Conference the non-socialist representatives of both countries
issued a vague resolution calling for a Franco-German *entente*. The SPD and SFIO
deputies issued a separate resolution which was more explicit in its condemnation
and requirements. This resolution was published in *L'Humanité* (12 May 1913).

The Germans remained sceptical,[34] but the French socialists considered the conference a great success. To them it was a beginning which made it possible to envisage the expansion and strengthening of interparliamentary action with the final objective of initiating a broadly based movement in support of a triple alliance between Britain, France, and Germany, 'the three great countries that guide human civilization', according to the Basle manifesto. That this was the International's main aim becomes clear also from a letter from Vaillant to Huysmans:

As regards the general crisis of armaments, militarism, and war, that causes such cruel ravages in France and Germany, the only remedy —as the International has recognized—lies in a Franco-German *rapprochement* leading to an alliance between Britain, France, and Germany. Britain which has been drawing closer to Germany and has struck up a friendship with France, can if she so desires achieve the Franco-German *rapprochement* that must of necessity precede the triple union for peace and civilization between France, Britain, and Germany.[35]

This was no new idea; in articles by Jaurès of this period we frequently find statements about the role which British democracy and its liberal foreign policy could and must play in easing international tension. After 1908 he conceived a plan by which the *entente cordiale* between Britain, France, and Russia would guarantee peace. In an open letter to Jean Jaurès, Rosa Luxemburg severely criticized the idea.[36] Subsequently

[34] As a German historian notes: 'Even Kautsky's commentary in *Neue Zeit* was devoid of pathos and false hopes.' See Gerhard Schulz, 'Die deutsche Sozialdemokratie und die Idee des internationalen Ausgleichs', in *Aus Geschichte und Politik*, Festschrift zum 70. Geburtstag von Ludwig Bergsträsser (Düsseldorf, Droste Verlag, 1954), 89–116.

[35] Vaillant to Huysmans, 9 July 1913, ISB archives. Among Albert Thomas's posthumous papers, Schaper has discovered the draft of 'a sort of arbitration treaty between France, England, and Germany.' He is of the opinion that this text (French in Albert Thomas's handwriting, German in typescript) dates from the end of 1912; cf. B. W. Schaper, *Albert Thomas*, 87. In my view this dating is questionable and needs careful examination.

[36] Rosa Luxemburg, 'Offener Brief an Jean Jaurès', *NZ* xxvi. 1 (1908), 588–92.

Jaurès modified his proposal to accord more with Vaillant's suggestions.

The vision of a Franco-British-German triple alliance, the vision of an ideal future, was cherished by the overwhelming majority of the International's leading personalities who had no illusions whatsoever about the time required to achieve this objective.[37] But in the summer of 1913 Vaillant believed that the moment had come to involve the leaders of the Labour Party in this struggle on the grounds that their action could 'determine the policy of the British Government in this matter'.

Vaillant tried at first to achieve immediate results through his old friend Keir Hardie. The latter expressed his willingness to put Vaillant's ideas to the Labour Party, but in order to make the initiative more effective he suggested the active collaboration of the ISB or rather of its Executive Committee which, as he said, 'had since Basle and Berne participated in all attempts to achieve a Franco-German *rapprochement*'.[38] Vaillant promised to obtain this support, and when in mid July Huysmans and Vandervelde went to a conference in London, convened for the purpose of initiating the unification of the British socialist parties, Vaillant urged them to impress

upon the Labour Party in the name of the ISB that intervention by Britain is the best means of achieving a Franco-German *rapprochement* in order to form an alliance between Britain, Germany and France which is so necessary for peace; and, depending on the circumstances, to exert pressure on the Lower House and on the British Government to the best of their ability with this end in view . . . There is nothing more imperative in this world . . . Even discussions on the subject with members of the British Government may be most useful.[39]

[37] Therefore the statement of the German and French socialist parliamentary groups and of the party leaderships of the two socialist parties was confined to the following generalizations: 'Since fortunately the antagonism created by imperialism between Britain and Germany has diminished, a Franco-German *rapprochement*, so fervently desired by the socialists, constitutes the most effective means of averting the threat of a European war and of creating by means of an alliance between Germany, France, and Britain the prerequisites for the development of human progress in lasting peace.'

[38] Vaillant to Huysmans, 9 July 1913, ISB archives.   [39] Ibid.

Huysmans and Vandervelde did as they were asked, but the Labour Party leaders received the suggestion cautiously. They promised to consider it without committing themselves. Vaillant continued to urge the ISB Executive Committee 'to do its utmost energetically and unremittingly to make the British section exert itself for a Franco-German *rapprochement*'.[40] But the authority of the ISB Executive Committee was insufficient to galvanize the Labour Party into action.

Month after month Vaillant returned to the point and in every letter he asked the ISB to put pressure on the Labour Party. As late as January 1914 he wrote to Huysmans: 'Always remember to insist on a British–German–French *rapprochement* with our friends in the British section.'[41] Vaillant confidently refused to interpret the silence of the British as a bad sign, or as proof of their inactivity, and continued his efforts to exert pressure on them. He successfully made the SFIO congress, which met at Amiens from 25 to 28 January and which was concerned exclusively with election tactics, include in its resolution a paragraph summarizing his views. Faced with this situation the Labour Party, whose annual congress at Glasgow began on the day that the Amiens conference ended, could no longer ignore Vaillant's proposal. A resolution was therefore adopted in Glasgow condemning the disastrous increase in naval expenditure and demanding a peaceful alliance between Britain, Germany, and France. In John Robert Clynes Vaillant found a spokesman who supported this proposal and who said that his party's efforts must be directed towards a British–French–German understanding that will ensure lasting world peace.[42] But the Labour Party did not enter into a definite commitment. In fact it did not take those ideas greatly into consideration—especially as at the beginning of 1914 there seemed to be every prospect of an early reconciliation between the three great powers. Mediation therefore appeared superfluous.

---

[40] Huysmans to Vaillant, 21 July 1913, ISB archives.
[41] Vaillant to Huysmans, 21 Jan. 1914, ISB archives.
[42] *Labour Party Annual Conference Report, 1914* (London, 1914), 97.

It would be a mistake, however, to see the Labour Party's lack of interest in Vaillant's proposals merely as further evidence of the traditional 'indifference' of British trade unionists and socialists to the affairs of the Continent. Its attitude was symptomatic of a frame of mind which in the spring of 1914 began to prevail in the International.

6

The *Détente* of 1914:
an Illusion

AFTER a long period of tension and ups and downs, the whole socialist world looked at the international situation with new confidence and felt sure that Europe was entering upon an era of lasting *détente*.

W. E. Walling, that well-informed observer, remarked that on the eve of the 1914 war 'a very strong tendency to modify the position held by the average socialist on the war problem . . . will be noted'.[1] The rare expressions of anxiety about local conflicts passed unnoticed. Pessimism gave way to hope, realism to illusion; the fatalistic expectation of a European clash, to an optimistic approach of economic determinism. In other words, a belief in the growth of pacifist tendencies within modern capitalism replaced the view of a conflict-breeding economic system.

This change was inspired by the leaders whose frame of mind in 1913–14 Charles Rappoport described as follows in his *Memoirs*. 'The most eminent of the International's leaders did not think war possible because it was too terrible. The most notorious Marxists exerted themselves to prove the economic impossibility of a world war.'[2] Only a left-wing minority battled

[1] Walling, 23.

[2] Charles Rappoport, 'Une vie révolutionnaire', typescript, Bibliothèque nationale, Paris, Department of MSS., fols. 184–9. In another version of his *Memoirs*, Rappoport is even more explicit: 'Everything considered, the spokesmen of international Marxism could not bring themselves to believe in the eventuality of a world war, incredible as this may seem to any sane mind. At the national and international congresses, Bebel and Victor Adler, the two outstanding leaders of the International, launched out—and for that they cannot be blamed—into such vivid descriptions of the horrors of a world war that they came to the conclusion that it was impossible.

Among the confirmed Marxists there were some like Weltmann-Pavlovitch (who died after the revolution in Moscow) who, echoing the English writer

against this deep-seated optimism—without much success. Rappoport's journal *Contre la Guerre* received no official support.[3]

The leaders of European socialism were unanimously of the opinion, expressed a year previously by Victor Adler, that for the moment it was in the interests of peace to let time do its work and to be extremely cautious and reserved about initiatives that would involve socialism in foreign policy. This applied particularly to a proposal made to the ISB by the Italian socialists in January 1914.

On 8 January 1914 the committee of the Italian socialist group in parliament sent an official letter to their French counterpart suggesting an early conference of Italian, French, and Austrian deputies in Italy or Switzerland 'to consider jointly ways and means to resolve the conflicts that cause tension between the three countries'.[4] This initiative was not received with any degree of enthusiasm. The French socialist parliamentarians decided to pass the letter to the ISB for comment on the expediency of such a meeting.[5]

The Italian proposal put the Austrian socialists on the spot. There had been links between the Austrian and the Italian socialist parties since 1905, and in 1911 in particular, the two parties had taken joint measures against the increase in military expenditure. It was therefore necessary to keep up the pretence, and also to preserve the freedom of manœuvre which the

Norman Angel, demonstrated how war was 'an *impossibility* in terms of economics'. As for Jaurès, who had a better knowledge of the international situation than Jules Guesde, one can say that until the very last day of his glorious life, he simply could not believe in the eventuality of such an absurd, criminal, and nonsensical thing as a war'. See 'Mon attitude envers la guerre qui m'a mené au conseil de guerre', typescript, 3 pp., Rappoport papers, Coll. Vogein.

[3] Apart from the support of the left-wing socialists mainly from the Balkan countries, like Rakovsky and Blagoev, this initiative had the support of the socialists on Jaurès's and Vaillant's side. See Harvey Goldberg, 'Jaurès et Rappoport', *Le Mouvement Social*, 73 (1970), 6–7.

[4] Communication from the committee of the Italian socialist parliamentary group to the members of the French socialist group in the Chambre des Députés, Rome, 8 Jan. 1914. (The original is in the Victor Adler Nachlaß (Vienna, Arbeiterkammer); and a typewritten copy is in the ISB archives.) See also the report of the French delegate to the ISB, submitted to the SFIO Congress at Amiens.

[5] Vaillant to Huysmans, 15 Jan. 1914, ISB archives.

Austrian socialists had always enjoyed. Hence their reply was sent only after much thought; it was cautious but in the main opposed to the Italian initiative.[6] The secretariat of the German social democratic workers' party of Austria questioned whether the moment was opportune for such a meeting, because the situation seemed too confused, particularly as regards Franco-Italian relations, for socialist action to have the desired effect on public opinion. The Austrians did not think that the peace between Austria-Hungary and Italy was threatened.[7] This circumspect reply expressed a frame of mind that was widespread in the International: a refusal to proceed to a further analysis of the uncertainties of the situation for fear that generalities would lead to optimism conducive to an attitude of wait-and-see. It was preferable to allow antagonisms to emerge clearly before taking action.

There is no trace of this cautious attitude on 6 June 1914, when the Italian socialist party, anxious about the diplomatic complications created by the Albanian frontier settlement, repeated its initiative—a step which, by the way, was in line with the recommendations of the resolution of Basle—and sent the following telegram to the SFIO secretariat, the Austrian social democratic workers party, and the ISB: 'Suggest meeting on 11 inst. in Milan with French, Austrian, and Italian parliamentarians to agree on joint action over the Albanian question.'[8] The proposal was no better received in Paris than in Vienna or Brussels. 'We disagree with such overhasty steps', declared Camille Huysmans, whose answer to Ciotti's inquiry whether the ISB could give any assistance, was a laconic 'no'.[9] As for the CAP, it thought that it would be of little use to send delegates to such a meeting 'as France is only indirectly interested in the Albanian question'; it thought that 'any meeting

---

[6] See the letter from the Secretariat of the social democratic workers' party of Austria to the ISB, Vienna, 20 Jan. 1914, typescript, 3 pp., ISB archives.

[7] On the relations between Austria and Italy, see W. C. Askew, 'The Austro-Italian Antagonism 1896–1914', in *Power, Public Opinion and Diplomacy: Essays in Honor of E. Carrol* (Durham, N.C., 1959).

[8] ISB archives.   [9] Huysmans to Dubreuilh, 8 June 1914, ISB archives.

of Italian, Austrian, and French delegates can be postponed until the end of August, when thay will all be in Vienna for the international congress'.[10]

At the time it seemed as though the uncertainty that had weighed upon the international situation had lifted. The International believed that the change in the balance of power had fundamentally altered the general situation and reduced diplomatic tensions. Victor Adler claimed that Russia had emerged weakened from the Balkan wars—an opinion shared by Vaillant —as had Austria, which was in the throes of an economic crisis caused by its armaments policy. On the other hand, everything contributed to strengthening the widely-held conviction that the conflict between Germany and Britain which, according to Bebel's prophecy, should have led to a European war in 1913,[11] was over. For these reasons the leaders of the International thought that the intrigues over the spoils of the Balkan wars, such as the quarrel over Albania, were of no great importance and could not affect the positive trend. For the first time for many years the International stated explicitly in May and June 1914 that the atmosphere was characterized by a general *détente*. A glance at the contemporary socialist press which painted the situation in Europe in very different colours from those used to portray the unrest of the year before, makes one appreciate the psychological transformation that began in 1913 and culminated in the spring of 1914. The socialists believed that after a succession of crises and diplomatic differences the world was entering upon a period of peace, possibly of lasting peace; they agreed with Jaurès who thought that international diplomacy was becoming increasingly civilized. The socialist press stopped being alarmist and called the militarists 'panic-mongers seeking to create a war psychosis'. The French Marxist journal *Socialisme et Lutte des Classes* claimed in May 1914 that

wherever one looks one is aware of the international *détente* . . . For years hardened chauvinists and militarists have tried to force upon

[10] Dubreuilh to Huysmans, 10 June 1914, ISB archives.
[11] Cf. *Victor Adler Briefwechsel*, 550.

us the conviction that war is imminent, that it will start in the spring. War has not started and it appears that the peace will not be disturbed, that it will last. [The proof:] The government's new slogan is peace and quiet; everyone uses conciliatory and peaceful language.

The socialist theorists explained the changes that had occurred by establishing a connection between the prevailing economic boom and the long-term economic trends. 'The causes of the international *détente*' was the title of an article[12] by the socialist historian and economist Paul Louis. He explained the governmental pursuit of a policy of peace in terms of economic factors. His line of argument was:

1. All powers have suffered 'real financial setbacks' because capitalist wastage has increased tremendously. To balance their budgets governments are forced to make considerable cuts in military expenditure.
2. The threat of armed conflicts continues as long as the great states quarrel over colonies. Now that the colonial spoils have been shared out governments seek to reap the benefits of their policy of conquest.
3. The world-wide economic crisis with its unpredictable social and political repercussions helps to minimize the chance of an early war.

On the basis of these three arguments Paul Louis comes to the following conclusion in June 1914: 'The capitalist régime preaches in turn the restoration of peace and war. At present governments are in favour of peace because the economic situation makes them cautious.'

Arguments such as these allowed the socialists to breathe a sigh of relief and banished the uneasiness that had seized them at the thought of having to accept responsibility for events of historical importance. This optimistic view, strengthened still further by a misunderstanding of the trends of international politics and imperialism (regarded, as we shall see, by a number of socialist theorists as a guarantee for peace), led to a false

[12] *Socialisme et Lutte des Classes* 7-10 (1 Apr.-1 June 1914), 196-8.

evaluation of the situation that had serious practical consequences (as subsequent chapters will show). Nor was the socialist Left any more clear-sighted.

There was evidence of this at the trial in June 1914 of Rosa
Luxemburg, who was charged with anti-militarist activities.
The accused attacked the autocracy prevailing in the German
army but made no reference whatsoever to a possible threat of
war.[13] Such differences of opinion as there were within the
socialist camp did not concern the evaluation of the general
international situation but only the issue of whether or not to
continue to collaborate with the bourgeois pacifists. In spite of
serious reservations Rosa Luxemburg, as the leading authority
of the Left, approved of this alliance with one proviso: the
bourgeois pacifists must vote against military credits.

The leading socialists were agreed that they must continue
to be vigilant because 'the International alone guarantees
lasting peace'. But because the governments had abandoned
their militant policy and because the immediate threat of
armed conflict no longer existed, the socialists thought that it
was inexpedient to make a special issue of the preservation of
peace, or to mobilize the masses for this objective by means of
pacifist agitation.[14] Their future task was to do everything to
bring about a *détente*. But how? The ISB provided no special
guide-lines. In view of the favourable light in which the future
was seen, the international congress in Vienna was expected to
lay down a long-term policy. Until then the ISB suggested:

1. Continuing existing activities, such as the campaign for
Franco-German *rapprochement*.

[13] *Rosa Luxemburg im Kampf gegen den deutschen Militarismus, Prozeßberichte und
Materialien aus den Jahren 1913 bis 1915* (Berlin, Dietz Verlag, 1960), 142–206. On
the trial, see J. Jemnitz, *A háboru veszélye és a II. Internacionale* (Budapest, 1966),
309–10.
[14] This view was widely held, even by the revolutionary syndicalists in France.
In June, in anticipation of the CGT Congress due to meet in September 1914 at
Grenoble, *La Voix du Peuple* announced how the unions had voted on topics for the
agenda. The 'English Week' had received 71 votes, 'Strikes and Social Actions'
followed with 57, 'The Problem of Foreign and Female Workers' collected 42
votes, and 'Anti-Militarism' brought up the rear with 35.

2. Using the favourable climate to promote yet more actively the spread of socialism and to strengthen the ranks of the International.

On the first point the leaders of the French and German socialist parties continued to agree. Hermann Müller said in January at the SFIO Congress at Amiens on behalf of his party executive: 'We are convinced that in this age of world imperialism we must collaborate ever more closely and that the links of Franco-German friendship must become ever firmer.'[15] The SFIO replied that Franco-German co-operation 'had advanced from theory to practice'—a fine phrase which did not, however, mean very much. On the French side the outcome of a year's joint struggle with the German socialists was rated positively. Not for years had the SFIO fought 'such an intensive and powerful campaign' as in 1913. Thanks to its efforts, and to the enthusiastic participation of the workers, the first goal had been reached. Socialism had successfully resisted 'the sudden offensive of militaristic reaction' which had threatened the whole of democracy, and forced it to retreat. The SFIO's election successes in the spring of 1914 were interpreted as representing a considerable strengthening of the democratic forces in general and of French socialism in particular.[16] Jaurès thought that the defensive struggle against the chauvinist Right had largely removed the military threat and that the obstacles that remained were not too formidable to overcome. As the immediate objective had been reached the two socialist parties could now go further and take action to achieve a real *rapprochement* between Germany and France which would lead to the implementation of the International's demand for general disarmament and a Compulsory Arbitration Court. The Franco-German Inter-Parliamentary Committee at its meeting

[15] *Onzième Congrès national de la SFIO tenu à Amiens les 25, 26, 27 et 28 janvier 1914. Compte rendu sténographique* (Paris [n.d.]), 16–24.
[16] Ibid. 367–71. The SFIO leaders believed that this election reflected some popular support; the Socialists' peace programme was very optimistic. A recent study sheds light on the limited and negative aspects of the SFIO victory. See E. Weber, op. cit. 136.

in Basle on 31 May 1914 agreed 'that the hour was propitious for a well-planned campaign to achieve a lasting *rapprochement* between the two nations'.[17] In future it would no longer be a matter of merely fighting the evil influence of nationalism on public opinion, but of urging the latter to liberate itself from the influence of 'small groups of militarists and financiers' and to participate in an active policy of *rapprochement*. Because of the important role that press propaganda would play in the campaign it was agreed that both the French and the Germans would systematically fight 'the provocations of the chauvinist press, which seizes on every incident and perpetuates every misunderstanding.

In tone and orientation this propaganda campaign was a continuation of that of the previous year. The main guide-lines had not changed and the themes and arguments remained the same. But the facts exploited in the campaign were of particular importance for the understanding of the hopes harboured at that time and for the attitudes of the leaders of the International during the critical period of late July and early August 1914. Three important factors substantially raised the standing of German social democracy in France, confirmed the conviction of all those who believed in a growth of international consciousness among the socialists on the other side of the Rhine, and made the accusations of the bourgeois press that 'the German socialists were jingoists, militarists, and chauvinists' seem 'impudent lies'. First there was the attitude of the socialist group in the Reichstag which, after the Zabern incidents, demanded an autonomous regime for Alsace-Lorraine.[18] Then there was the trial of Rosa Luxemburg, accused of having said at a meeting in Frankfurt: 'The last thing the German worker wants is a war

[17] Alexandre Zévaès, *Un Apôtre du rapprochement franco-allemand, Jean Jaurès* (Paris, Aux Armes de France, 1941), 173–4; see also Rosa Luxemburg's commentary on this conference, 'Die Basler Aktion', *Sozialdemokratische Korrespondenz* ii. 66 (June 1914), 1–2.

[18] On the provocative behaviour of the German officers at Zabern and the resulting crisis in Franco-German relations, see G. Zibura, *Die deutsche Frage . . .*; Jemnitz, op. cit. 293–8. On the socialist exploitation of the Zabern affair, cf. Walling, 83–90.

of aggression against France. When we are expected to take up weapons against our French brothers, or other foreigners, we shall say: "No, we are not prepared to do this!" ' Finally in May, in the course of the Reichstag debate on the foreign affairs budget, the socialist deputy Wendel made a speech that was a moving avowal of Franco-German friendship, a solemn proclamation of the determination of the German working class 'to achieve lasting understanding with France'.[19]

These facts were amply exploited by the SFIO during the big election campaign in the spring of 1914. A special section of its election programme dealt with 'the German socialists' fight against war and militarism'. It said: 'Determined like us to defend the national independence of their country if threatened by attack . . . the German socialists fight unceasingly against insatiable militarism and disastrous war and for mutual understanding and lasting peace between France and Germany.'[20]

This paragraph is instructive. It shows the extent of the links between the French and the German socialists and reveals the limits of their collaboration. As the underlying principle we find, instead of internationalism, anti-militarism (as defined by Jaurès in *L'Armée Nouvelle*) seeking to reconcile the Jacobinical patriotism of those who wanted to defend their threatened country (*patrie en danger*) with the traditional Marxist postulate of defensive war. Jaurès, the probable author of the SFIO election programme, was conscious of the limitations of this attempt but did not admit that the two concepts conflicted. It was not until the principle was tested by reality that differences emerged. The ISB saw the campaign for Franco-German *rapprochement* from both a political and a tactical angle: as a contribution towards a *détente* and also as an effective means of strengthening the influence of the International as a whole. Like the SFIO which in 1914 believed that by opposing the

[19] This celebrated speech was published extensively by the contemporary French press; cf. *L'Humanité*, 15 May 1914; and *Le Mouvement socialiste* 261–2 (Mar.–Apr. 1914), 385–7.

[20] Quoted from the text published in *Le Mouvement socialiste* (ibid.), 231–4.

military threat it had 'considerably increased its moral prestige',[21] the International was happy to have emerged strengthened from past diplomatic crises. Its secretary, speaking of the International's progress, said in April 1914 in Bradford: 'When we distribute the reports of the affiliated parties in Vienna you will see that we have reason to be proud of what has been achieved in these last three years. Socialism is developing in the face of our opponents and with them.'[22] The parties' pacifist efforts had proved effective and successful.

The International increased its numbers, and its political standing rose. In 1914 the socialist parties of the world had a total membership of 4,200,000, almost twice as many as at the time of the Copenhagen Congress when there were 2,400,000 party members.[23] The election successes of 1913 and 1914, the most striking of which were those of the Italian party in the autumn of 1913 and the SFIO in the spring of 1914, were also credited to the International as pacifist victories.[24] On the eve of the First World War there were about 700 socialist deputies in the various parliaments.[25] Socialism expanded beyond the

[21] Report of the SFIO secretariat to the National Congress at Amiens (cf. *Compte rendu sténographique* of the Congress, 26).

[22] April 1914, ISB archives.

[23] These figures are approximate. For 1910, see the report which the secretary of the ISB submitted to the Congress at Copenhagen, *Von 1907 bis 1910. Bericht über die Arbeiter- und sozialistische Bewegung, dem Internationalen Sozialistischen Bureau vorgelegt von den angeschlossenen Parteien*, Vorrede des Sekretariats des ISB (Brussels, 1910), 8; the figures for 1913 are taken from Longuet, 627.

[24] Interesting in this connection is the report (six typewritten pages) of the secretary of the SFIO, Louis Dubreuilh, to the ISB, which is in the ISB archives. The report ends as follows: '. . . it is superfluous to go further into the significance of our success. This was so apparent and so overwhelming that even our enemies were enviously compelled to admit it. They have emphasized repeatedly that we are the only victorious party.' On the political atmosphere in which the election took place see G. Tétard, *Essais sur Jean Jaurès* (1959), 100. For an optimistic appraisal of the socialists' success at the elections of 1913 in Italy and Bulgaria with a view to peace, cf. *The Socialist Review* (Jan. 1914), 57–9.

[25] The statistics are inexact and contradictory; compare, for instance, those established by the American Morris Orans, in W. E. Walling, J. G. Phels Stoke, J. W. Hughan, and H. W. Laidler, *The Socialism of To-day, A Source-book of the Present Position and Recent Development of the Socialist and Labor Parties in all Countries*, consisting mainly of original documents (New York, Henry Holt, 1916), 24–6, with the figures given by Longuet (p. 627) or the statistics published recently by I. M. Krivoguz, *Vtoroj Internatsional* (Moscow, 1964), 354.

frontiers of the old continent. Reports flowed into the ISB from Latin America of socialist parties being set up and sending deputies to parliament; socialism was also penetrating South Africa and Asia where it began to take a foothold in Japan, Indonesia, and even China and Iran.[26]

Now it was a matter of using the advantages gained. The ISB tried to use its mortal authority in order to re-establish unity among some of its affiliated parties.[27] It saw anti-militarism as the common denominator of the divided movements and believed that the strengthened moral standing of the International would make it possible to restore socialist unity in Britain, Russia, Poland, and Bulgaria before or during the congress in Vienna. Hence the urgent initiatives taken by the ISB after 1913: first the conferences with representatives of the three socialist parties of Great Britain (agreement seems to have been reached on the principle of a gradual merger to be achieved by 1915);[28] then the urgent appeals to the two groups of Bulgarian socialists to end their rivalries;[29] and finally the energetic preparations for the unification conference of the Russian (and Polish) socialists, to be held in mid July in Brussels. Because of this conference, the Chairman of the International, Vandervelde, visited Russia in June 1914, a journey interpreted by the socialists as an indication of a more conciliatory attitude on the part of the Tsarist authorities.[30]

[26] G. Haupt et M. Rebérioux, eds., *La Deuxième Internationale et l'Orient* (Paris, ed. Cujas, 1967), 200 ff.

[27] Speech by Camille Huysmans on 11 Apr. 1914 in Bradford at the 'Special Coming of Age Conference . . .', ISB archives.

[28] Manifesto of the ISB to the socialist organizations of Great Britain, *Le Mouvement socialiste* 259 (Jan.–Feb. 1914), 58 ff.; see also the ISB report on the session held in London on 13 and 14 Dec. 1913 in *Supplement to the Periodical Bulletin of the ISB*, v. 11 (1914), 2–10.

[29] G. Haupt, *La Deuxième Internationale*, 337.

[30] *Vorwärts* commented in its account of this mission that 'with Vandervelde's visit to St. Petersburg the ISB has taken an extremely important step', and Vaillant was of the opinion that 'these discussions in St. Petersburg even with the disunited groups of Russian social democracy' were the best preparation for the conference to be held from 16 to 18 July 1914 in Brussels (Vaillant to Huysmans, 5 July 1914, ISB archives).

On the basis of these facts Kautsky claimed in July 1914 that the International had never before been as strong or as united.[31] It had certainly become stronger from an organizational point of view. But as regards its political and theoretical nature it suffered from a profound malaise, the symptoms of which were pointed out by Kautsky himself. He hoped, however, that the Vienna congress would find a cure.

To sum up, the successful pacifist struggle of the years 1911–13 strengthened the vision of a promising political and social future for the International. Everything pointed to a quiet summer ahead. Predictions of a European clash gave way to the illusion that a period of peace lay ahead. The nature of capitalism—so the socialists claimed—had not changed but some of its principles had perforce been revised: reason had triumphed over imperialist arrogance and the spectre of revolution had put an end to all desire for military adventures.

Nothing illustrates better the attitude adopted by the International after the anguish in Basle in 1912, the turning-point, and the confidence with which the socialist movement now saw the European situation, than the reports prepared for the congress to be held in Vienna in August 1914. As primary sources they are an authentic expression of top-level socialist thought at the eve of the war, of its main preoccupations and its tragic mistakes.

In the light of those documents one can understand the optimistic atmosphere which characterized the preparations for this congress which never met and whose keynote the leaders of the International intended to be peace.

---

[31] '. . . the structure of our international organization [has never been] as firm and as solid as now. With each congress international co-operation becomes closer' (Karl Kautsky, 'Die alte und die neue Internationale', in Festschrift des *X. internationalen Sozialistenkongreßes, Wien 1914*, 4). This text is also published in G. Haupt, *Der Kongreß fand nicht statt* (Vienna, Europa Verlag, 1967), 285–7.

7 On Imperialism: the Debate which Failed

By the end of 1913 socialist circles were mostly concerned with making preparations for the Vienna Congress. Indeed, it was only a stage in the whole process, but one that provides insight into the atmosphere and the psychological climate which prevailed in the International on the eve of World War I.

In September 1912, the Dutch delegate to the ISB, Troelstra, called the attention of the socialist leaders to the need to enhance the prestige and range of their international sessions: 'It is becoming ever more difficult to imbue our congresses with the propaganda efficiency which they had at first . . . Now, we must seize every opportunity of giving every congress a more topical and propagandist tone. And the congress to be held in 1914 will provide such an opportunity.'[1]

A balance-sheet of the situation was to be drafted on the occasion of the fiftieth anniversary of the International and the twenty-fifth anniversary of the Paris Congress. It explains why seriousness characterized the preparations for the Vienna Congress was the keynote.

The thirteenth session of the ISB which met in London on 13 and 14 December 1913 considered the agenda of the forthcoming international congress. Thirteen proposals which various parties wished to discuss in Vienna were submitted to the secretariat before the opening of the session.[2]

The threat of war had been averted several months ago and the international situation seemed calm. In choosing topics for discussion at Vienna the ISB therefore gave priority to problems

[1] Cf. letter from van Kol and Troelstra to the ISB, September 1912, ISB archives.

[2] Cf. report published in *Supplement to the Periodical Bull. ISB* 11 (1914), 1–5.

within the European workers' movement where disquieting signs of malaise could be discerned. Two months before the session Kautsky estimated that the workers' movement had reached the phase described by him in his book *Der Weg zur Macht* (The Road to Power) as the 'end of progress through the trade union struggle and the worsening of class-antagonism'.

But the consequences of this phenomenon were not what he had expected. On 18 October 1913 he wrote to Victor Adler: 'Instead of a greater revolutionary drive behind the political struggle we find widespread apathy, despondency, and disquiet.'

Kautsky further observed that there was among the German social democrats a 'widespread sense of unease, a feeling of being in a dilemma, of wanting to act and of not knowing what form the action should take'. New approaches were being explored without much hope and it was felt that 'something new [was] bound to take place'.

In this atmosphere the differences between the various trends within the party became more marked, and the Left, with Rosa Luxemburg at its head, began a violent offensive against the party executive which it accused of being responsible for the quandary the SPD was in. It was the passivity of the leaders alone that discouraged and demoralized Germany's social democratic masses.

Kautsky replied by stressing the international character of the malaise which according to him could not be blamed on either the party leadership or the direction in which the party was moving, but on retrograde political trends.[3]

Kautsky's view of the situation prevailed at the ISB session in London and determined the choice of questions to be discussed in Vienna. It was agreed that there should be a thorough examination of the economic, social, and political aspects of contemporary capitalist society. Therefore arrangements to prepare the organization and agenda of this congress were made more carefully than for the previous ones. The wish which Jaurès had expressed as long ago as 1902, that the international

[3] *Victor Adler Briefwechsel*, 582.

congress should undertake 'a careful and thorough analysis of the facts, a criticism of prevailing ideas, and a thorough examination of the solutions', seemed at last to have become a reality.

There was an organizational improvement;[4] there was progress too as regards the programme: not only was the agenda shorter (there were only five items as compared with twelve at Copenhagen), but wider issues were raised and there was an increasing awareness of the need to consider topical problems. While at past congresses attention had been focused on the immediate political situation, at Vienna the International proposed to examine the structure of capitalist society.

As a concession to the chairman of its Executive Committee, Émile Vandervelde, the ISB placed the struggle against alcoholism on the agenda. Although of minor importance, this was a problem which preoccupied the socialist world of the period and which throws light on pre-1914 social democratic ethics. A question of burning topicality was also to be considered, namely the situation of political prisoners in Russia.[5] As regards this problem, the International had—for years—denounced political terror in Russia and tried to arouse public opinion against the Tsarist regime.[6] In 1913 two factors made this a

---

[4] For each item the ISB set up in advance a commission and appointed three or four experts to prepare reports. The idea was to print the reports before the congress met and to use them as a basis for the commissions' discussions. The various spokesmen were chosen from among the most representative and most expert personalities of the International. It was their duty, on the basis of the information provided by the national parties for the ISB, to submit concise reports on the items on the agenda.

[5] The fate of Russian political prisoners had preoccupied European public opinion since 1913. In that year, on the initiative of the German socialists and syndicalists, an appeal was made on behalf of Russian political prisoners and those exiled by the courts. It was signed by many leading socialists including Bebel, Jaurès, de Pressensé, Sembat, and others, and by literary and academic figures, such as Anatole France and Octave Mirbeau. Cf. Francis de Pressensé, *Les Atrocités dans les prisons russes. Discours prononcé à la Salle des Sociétés savantes sous la présidence de Vera Figner le 13 février 1913* (Speech delivered at the Salle des Sociétés savantes under the Chairmanship of Vera Figner on February 13th, 1913) (Paris, 1913).

[6] In London, Francis de Pressensé, chairman of the League for the Defence of Human Rights, had been asked to report on that question. After his death, in Jan. 1914, there was thought of entrusting Jaurès with this task, but since he refused, Karl Liebknecht was chosen. Liebknecht, whose name was revered

major issue: the new growth of the workers' movement in Russia and the crisis of Russian social democracy. Unable to intervene directly in internal party affairs, the International tried to raise the question of socialist unity in Russia indirectly at the 'International Socialist Parliament'.

The three big problems which headed the agenda, unemployment, the increase in the cost of living, and imperialism, formed an organic whole, and the subject-matter of the reports is evidence of the International's determination to be thorough in its analysis of these problems.

The preparation of the reports on unemployment was entrusted to the representatives of the three most important western parties. Édouard Vaillant, the veteran of the International, the most active delegate to the ISB, and a leader of international repute,[7] was appointed for France at the insistence of Jaurès.[8] The report for Germany, where unemployment had been the cause of serious unrest and the subject of debates in the party and trades union congresses, was entrusted to the secretary of the SPD, Hermann Molkenbuhr. This former tobacco worker and Reichstag deputy who had been a member of the party as far back as the heroic days of the 'Anti-Socialist Laws' was considered an expert in his field and had in the past prepared papers on social policy and workers' insurance for two of the International's congresses—in 1896 in London and in 1904 in Amsterdam. Ramsay MacDonald, the secretary of the Labour Party, was supposed to write a report on conditions in Britain. When he failed to do so a substitute paper was submitted at the last minute by the Belgian workers' party.

among the Internationalists as that of the son of one of the founders of the SPD, adhered to the left wing of the party. Besides the fact that he was the founder of the International Socialist Youth and a consistent anti-militarist, he was well informed about Russian political prisoners since he kept in close contact with Russian political exiles, many of whom settled in Germany. Liebknecht, as a lawyer and deputy in the Reichstag, undertook their defence against the enactments of the German and Russian police. Cf. B. Brachman, *Russische Sozialdemokraten in Berlin, 1895–1914* (Berlin, Akademie Verlag, 1962), 88.

    [7] On Vaillant, cf. M. Dommanget, *Édouard Vaillant*, op. cit.
    [8] Vaillant to Huysmans, 22 May 1914, ISB archives.

Since 1908, the rise in the cost of living had preoccupied the International and the socialist parties and the trade unions were busily campaigning against this rise all over Europe. Was this an inevitable consequence of economic policy? What was the result of the rise in the cost of living? What fundamental trend of capitalist society did it express? To all these questions the delegates assembled in Vienna were going to find clear answers in the reports prepared by three intellectuals who were considered experts. First there was Sidney Webb,[9] one of the founders and theorists of the Fabian Society, a famous political economist and trade union expert. The second was Dr. Juan B. Justo, the leader of the socialist party of Argentina, a pioneer of Marxism in Latin America, the translator of Marx's *Das Kapital* into Spanish.[10] Then above all there was Otto Bauer, already internationally famous for his masterly dissertation on the nationalities question and his numerous works on various theoretical and political subjects.[11]

Among the four speakers on the main topic, imperialism, were the two men who, in 1913, after the death of Bebel, always regarded as 'the moral dictator of the International', might have stepped into his shoes—Jean Jaurès and Hugo Haase.[12] But Haase, Bebel's successor as chairman of the German party,

[9] On Sidney Webb, cf. Mary M. Hamilton, *Sidney and Beatrice Webb* (London, Sampson Low, 1934); Margaret Cole, ed., *The Webbs and their Work* (London, Frederick Muller, 1949); A. M. McBriar, *Fabian Socialism and English Politics 1884–1918* (Cambridge U.P., 1962).

[10] A biography of Dr. Juan Justo was published in *L'Humanité* (25 Aug. 1910), 1; cf. also Victor Alba, *Le Mouvement ouvrier en Amérique Latine* (Paris, Les Éditions Ouvrières, 1953), 88–90; Luis Pon, *Justo y Marx. El socialismo en Argentina* (Buenos Aires, Monserrat, 1964, 173 pp.).

[11] See Julius Braunthal's biographical study in his preface to *Otto Bauer, eine Auswahl aus seinem Lebenswerk. Mit einem Lebensbild Otto Bauers* (Vienna, Verlag der Wiener Volksbuchhandlung, 1963), 5–60.

[12] In a letter to Victor Adler of 13 Feb. 1914, Kautsky, speaking of possible successors to Bebel in the International, gives his views on Haase and Jaurès: 'Haase is a very clever and honourable man for whom I have the highest regard, but he lacks as yet the prestige required of a leader. Apart from you, Jaurès is the only one who has international prestige, but he does not know the world outside France, even though he knows it better than the average Frenchman' (*Victor Adler Briefwechsel*, 592).

as yet lacked the necessary authority.[13] And the leader of French socialism, Jaurès, was not, in spite of his great international prestige, accepted by the International as an arbiter. Nevertheless the opinions of these two men would count for much during the consideration of disputed questions at the Vienna Congress. The two other speakers were the chairman of the reformist social democratic party of Holland, Vliegen, and the veteran of British socialism, Keir Hardie,[14] whose role it would have been to defend the motion on the general strike.

By the end of June 1914, most of the speakers had completed their tasks and the ISB secretariat printed their reports which were of varying importance and scope: there were investigations,[15] analyses, and outlines of resolutions. The three reports on 'involuntary unemployment' are richly documented papers which above all offer solutions, inspired by trade unions, of the unemployment problem and its social effects at international level.[16]

The choice of the speakers was no less significant than that of the topics for discussion. At first glance all Marxist and socialist trends and schools of thought were represented. But in fact the radical Left was present only symbolically in the person of Karl

[13] Trotsky describes H. Haase in these terms: 'Mild and considerate in his personal relationships, Haase, up to his very last day, behaved in the realm of politics according to his very nature: the average mediocrity of an honest provincial democrat lacking theoretical scope as well as revolutionary temperament' (L. Trockij, *Sochinenija* (Moscow–Leningrad, Gosizdat, 1926, vol. viii), 73).

[14] Cf. W. Stewart, *J. Keir Hardie, a Biography* (London, ILP, 1925); J. Maxton, *Keir Hardie, Prophet and Pioneer* (London, Francis Johnson, 1939).

[15] See e.g. Liebknecht's report, 'Les horreurs des prisons russes', in Haupt, *Le Congrès manqué*, 239–48.

[16] All three authors were agreed on the principle and the measures to be taken: social insurance and unemployment insurance. Vaillant suggested the largest number of remedies. Like the others, he insisted on the idea, considered revolutionary by him, of statistics on workers which were already in use on a large scale in Germany, and on the plan for the 'co-ordination and methodical execution of public works' to which he attached great importance. It was only on details that the three reports differed, as for example on the subject of relief works, the value of which Vaillant rated very highly in the 1848 tradition, whereas Molkenbuhr regarded them as useless and outdated in view of increased specialization on the part of workers. Cf. International Socialist Bureau, *International Socialist Congress of Vienna (Aug. 23–9, 1914). Documents. 1st Commission*, report by Vaillant (Brussels, Co-operative Printing Office 'Lucifer').

Liebknecht, and the centre Left had only Haase and Wurm as its spokesmen (on the question of alcoholism). Most of the speakers and particularly those dealing with the basic questions did not come from the ranks of the 'orthodox Marxists', as witness the three speakers on the increase in the cost of living: Juan Justo was an avowed reformist, Sidney Webb was no Marxist, and Otto Bauer—the most respected representative of 'Austro-Marxism'—was also an advocate of 'passive radicalism'. The choice of the speakers on imperialism was even more heterogeneous. In Vliegen reformism found its most active spokesman.

This representation faithfully reflected the strength of, and the connection between, the various factions within the International and the reports clearly revealed the prevailing trend. In the context of the international socialist movement the Vienna Congress would have marked an important stage in the struggle between various conflicting trends within the International.

Because of the urgent need to evaluate the extent of the changes that had occurred in capitalist society, and to choose between what seemed new and inescapable and what should be preserved of the classical concepts, as well as to extend socialist horizons and to change the methods and theoretical interpretations which formed the basis of socialist policy, the revisionists and the radical leftist minority demanded a survey, while differing profoundly on the nature of the adaptations required.

It was in this context that the problems of the cost of living and of imperialism were to be examined, the two being interconnected and giving rise to common consequences at the social and political level. This connection had been revealed during the debates concerning the tactics to be adopted, in particular the mass strike, between 1910 and 1913 at the SPD annual congresses. In the opinion of the left-wing radicals, according to Pannekoek's analysis:

There are new dangers and catastrophes with which imperialism threatens the masses—the lower middle classes as much as the workers—, and by which it rouses them to opposition; taxation, increases in the cost of living, and threats of war make fierce resistance essential. But these dangers are only partly the result of parliamentary decisions and can therefore only partly be fought in parliament . . . Hence mass campaigns are a natural consequence of the imperialist development of modern capitalism and provide more than ever the essential tool in the struggle against this [form of] capitalism.[17]

The general malaise then inherent in the socialist parties was caused, according to the Austrian socialist Ellenbogen, by

the continual increase in prices which kept provoking disorders and made it necessary for the Party to organize a series of demonstrations in order to keep the movement under control. But the deep dissatisfaction which prevailed among the masses could not be contained within the confines of organized meetings and caused spontaneous virulent demonstrations.[18]

It was above all in Britain and Austria that the protest movement achieved major dimensions and encouraged radical tendencies. In Austria the campaign transgressed the party's orders; in September 1911 in Vienna it led to 'savage' street clashes of exceptional violence which were brutally repressed by the police.

The German Left, realizing the scope of such agitation, submitted the problem of the cost of living to the International in order to take the discussion on a mass strike beyond the SPD's confines, thus giving it a wider range.

At Rosa Luxemburg's request the question had been placed on the agenda of the ISB meeting of 23 September 1911 and her resolution on the subject had been adopted. In its statement the ISB noted 'the disastrous rise in the cost of living which provokes the starving masses to violent protest campaigns in one capitalist country after another'. It was said to be 'the result of the tariff policies pursued by most European states' and also of the 'criminal protectionist policy of the agricultural pressure groups'. The text of the resolution dwelt on this point at some

---

[17] Cf. A. Pannekoek, 'Massenaktion und Revolution', *NZ* xxx. 2 (1912), 541.
[18] Cf. Wilhelm Ellenbogen, 'Vierzig Jahre seit Hainfeld', *Archiv, Mitteilungsblatt des Vereins für die Geschichte der Arbeiterbewegung* viii. 4 (1968), 101.

length. 'The increase in the cost of living is a result of the manœuvres of capitalist cartels which are the worst enemies of the
proletariat and of its struggle for emancipation.' A year later in
the Basle manifesto reference was again made to this state of
affairs and a rider added that 'by pushing up the cost of living
the universal armament frenzy has greatly increased class
differences and created intolerable tension among the working
class'.[19]

Structural crisis or sheer contingency? The fact that the
reports on the cost of living aimed to examine the vital organisms
of the capitalist economy gave their diagnosis fundamental
range and theoretical importance.

Justo's report, however, is disappointing. It contains nothing
new either on the price rises or on the controversy between
Marxist economists on the value of the gold standard and its
influence over the increase in the cost of living. (It was Otto
Bauer who in 1912, in the columns of the *Neue Zeit*, had fought
over this controversy with Karl Kautsky, Rudolf Hilferding,
and Eugen Varga.) But the report of Webb and in particular
that of Bauer are two highly important documents which both
stand out for their clarity. What is remarkable is that the two
authors, although they deal with the same subject-matter,
supplement each other without duplication. Each seeks to
examine different aspects of the question. Webb highlights what
seemed to him the essential problem: that during the preceding
twenty years wages had not risen as fast as prices. He therefore
concentrated his exposé on the causes of the fall in real wages
and on remedial measures.

Otto Bauer, one of the leaders of the Austrian Marxist school
of thought, had already published in 1910 a voluminous
analysis of the cost of living—an acutely felt reality in Austria.
After the very agitated period in September 1911, his party had
come to the conclusions which Ellenbogen summed up as
follows in 1968:

This demonstration damaged the Party's cause: it set limits to the

---

[19] Cf. *Periodical Bull. ISB* iii. 8 (1912), 128.

worker's combativeness and aroused the enemy's brutality. It proved that in a great party mass action must be based on a common feeling of responsibility and that the biggest mistake in politics consists in wrongly estimating one's own strength and that of one's opponent.[20]

Did Bauer share this view? In his very cautious report,[21] he avoids formulating any definite position. Although he speaks as a Marxist and takes up his own early analyses—other influences are also discernible: those of contemporary economists, in particular the marginalists. He based his work on the results of the market research undertaken on a large scale in Germany at the time. The ideas developed in his report were not new. What he succeeded in doing was to summarize the latest works of the economists of the period and to provide an answer to the major question, that of the nature of the crisis. He began his report with an investigation into price changes and noted that the great expansion of capitalism was connected with a rapid rise in prices. This he saw as a characteristic feature of the economic progress of the nineteenth century, which came to an end with the crisis of 1873 and resulted in a period of stagnation and difficulties with a distinct trend to a lowering of prices. After 1895 capitalism experienced a new period of unrestricted growth which brought with it another rise in prices. For Bauer price movements were the expression of the dynamism of the capitalist economy, and this approach led him to assume that existing trends would continue, particularly as during the preparation of his report, in May 1914, prices went on rising.

Having examined the factors that boost the capitalist economy and investigated the considerable backwardness of agriculture, Bauer proceeded to analyse imperialism as an economic phenomenon. The last part of his report, particularly the chapter on the structural changes in industry (cartels, trusts,

---

[20] Cf. W. Ellenbogen, art. cit. 102.
[21] Cf. International Socialist Bureau, *International Socialist Congress of Vienna. Documents. 2nd Commission: the High cost of Living*, report by Otto Bauer (35 pp.).

and monopolies), was based on his own former works and on Hilferding's book whose conclusions it repeated. Therefore it is unnecessary for us to summarize still further what in the report was necessarily presented in summary form.

As for Bauer, he saw in the imbalance between rapid indust-rial development and a backward agriculture one of the reasons for the increase in the cost of living, one of the most important but not insurmountable problems of contemporary capitalism. Agricultural production could no longer satisfy the constantly growing requirements of industrial society. What Bauer called the 'urbanization of the peasant masses' was a factor of progress which created conflicts that could be overcome, as soon in fact as east European agriculture increased its productivity under pressure from the world markets.

What then were the social consequences of this phenomenon? Bauer's conclusions are both cautious and vague. He notices some changes in the situation of the working class: after benefiting from the powerful industrial development which took place during the last twenty years of the nineteenth century, it was again exposed to intensified exploitation. Thus, the cost of living had become a ferment to the workers' great restiveness and even 'outside the industrial capitalist states the cost of living is a prime factor in the social and national move-ments'. As a result of this agitation, the reformist illusions were dissipated and the Marxist notion of the class struggle re-habilitated.

But as Bauer saw it, capitalist society was not threatened by an immediate crisis but undergoing structural changes which, while widening existing gaps, merely increased its growth rhythm.

The ever more marked differences between the classes within imperialist states and the strengthening of revolutionary move-ments in Asia and in colonial countries—'prerequisites for the suppression of capitalist domination'—are considered long-term processes. The cost of living which gave a new impulse to the antagonism between workers' and employers' organizations resulted in a renewed offensive by the trade unions: 'the cost of living obliges the working class to fight for higher wages', or more precisely, to bar the way to trends towards a lowering of living standards.

Taking as his example Britain, where the cost of living had reached its peak in 1914, and where the situation of the working class was becoming particularly difficult, Sidney Webb was less affirmative. His report sought to explain primarily that the growth of monopolies had led to a fall in real wages because of the artificial increase in the price of consumer goods. He too thought that the fall in real wages was relative; the fact that the workers' purchasing power had been reduced was an isolated phenomenon in an over-all development, characterized nevertheless by a rise in living standards. Webb formulated most clearly the ideas common to all the reports: that it was possible for trade union organizations to achieve a degree of effectiveness sufficient to force the monopolies into a new distribution of surplus values. This line of reasoning contradicted the theory of the Left that imperialism intensified class differences and necessitated the use of revolutionary tactics. It was not the hour of revolution and mass strikes but the hour of reform and of trade union struggle which would allow the working class to benefit from this accelerated development.

All the reports dealing with analyses of capitalist trends in economics reflect what later on Lukàcs called 'capitulation to capitalism both ideologically and economically':[22] the belief in the cohesion of well-regulated production within a capitalist system whose expansion makes it capable of overcoming economic crises. The reports on unemployment agreed unanimously with these conclusions. Unemployment had increased on a limited scale and was much less than the International had foreseen. If there were any signs at all of a depression or even of a crisis due to over-production, they could be found in Germany, and particularly in one sphere, the building industry.

[22] Georg Lukàcs, *Histoire et conscience de classe* (Paris, Éditions de Minuit, 1960), 59.

On the agenda of the Vienna Congress the reports on the cost of living formed a bridge, so to speak, between the examination of prevailing economic and social conditions and the important question of the political consequences arising from any structural transformation, and the changes produced by imperialism in its international policy.

As a result of a proposal of the SPD an international socialist congress was called to debate imperialism. The seemingly clear term 'imperialism' in reality concealed two problems. On the one hand there was the need to define the nature of the differences between the great powers and to decide whether the threat of a European clash still existed. On the other hand it was necessary to determine exactly what measures were to be taken to prevent war from breaking out: to resort to a general strike or simply to reproduce the arbitration formula. After a short exchange of views at the ISB meeting in December 1913, the German and Austrian delegates actually agreed to put 'the Keir Hardie–Vaillant proposal on the agenda of the congress at Vienna and to link it, as also the arbitration issue, with the wider question of imperialism'.[23]

In the socialist vocabulary of the nineties 'imperialism' was used to describe the great powers' new policy of expansion and aggression.[24] After 1900 left-wing socialist opinion regarded imperialism as 'the policy of a dying capitalism', defined by G. Ledebour as 'a phenomenon inherent in the highest stage of capitalism'. Although imperialism was on the agenda of the

---

[23] Vaillant to Huysmans, 26 May 1914, ISB archives.

[24] The expression 'imperialism' was used for the first time around 1880 by a group of English publicists and colonial officials intent on strengthening and extending the colonial empire. Imperialism was what they called the policy which they advised their countrymen to pursue. In the following thirty years the expression became part of political terminology and was used in a much wider sense.

For an interesting and extensive discussion of the historic and semantic development of the word 'imperialism', see Richard Koebner and Helmut D. Schmidt, *Imperialism: the Story and Significance of a Political Word, 1840–1960* (Cambridge, 1964); especially ch. 10: 'From Sentiment to Theory'; cf. also George W. F. Hallgarten's important work, *Imperialismus vor 1914. Die soziologischen Grundlagen der Außenpolitik europäischer Großmächte vor dem ersten Weltkrieg* (Munich, 2nd edn., 1963, vol. i), 30 and *passim*.

ISB sessions in 1901 and 1902 and was the subject of numerous articles, it was always the traditional aspect that was considered, the threat to world peace created by the great powers' determination to rule and partition the world.

We find no reference in socialist writing of the period to the works of the English economist J. A. Hobson. In his famous book, *Imperialism*, published in 1902, Hobson defined the concept in a completely new way, emphasizing not the political aspects of expansion but the effects of such expansion on imperialist society itself. In so doing he stressed the exploitation of the 'backward' nations by the so-called 'advanced' nations and the development of what he later called 'parasitism'. These concepts penetrated only very gradually into socialist theory. It was not until about 1909 that the emphasis shifted from the political to the economic significance of the phenomenon, and the term 'imperialism' came to describe the struggle for markets, sources of raw materials, and opportunities for investment. Henceforth these issues increasingly preoccupied socialist theorists. But neither the importance of their output nor the intensification of the debate in various journals can be interpreted as evidence of a clarification for the militants, or an assimilation of the concept by the potential leaders. For example, Morris Hillquit, one of the American socialist leaders, wrote in 1914: 'Imperialism is a comparatively new term in the political dictionary of Europe, and its definition is somewhat vague.'[25]

The starting-point for the discussions and investigations which were to lead the Vienna Congress to its political conclusions was the important work of the Austrian Marxist, Rudolf Hilferding, *Das Finanzkapital* (Finance Capital).[26]

---

[25] Cf. Walling, 22.

[26] The book produced many commentaries and violent discussions in contemporary Marxist journals. Whereas Bernstein rejected Hilferding's statements and conclusions, Kautsky welcomed the work as a continuation of *Das Kapital*. He dealt himself with the problem of imperialism and published a number of important studies in *Neue Zeit*. On the discussions within the SPD on imperialism see Kurt Mandelbaum's dissertation, *Die Erörterungen innerhalb der deutschen Sozialdemokratie über das Problem des Imperialismus, 1895–1914* (Frankfurt am Maine 1930, 140 pp.); Schorske, 241–50. Cf. also Hans-Christoph Schröder's recent work,

This 'masterly work', as Jaurès described it, was subtitled *'Eine Studie über die jüngste Entwicklung des Kapitalismus'* (A study of Recent Developments of Capitalism) and published in Vienna in 1910. Hilferding went further than Hobson in his definition. Consciously leaning on Marx's *Das Kapital*, he saw imperialism as an important part of the capitalist economic system. According to Hilferding imperialism originated in finance capitalism and was the certain outcome of the universal struggle of industrial and financial monopolies for maximum profits, contradictions which made armed conflict inevitable. But in his view there was no need for capitalism to degenerate into aggressive imperialism, because the international financiers could arrange peacefully to share out the colonial spoils. 'The dramatic phase of capitalist concentrations and imperialist rivalries is but a stage in the dialectics of the historical process of capitalism.'[27] In other words the trends towards international competition could be counteracted by the expansion of imperialism characterized by a concentration of international monopolies.

Hilferding's analysis was stimulating and gave rise to a fierce controversy.[28] Neither the interpretations nor the conclusions agreed. The argument which was advanced in socialist journals between 1911 and 1913, and which gained widespread acceptance in 1914, was that the new features of capitalism—which was a world-wide phenomenon—neutralized the contradictions that could create conflict, and that the interests of

Sozialismus und Imperialismus. Die Auseinandersetzung der deutschen Sozialdemokratie mit dem Imperialismusproblem und der 'Weltpolitik' vor 1914 (Hanover, Verlag für Literatur und Zeitgeschehen, 1968, vol. i, 226 pp.).

[27] Cf. Pierre Souyri's short but compact analysis, *Le Marxisme après Marx* (Paris, Flammarion, 1970), 23–8 (coll. 'Questions d'histoire').

[28] This controversy has been variously interpreted. Brynjof J. Hovde's article, 'Socialistic Theories of Imperialism Prior to the Great War', *Journal of Political Economy* 36 (Oct. 1928), 569–91, is only of bibliographical value. Paul M. Sweezy stresses the dynamism of this study which he regards as a contribution to the great debates on reformism, and as a continuation of the discussion and the theory of the collapse of capitalism initiated by Bernstein's critics. Cf. Paul M. Sweezy, *The Theory of Capitalist Development: Principles of Marxian Political Economy* (New York, 1968), 202–7. For a general survey see George Lichtheim, *Marxism, an Historical and Critical Study* (London, Routledge, 1967), 304–22.

capitalism reduced the threat of a European war. These diffuse ideas were put into shape by Kautsky who was beginning to crystallize his theory of 'ultra-imperialism'. He argued that if imperialism had characteristics

that are sufficient to unleash wars (competition between states . . . set up by powerful capitalist organizations such as cartels and trusts . . .), there are at present in the same society conflicting elements which are economically interested in the preservation of peace and which thus discourage the growth of the other features.[29]

He did not see imperialism as synonymous with the natural and necessary trend of capitalism towards expansion, but regarded the violence displayed by the capitalist nations in their efforts to gain control of agricultural preserves as a particular expression of this trend. As the armament race was in no way based on economic necessity, it was important to stress the pacifist theories contained in imperialism whose main attraction was the prospects of profit. Instead of struggling to compete, states would form cartels. If imperialism refused to take the non-violent road it would sign its own death warrant and would give way to socialism. At the practical level, the belief in the possibility of a crisis which might degenerate into a military conflict was narrowly connected with the estimate of the evolution rhythm of capitalism. According to Kautsky, the obvious trends of concentrations on an international scale preceded the end of the critical phase. This view was shared by Bebel, who during the Agadir crisis in a speech in parliament described the world-wide involvement of capitalism as one of the strongest barriers against war: 'I say openly that the greatest

---

[29] P. Angel is of the opinion that the origins of Kautsky's views on 'super-imperialism' must be sought in the outcome of the Morocco crisis. In the ranks of German social democracy 'great hopes are aroused by the example of Morocco where after serious tension between the two countries French and German cartels have found a basis of understanding. This seems to prove that the representatives of big economic concerns are better at reaching agreement than the diplomats of great nations' (Pierre Angel, *Édouard Bernstein et l'évolution du socialisme allemand* (Paris, Didier, 1961), 345). On Kautsky's views about the 'pacifist tendencies' which he felt to be inherent in imperialism, see Schorske, 244–72.

guarantee for the preservation of world peace today is found in the international investments of capitalism. These investments make war so dangerous for both sides that it would be pure madness for any government to push things to the brink over Morocco.'[30]

It was in this spirit that the party leadership put the problem to the SPD congress at Chemnitz in September 1912. For the first time in the history of socialism imperialism was transferred from the columns of the press to the agenda of a congress, and that of a 'great power' of the International into the bargain. This development showed that the problem was being taken note of, but it also provided an opportunity for the differences to come out into the open. Haase, who acted as *rapporteur* to the congress, strongly condemned the militant policy of imperialism. But at the same time he saw in the English proposal for an armaments limitation proof of the fact that to arm to the utmost was not vital for capitalism which had other economic trends. Starting from the ideas of Kautsky and Bebel, Haase drew a picture of international solidarity, the objective of which was to preserve capitalist peace:

Within the international framework the capitalist groupings of different countries are closely linked and depend on each other. They regard it as more advantageous to divide marketing areas than to exhaust themselves in struggles the outcome of which, as regards profits, is doubtful and dangerous.

According to Haase, capitalism's aggressive tendencies were restrained by three major elements. First there was 'the collaboration of British and German capital in the world markets', which was the best way of overcoming Anglo-German differences; then there was 'the fraternal solidarity of the international proletariat' as a guarantee for peace; and thirdly there was the fear of the consequences of a conflagration which stopped governments from embarking on war. A war would cause so much discontent and misery that it would inevitably lead to the

---

[30] Quoted in Drachkovitch, 267.

collapse of the capitalist system. Of this the ruling classes were aware and acted accordingly.[31]

As we have seen these views were shared by the French socialists. Such disagreements as occurred were caused by the situation rather than by principles.

In the speech which he made on 20 December 1911 in the Chamber of Deputies, on the occasion of the ratification of the Franco-German agreement on Morocco, Jaurès developed the same idea as Bebel. The links created by modern industrial and financial capitalism between various countries were so close that from them might spring the 'beginning of capitalist solidarity', 'the principle of capitalist expansion without territorial monopoly, without industrial monopoly, and without tariff monopoly'. Under these conditions capitalism would be transformed and become 'an open door through which business transactions can undoubtedly be made but through which peace must also enter'.[32] But according to Jaurès there were factors other than those based on economic determinism that safeguarded peace; there was the moral element, as exemplified above all by the manner in which the sensible sections of humanity—among the ruling classes as among the international proletariat—resisted militaristic trends. It was Jaurès's view that inherent in the rapaciousness of finance capitalism there was the constant threat of war. The danger came not from local conflicts but from the manner in which these were conjured up and exploited by the imperialists:

European civilization has so completely transcended the age of genuine national conflicts that where archaic differences of religion and race persist they flourish only if brought out by the new interests and forces of finance imperialism, of shameless and rapacious colonialism.[33]

[31] Cf. *Protokoll über die Verhandlungen des Parteitages der SPD, abgehalten zu Chemnitz 1912* (Berlin, 1913), 403 and *passim*.

[32] Cf. Madeleine Rebérioux's introductory study in *Jean Jaurès. Textes choisis* (Paris, Éditions Sociales, 1959), 30 ff. See also Harvey Mitchell, 'Jean Jaurès: Socialist Doctrine and Colonial Problems', *Canadian Journal of History*, i (Mar. 1966), 31 ff.

[33] *Œuvres de Jaurès*, vol. iv, 460.

Hence the need to guard constantly against these influences. It was on this point that Jaurès's pacifism became radical.

The theory of 'ultra-imperialism' as well as the perspective of a new stage in the peaceful development of imperialism were categorically rejected by the Marxist Left. The controversy and the differences reached their peak at the Chemnitz Congress; the representatives of the various trends disagreed fundamentally in their interpretation of the imperialist phenomenon and the tactics to be pursued and the Left itself was divided.

The extreme Left to which Lensch, Radek, and Pannekoek belonged saw imperialism as a 'necessity immanent in the further development of capitalism', the 'ultimate and highest stage' in which the armaments race was an inevitable, economically necessary phenomenon. For them any efforts to achieve disarmament, to persuade governments to enter into agreements for that purpose, were utopian and bound to fail. Liebknecht rejected this analysis. He saw disarmament and understanding between nations as an opportunity to preserve peace.

Whatever the differences of nuance or the basic disagreements among the Left radicals, they illustrated above all the doctrinal difficulties presented by the imperialist phenomenon, and they vanished in the face of the unanimity that existed as regards the tactics to be adopted: to fight against imperialism with these very weapons it provided, such as mass campaigns 'to educate the masses about the nature of imperialism' in order to encourage them to wage a conscious anti-war offensive. Thus Pannekoek wrote in 1912:

The development of modern capitalism has imposed upon the conscious masses of the proletariat new ways of acting: threatened by imperialism with the worst dangers, struggling for greater power, for more rights, it is a necessity to make its [the proletariat's] will prevail against the various trends of imperialist power—and this, in a more energetic way than its representatives in Parliament can do . . . When we talk about mass actions and their necessity, we mean extra-parliamentary intervention by the organized workers who should intervene *directly* at political level, and not *through* their delegates.[34]

The agreement on the attitudes to be adopted ended up in an animated criticism of the Executive Committee's defensive tactics and the parliamentary group's attempts to give the Reichstag full charge in the political struggle.

In its counter-attack, the party executive disagreed with both the prognosis and the diagnosis of the condition of capitalist society; it disagreed even more with the conclusions concerning the immediate objectives of the workers' movement and the need for a radical line and for revolutionary methods. The Chemnitz Congress reached a deadlock. 'Almost every speaker emphasized that the examination of the problem was only at its starting-point, that there was as yet no clear definition of the issues, that no equivocal stands had been adopted.'[35] It was in order to throw new light on the situation or, as she said in her preface, to 'serve the struggle against imperialism better' that in January 1913 Rosa Luxemburg, who had been missing from the Chemnitz Congress, published her book *Die Akkumulation des Kapitals* (The Accumulation of Capital)—a work which reveals the real nature of the disagreements and controversies.

In her analysis of capital expansion into the 'non-capitalist area' Rosa Luxemburg covered the imperialist manifestations of her age; in the final chapter, with spirit and skill, she made a passionate attack on 'the horrors of imperialism'. Her theory was designed not merely to explain the inevitable collapse of capitalist society because of the revolutionary implications of imperialism, but to prove that the system's breakdown had become an historical datum. The socialists must therefore be ready to take up the succession, not only by awaiting the collapse

---

[34] Cf. S. Bricianer, *Pannekoek et les conseils ouvriers*, 110. As early as 1909 Pannekoek analysed the leap of capitalism into monopolism and imperialism, which necessitated the adoption of a new strategy; the socialist movement would have to pass from its parliamentary stage into that of mass action.

[35] Drachkovitch, 286.

but by going over to the offensive in order to hasten the death-throes of capitalism.

Rosa Luxemburg's theory was received cautiously, even with hostility, and sparked off a heated discussion. Mehring said: 'Although the book is only a few months old it already has a past and a pretty lively one at that. Written from the Marxist point of view it has become the object of vigorous discussion in Marxist circles.'[36]

Thus Rosa Luxemburg's book, published in January 1913, was at once attacked by Pannekoek (who was to refute his schemes later on), Eckstein, and Otto Bauer.[37] These criticisms had the approval of Lenin who himself publicly declared the book to be 'a false interpretation of Marx's theory'. In March 1913 he sent a letter to Kamenev, the editor of the Russian party organ *Social Democrat*, in which he said: 'I have read Rosa's book *Die Akkumulation des Kapitals*. She is an impudent liar, who has mutilated Marx. I am delighted that Pannekoek, Eckstein, and Bauer have unanimously accused her of the same things of which I accused the Populists in 1899.'[38] Rosa's theory of imperialism was attacked by the radical and the orthodox Marxists as well as by the Revisionists.[39]

[36] *Archiv für Geschichte des Sozialismus und der Arbeiterbewegung* (1914, vol. iv), 356.

[37] Cf. Otto Bauer, 'Die Akkumulation des Kapitals', *NZ* xxxi. 1, no. 23 (1913), 831–8; and ibid., no. 24 (1913), 862–74; see Gustav Eckstein's highly critical review in *Vorwärts*, 16, 3rd supplement (3 Feb. 1913), 1; as well as A. Pannekoek's in the *Bremer Bürgerzeitung*, 24 (29 Jan. 1913); and ibid. 25 (30 Jan. 1913). On this controversy see also Lucien Laurat, *L'accumulation du capital d'après Rosa Luxemburg* (Paris, 1930).

[38] Lenin, *Sočinenija*, vol. xxxv, 63; and also the notes which Lenin made as he read the book, published in *Leninskij sbornik*, vol. xxii, 346–90. See also J. P. Nettl, *Rosa Luxemburg* (Oxford U.P., 1966, vol. ii), 532 ff.

[39] Lukàcs, who did not share Lenin's views, published in 1921 a study on the controversy over *Die Akkumulation des Kapitals*. On her methods he wrote, 'Rosa Luxemburg does not abandon the Marxist tradition', whereas her critics, in particular the severest of them, Otto Bauer, 'while using Marxist terminology [were] by the nature of their theory Proudhonist'. According to Lukàcs, Bauer and his supporters, whom he described as 'Centrist', had become the ideological spokesmen of the sections that 'hope for . . . a highly developed capitalism without imperialist "excrescences", "regulated" production without the "disturbances" of war'. He completely shared the opinion of Rosa Luxemburg who in her reply to Bauer said: 'According to this interpretation the bourgeoisie must be persuaded that

The SPD on its part meant to take the discussion out of the sphere of theoretical dispute and to submit it to the International. As a general rule the congresses of the International avoided pronouncing on differences within the national parties. The only exceptions were matters of principle, such as the case raised by the 'Millerand affair' in 1900. It was this kind of case and issue that the SPD was trying to raise in 1914. But the Executive groped its way very carefully because of the complications that could be brought about by the ambiguity of the concept of imperialism as formulated on the agenda of the congress—and considering that the Vaillant–Keir Hardie motion was being propped up. In this context, Bauer's report served both as a key document and as a pretext.

Socialist opinion of the period therefore expected from Bauer, who was considered 'the leading Marxian authority [after Kautsky]', a theoretical clarification of the question of imperialism. Walling, who had probably seen the printed report, wrote in 1915:

The all-important problem of imperialism was to have been discussed at the proposed international socialist congress that was to have been held in Vienna. Otto Bauer, undoubtedly the most eminent of the Austrian socialists after Victor Alder, was to have reported to the international congress on this subject and to have submitted a resolution which would have been the most important of all socialist pronouncements on the causes of war.[40]

Bauer was entrusted with translating into clear political alternatives the views expressed, with varying degrees of clarity, by the party leaders and with giving them the theoretical justification required to satisfy the militants' need for orthodoxy.

imperialism and militarism are damaging to its own capitalist interests, thereby isolating the alleged handful of beneficiaries of this imperialism and forming a bloc of the proletariat and broad sections of the middle classes with the object of "curbing" imperialism . . . of "drawing its sting". When liberalism is on the decline it turns from what it sees as a badly informed monarchy to one that it hopes can be better informed; similarly the "Marxist Centre" . . . instead of appealing to a badly advised bourgeoisie proposes to address itself to a bourgeoisie which is capable of learning.' (G. Lukàcs, op. cit. 58.)

[40] Cf. Walling, 19.

But he did not carry out his task as expected. Being aware of the difficulties, he chose caution. He was evasive and equivocal concerning the solution of the theoretical problems and refrained from attacking Rosa Luxemburg—although he had been the first to criticize her. None the less his report was an indirect answer to Rosa and the Left as a whole. He suggested—without mentioning names—that she should be opposed and that there should be no mention of disagreements, no polemics.

On the question of 'imperialism' as it appeared on the agenda, the *rapporteurs* in fact proposed to wait for the views of the Congress, and the historian of today is therefore deprived of three important texts. Jaurès did not produce his report for reasons which will be examined further. Keir Hardie had promised to send the text of his report after the meeting of the British section of the ISB (composed of representatives of various British parties affiliated to the International) but it seems that this document never reached its destination. Hugo Haase, who two years earlier, in September 1912, had presented a report on this subject to his party assembled at Chemnitz, found it more difficult to evade his task. But instead of providing a detailed exposé he cautiously contented himself with submitting for the Vienna Congress a draft of the very resolution which had been adopted at the end of June 1914 by the party executive.[41] The document was apparently a watered-down variant of the resolutions adopted at Chemnitz. But closer examination shows that the author's reappraisal of the international situation has led to a change of substance. Without actually spelling out the idea Haase's new report suggests that there had been a considerable relaxation of political tension because of the disappearance of differences and the *rapprochement* between Germany and Britain.

While Haase in his capacity as party chairman thought it necessary, in view of the recent repressive measures of the

[41] Haase to Huysmans, 22 June 1914, ISB archives; the report reached Brussels only on 6 July. Cf. International Socialist Bureau, *International Socialist Congress of Vienna. Documents. 3rd Commission: Imperialism and Arbitration*, report by H. Haase (4 pp.).

German Government, to be careful and restrict himself to generalizations, the Dutch *rapporteur*, Vliegen, could take greater liberties.[42] Of the texts intended to serve as the basis for the work of the 'international socialist parliament' gathered in Vienna, his report is second in interest only to Bauer's analysis.

Of course we must not exaggerate the range of Vliegen's observations or their influence. The theory which he developed was not a personal view, nor was it an isolated one. He expounded openly the ideas on imperialism and war current among German and Austrian social democrats, and presented a coherent exposé of the reformist theses on imperialism and the theory of ultra-imperialism which he had carried to its logical consequences.

While Bauer in his economic analysis sought to show the basic characteristics of capitalism in full growth and the resulting process of structural change, Vliegen investigated the effects of this development on international politics and formulated the theory of the improbability of a European war. Although their starting-points and approaches differed, there was some connection between Bauer's analysis and Vliegen's theory. If capitalism could solve its economic contradictions, it was logical that in the long run it could also eliminate the factors that caused wars. It was no less possible to tone down inequalities in capitalist society, and even to do away with them completely by reform, than to localize international political crises and reduce their impact gradually with pacifist policies. The role of socialism was therefore to exert pressure; in the social sphere it must defend the interests of the workers, in the domestic sphere it must check all militaristic trends and strengthen the anti-war movement.

Vliegen did not deny that the militaristic trend and the armaments race presented 'a growing threat to the world and to civilization', but he looked confidently into the future, convinced that in the international sphere 'there is a complete

[42] Ibid., report by W. H. Vliegen, 'The Socialist International and Arbitration' (10 pp.).

absence of the real and tangible interests that could justify a war'. Vliegen made this observation in June 1914. What made him think so? In the first place, he believed that even from the capitalist point of view war was undesirable because it could only lead to economic ruin without benefiting any nation, even if it emerged victorious. In the second place he thought that the main causes for which nations had fought each other had arisen from the wrangle over colonies and that, because the division of the world had been completed, these factors no longer operated. The conflicts which resulted from the struggle of the great powers for political predominance in certain parts of the world did not, as the Russo-Japanese war and the Balkan wars had proved, assume dimensions sufficient to spark off a general war. Finally he thought that pacifist elements were in the ascendancy, even among the ruling classes, and that the governments were anxious to avoid war so as to counter a twofold threat. They appreciated the incalculable dangers inherent in modern armaments and realized that 'any attempt to reach a decision by the use of force will be energetically resisted by all socialist parties, thereby increasing the risk for the ruling classes'. He said that the idea of an arbitration tribunal was about to be accepted by both public opinion and government circles.

The importance of Vliegen's report lay less in its optimistic vision than in its attempt to revise the basis of international foreign policy as formulated in the manifesto of the Extra-ordinary Congress at Basle. This was neither an isolated attitude nor a personal one. If one scrutinizes the literature of the period one realizes that the Basle resolution had quietly been modified and reinterpreted from 1913 onwards. Without sensational announcements a reappraisal of the international situation and the trends of imperialism, as formulated at Basle, was made in socialist theoretical journals and in the documents of the national party congresses.

The Basle manifesto had started from the postulate that because of the 'policy of the competing great powers' a European war constituted an objective in the sphere of capitalist imperialism and dynastic interests. But in Vliegen's view the development of the previous two years had shown that the basic characteristics of modern capitalism did not lead to a strengthening but to a noticeable decrease of existing differences. He found proof of this in the change of relations between Germany and Great Britain. The Basle Congress had in fact regarded the 'artificially preserved hostility between Great Britain and the German Reich' as the greatest threat to peace; but according to Vliegen the visible *rapprochement* between those two powers had now banished that danger. The idea was not an isolated one, it was found also in Haase's reports and Jaurès's writings.

All in all, the importance of Vliegen's report and the idyllic picture he painted, lay essentially in the fact that he had made himself the spokesman of a view of the future widely held in 1914, of a reassuring analysis of capitalism, an approach that was questioned only by the Left. Fatalistic pessimism was succeeded by deterministic optimism, and the practical consequence was a policy of wait-and-see. On this very point a group of French socialists, Jaurès among them, took a fundamentally different line. Opinions were divided, particularly as regards the question that had remained unsolved at the international congress of Copenhagen: the possible need to define the means that should be used to prevent war. The Congress at Vienna would tackle this question.

8 The General Strike Once More

THE aim of the Congress in Vienna was not only to reappraise the situation but to draw up an international socialist policy, and, more particularly, to decide on concrete anti-war measures. This, however, was likely to prove very difficult because of the differences in approach between the French socialists and the German social democrats.

The new optimism with which the majority of leading socialists viewed the international situation (given a preventive strategy) was a further reason to consider only solutions that remained within the traditional and parliamentary framework. The reports of Haase and Vliegen were pleas for the idea of international arbitration. They limited themselves to what had been said and recommended at previous congresses. But they redefined socialist foreign policy to the extent of regarding arbitration not merely as desirable but as an immediate political aim. In these circumstances the open rejection of the general strike as a weapon could only be reaffirmed.

Considerations of a political nature were added to the earlier theoretical and ideological arguments advanced by the Germans and expressed unequivocally by Vliegen: 'As with so many other resolutions passed at international congresses here [in the field of anti-war activities] the socialist parties of all countries must be free to choose the means which will enable them to realise their objectives.' However, in 1914 most of the French socialists were firmly determined to get the international congress in Vienna to adopt the proposal submitted by Vaillant and Keir Hardie at Copenhagen. The extraordinary SFIO congress which met in Paris from 14 to 16 July for the purpose of preparing for the forthcoming international congress accepted a proposal submitted by Jaurès to the effect that the general strike should be adopted as a weapon in the struggle for peace.

The documents prepared for the Vienna Congress thus confirm at a glance the view widely held by historians that in 1914, at a decisive moment and on a matter of burning topicality—the general strike as a weapon in the anti-war struggle—the French and German socialists were divided and that this disagreement added to the already existing differences.

As mentioned earlier the German social democratic leaders made no secret of their opposition to the Vaillant–Keir Hardie proposal.[1] In their view a general strike was of no help in preventing war, primarily because the successful calling of a general strike required far more internationalist convictions than existed among the national sections. Such a decision could only 'ensure the defeat of the country whose proletariat is the best organized and the most loyal in implementing the decisions of the International, to the advantage of the least socialist, least disciplined country'.

Moreover, a general strike would place many socialist parties, above all the SPD, in a dangerous situation by exposing them to persecution or by serving as a pretext for emergency legislation 'against organized labour'.

Finally the Keir Hardie–Vaillant amendment was not a constructive contribution towards an international *détente* because it made it impossible to exert a positive influence on governments

---

[1] See above, Ch. 4. At the ISB meeting of 23 Sept. 1911 the proposal advanced by Vaillant provoked a new debate on the subject of the general strike, which led to a crystallization of the various trends. With the open support of Adler and Stauning, the Danish delegate, Bebel, expressed his anxiety that plans might be disclosed which could expose the socialists—especially the SPD—to governmental reprisals. The Guesdist delegate, Rousset, stressed another point: the parties had no influence whatsoever on trade unions. 'Actually, in France, the socialist party could not take upon itself to set off the general strike.' As for Rosa Luxemburg, she did not disagree with the leading idea of having recourse to the general strike but with Vaillant's own proposal: that a railway strike should be started after the outbreak of war. 'Once war is declared . . . there will be no opportunity for the railway services to go on strike, except in private sectors; which would not apply to Germany' (notes taken by Plekhanov, Arkhiv Doma Plekhanova, Leningrad).

and to induce them to continue to work for closer ties and mutual understanding.

Those were the main objections advanced in public. But behind the negative attitude of the German party executive, which did not hide its view that French and British radicalism was purely rhetorical, were a variety of other, hidden purposes. In the opinion of the Germans there was always something unplanned and anarchistic about a military general strike.[2] To Kautsky it was 'a heroic folly'.[3] To Otto Bauer the idea of wanting to stop war by this means was utopian.[4] The theoretical objections and political suspicions of the social democrats grew in 1913 and 1914 when a mass strike became the hobby-horse of the SPD's militant Left. Having won the controversy at the Jena Congress[5] in 1913 it was therefore unlikely that the German party leadership would at the international level support the Vaillant–Keir Hardie proposal. After all the formulation of the amendment was such that the Left, which was hoping for revenge, might seize upon the opportunity of reopening the dispute within the SPD.

This résumé delineates the main points of the generally accepted interpretations. Does it agree with the facts? Apparently it does, if we keep to the publicly expressed views. But an attentive examination of the documents reveals the artful manœuvres which took place behind the scenes, particularly in 1914, which force us to abandon the traditional view and to come to more subtle conclusions.

After sifting the relevant source material from the conflicting

[2] Cf. Richard Hostetter, 'The SPD and the General Strike as an Anti-war Weapon, 1905–1914', *The Historian*, xiii (1950–1), 27–51.

[3] Cf. Karl Kautsky, 'Krieg und Frieden', *NZ* xxix. 2 (1911), 104.

[4] Otto Bauer was of the view that 'war is the last step of capitalist competition, the last outlet of the capitalist way of production. It cannot be prevented by the mechanical withdrawal of labour. The general strike is feasible only if the intention is to follow it up at once with revolution, with armed revolt . . . In the circumstances that exist today the prevention of war by a general strike is a utopian idea' (Heinrich Weber [Otto Bauer], 'Der Sozialismus und der Krieg', *Der Kampf* 3 (Dec. 1912), 105. Quoted in Norbert Leser, *Zwischen Reformismus und Bolschewismus. Der Austromarxismus als Theorie und Praxis* (Vienna, Europa Verlag, 1968), 267).

[5] Cf. Schorske, 274–6.

party pronouncements, the historian must interpret what really was behind the strike issue in which ideology, diplomacy, strategy, and tactical considerations were all mixed up.

It is generally stated that in the atmosphere of general *détente* that prevailed at the end of 1913, the German party leaders thought that the Vaillant–Keir Hardie proposal had lost its topicality. They therefore hoped that the sponsors of the proposal would withdraw it from the agenda of the forthcoming international congress or relegate it to a less important place. 'We do not expect the mass strike question to be dealt with in detail, and if it does come up we shall be bound by our party decisions,' Haase stated on 11 December, two days before his departure for London, at a meeting of the SPD party leadership and the general committee of the trade unions[6] dealing with the agenda for the next international congress. The meeting was rather stormy and Haase met with fierce opposition from union leaders. Legien in particular mounted a violent attack on the party leadership, asking it to adopt an unequivocal position at both international and national level:

The trade unions are most anxious to see the mass strike question settled in their own interests. Therefore the party executive must examine whether the party and the trade unions can make common cause against the countries campaigning for a general strike. The party executive must of course take a firm stand against the advocates of a general strike in our midst in Germany.

Was this an ultimatum or a clever manœuvre to force the party to adopt a rigid attitude? The trade union leaders were determined that the proposal should not receive international support, thereby cutting short the offensive within the SPD of those whom Legien called 'our great general strike fanatics'. The opposition could not be ignored because, according to an agreement reached at the Congress of Mannheim in 1906, all

---

[6] Minutes of the joint session of the party executive and the General Committee of the Trade Unions on 11 Dec. 1913; prepared by von Diener, 15 Dec. 1913. Brandenburgisches Landes-Hauptarchiv, Potsdam, Prov. Brand., Rep. 30, Berlin C, Polizeipräsidium, Tit. 95, Sect. 7, Lit. J, no. 2, vol. iii.

decisions affecting both the party and the trade unions had to be taken jointly by the two leaderships.[7] Moreover the general strike had been the starting-point of trade union pressure upon the party leadership. At the end of 1913 the SPD Executive Committee therefore found itself caught in a cross-fire. It did not want its hands tied at home if it was to preserve its freedom of manœuvre in the International. Hence Haase adopted a very cautious attitude and tried to frustrate the discussion with the trade unions. The Executive Committee maintained its stand and sought to have the item removed from the agenda of the next international congress.

Ebert and Haase, the German delegates to the ISB session in London in December 1913 therefore passed quickly over the strike issue when the meeting came to discuss the agenda for the Vienna Congress. They hoped that by displaying indifference they could avoid a discussion of whether to put the proposal on the agenda or to replace it by another item—'imperialism and the arbitration Court'. They were certain of success because in their opposition to the Vaillant–Keir Hardie proposal they had the support of many parties, above all that of the Austrian party and of Victor Adler, in whom they found an important and determined ally. They were further supported by the parties of the Scandinavian countries, by the socialist party of Holland, and by the Guesdists who openly agreed with the SPD's point of view and informed the ISB that they were utterly opposed to the proposal.[8] The Russian socialists, the Bolsheviks included, were also for various reasons suspicious of the general strike as an anti-war weapon. The representatives of the small parties, that of Serbia for instance, refrained from making their opinion known and left the decision on this issue to the parties with experience and extensive parliamentary influence.[9] In spite of Keir Hardie's efforts the important British section displayed a barely disguised indifference because it

---

[7] Schorske, 49–53.   [8] ISB archives.
[9] Cf. Dusan Popovič's reply of 1912 to the ISB on the subject of the Vaillant–Keir Hardie motion, ISB archives.

regarded the discussion as purely academic and unrelated to reality.[10]

But the calculations of the German delegates proved mistaken and their manœuvres failed. Vaillant was more determined than ever that his proposal should be discussed in Vienna and adopted. The French socialists, however, underestimated the strength of the opposition which the proposal encountered. They were inclined to think that there were no basic objections, merely reservations about the wording. It was not until the preparations for the Vienna Congress were well advanced that it became possible to appreciate the confusion and the misunderstandings on both sides.

In May 1914 Vaillant not only re-submitted his proposal but tried repeatedly, through ISB intervention, to gain the support of the German socialist leaders for it. First of all he asked the secretary of the SFIO, Louis Dubreuilh, to make the chairman of the ISB 'use his influence with the German and Austrian sections to ensure that the Keir Hardie–Vaillant proposal, or a new formulation as close to the original as possible, is accepted before the Congress of Vienna'.[11] In spite of his efforts Dubreuilh had no success. Vandervelde replied evasively that 'there would be time in Vienna' to settle differences of opinion. Dissatisfied, Vaillant, on 20 May 1914, approached the ISB direct and urged its secretary to persuade the German and Austrian sections to reach a preliminary agreement. He believed that

it is very important in the joint interest of all sections of the International, and even more in the interest of the International and of peace, that it shall not be thought that the sections labour for peace with varying degrees of enthusiasm; on the contrary all must appear determined to act jointly and to comply with the provisions of the Basle manifesto with equal energy.

Certain comments have made one believe that this was in fact the view taken by our Austrian and German friends and it seems important

[10] Of the hundreds of questionnaires sent to the trade unions asking them their view on the Keir Hardie–Vaillant proposal only eight were answered. Cf. Max Beer, *Sozialistische Dokumente des Weltkrieges* (1915, vol. iii), 12; and Steward Reid, *The Origins of the British Labour Party* (Minneapolis, University of Minnesota Press, 1955), 206.   [11] Vaillant to Huysmans, ISB archives.

to me that their reports on militarism and on the Keir Hardie–Vaillant proposal must, by the date agreed upon, 1 June, lead to this highly desirable agreement.[12]

Vaillant placed the ISB Executive Committee in a difficult position. It could neither do what he asked nor refuse his request, particularly as at this very time, by pursuing an appeasement policy, the Executive Committee had made several inept moves which had affected Vaillant and made him question the loyalty of the Belgians. For instance, when Vaillant, at the end of May, read the report of the last ISB session as published in the *Periodical Bulletin of the ISB*, he noted that this official document made no reference to his proposal being placed on the agenda of the Vienna Congress. Huysmans rectified this at once and the affair was dismissed as an 'accidental omission'.[13] He also found a way of solving the difficulties created by Vaillant: he sent a copy of Vaillant's letter to the SPD Executive without comment, thereby achieving the desired effect. The German party executive realized that Vaillant was not giving way and that they had no alternative but to examine this thorny proposal. A solution had to be found because time was short and complications might now take a political turn. With the approach of the Vienna Congress attitudes were in fact hardening in favour of the Vaillant–Keir Hardie proposal and public opinion was watching with interest to see what line the German social democrats would adopt. Socialists of all shades discussed the situation openly in the press. Paul Louis wrote early in June 1914:

As part at least of the French and British socialists are in favour of the proposal signed by Vaillant and Keir Hardie, the eyes of the world—and not only of the workers—are focused on Germany. It is up to German social democracy to help this proposal to victory or to bring about its defeat. On the Germans depends the International's decision.[14]

---

[12] Ibid.

[13] See Vaillant to Huysmans, 26 May 1914, and the reply of the secretary of the ISB, ISB archives.

[14] Paul Louis, 'L'impérialisme', *Socialisme et Lutte des Classes* 13 (1–5 July 1914), 290.

M

German social democracy thus carried a very heavy responsibility, particularly since in the political circumstances of 1914,
with the joint campaign for a Franco-German *détente* as the focal
point of socialist propaganda, any disagreement between the
two parties was easily exploited by their political opponents.
The party executive had the choice between three solutions: (1)
to oppose the proposal categorically, (2) to make Vaillant abandon the idea of submitting it to the Congress, and (3) to find a
compromise solution. The first alternative was too risky, the
second improbable. There remained only the third. With tactical skill the German party leadership began to toy with the first
two alternatives so as to gain as many concessions as possible for
the third, the only sensible one—particularly as it knew that
Keir Hardie, the co-author of the motion, had been ready
for a compromise since 1912 and was extremely conciliatory. In
August 1912, Keir Hardie, together with the other delegate of
the British section, Henderson, had explained the proposal to
the British trade unions: 'Those who support the anti-war strike
do not [see it as] an alternative to political action but as sup-
plementing that action and as a weapon only to be used as a
last resort if political action is not yet effective enough to prevent
war.'[15]

Haase's reply to Vaillant (at the end of May 1914) took these
factors into account.[16] A subtle document, it was at the same
time a refusal and an attempt, if not to convince Vaillant, at
least to make him adopt a less intransigent stand.

Haase rejected certain details of Vaillant's proposal: the paralysing of supplies by a strike of transport workers and the general
strike as a reply to war. As regards the principle of the general
strike as a weapon in the struggle for peace the letter was conciliatory. Haase obviously wished to preserve the *status quo* as
defined in the Basle resolution, namely to allow 'each of the
parties affiliated to the International freedom in the choice of
means with which to resist the threat of war'.

[15] Cf. Walling, 51.
[16] The letter was published by E. Haase, *Hugo Haase*, 102–3.

But he did not exclude the possibility of a compromise, as emerged from the concluding words of his letter:

Why should we create the impression of disunity in Vienna when we are all without exception agreed that we must redouble our efforts as the threat of war grows and that the means at our disposal change with the political situation and with the strength of the proletariat. I shall be delighted to come to an understanding with you and to avoid having to reject a proposal made by you.

Haase's suggestion therefore was that they should come to an understanding before the Vienna Congress. In his letters to the ISB Vaillant, who for long had taken an uncompromising stand, revealed that this was his wish also.

Indeed, Haase expressed a moderate line that began to emerge within his party in the spring of 1914. Although Kautsky remained a determined opponent of Vaillant's proposal, the majority of the executive was even more conciliatory than its chairman. This was revealed by a police report on a joint meeting of the Party Executive with the social democratic group in the Reichstag held a month before Haase's letter, on 28 April. At the meeting, which discussed the forthcoming international congress, Molkenbuhr proved to be accommodating with regard to the Vaillant–Keir Hardie motion[17]—which denotes the SPD's will to reinforce its influence in the International. Emphasis was placed on the need to strengthen preventive policy. If this should prove ineffective, the SPD was willing to make every sacrifice in case of war. Henceforth, it no longer flatly rejected measures like a general strike or desertion. This was a declaration of principle. As for their application, Molkenbuhr stressed that his party, as in the past, remained firm on one point of major concern: it would

[17] Police report: Brandenburgisches Landes-Hauptarchiv, Potsdam, Prov. Brand., Rep. 30, Berlin C, Polizeipräsidium, Tit. 95, Sect. 7 (files of Section VII-4 of the Royal Police Headquarters in Berlin, on international social democratic movements and congresses). This report mentions an unknown fact: the wish of the Germans to transfer the International Bureau to Berlin to ensure the co-ordination of the Socialist International and the International of the trade unions; this wish was said to have been discussed previously. There is no mention whatsoever of this in the ISB correspondence.

refuse to agree to compulsory, uniform, and precisely prescribed tactics and would not be tied down. But to the SPD Executive the question of what tactics to adopt was an essential point so far as the Vaillant–Keir Hardie motion was concerned. How then could the dilemma be resolved, the misunderstandings removed, and the work of the international congress be made easier? This is where the police report contains a second surprise. Molkenbuhr's idea was to submit to the Congress another proposal, namely to establish a war council at the ISB, whose duty it would be to provide the ISB 'according to the state of the individual nations with a basis for action if any decision was required'. This is indeed surprising, because neither the printed sources nor the archives contain any reference to such a proposal. The idea of an ISB 'war council' appears here for the first time.[18] It is remarkable that there is no reference to this proposal in the ISB correspondence, that it is not mentioned in Haase's letter nor in the report which he prepared for the Vienna Congress.

According to the police report the speakers in the brief discussion that followed Molkenbuhr's introduction indirectly expressed themselves in favour of a compromise with the French. Hoch said: 'The main thing is to reach some basic measure of agreement and to decide on the means to be used by the

[18] Molkenbuhr said: 'The Keir Hardie–Vaillant amendment will lead to lively controversy. We are fully aware that a war between the great powers of Europe must be resisted with every means. Refusal to join the army and the general strike must be used in such an eventuality. The purpose of the proposal is to come to an international understanding on this point. Vaillant clings to his old principle: "Plutôt l'insurrection que la guerre". Our view is that it is necessary to eliminate from the start any possibility of war. But if war does break out we shall make every sacrifice to carry out the decisions of the International. I want to emphasize, however, that we do not wish to enter into commitments which we cannot carry out. Therefore we shall ensure that we have the maximum flexibility in deciding on the means of resistance in case of war. In no circumstances shall we therefore commit ourselves to a definite strategy. Here the congress faces a very difficult task. It will give prominence to anti-militarism and to the solidarity of the working class which makes it the unyielding enemy of war. A discussion of the methods will be necessary for all nations and will remove misunderstandings. Therefore we shall support the amendment to the extent of favouring the establishment of a war council which, while bearing in mind the position of the individual nations, can act in case a decision is called for.' (Applause.) (Ibid.)

individual countries. It would be expedient to set up a so-called war council to assist the International Bureau.' And Albrecht said: 'Provided we do not tie ourselves down too much I too am in favour of examining the means to be used in the event of war. Let us hope that the German delegation and the entire congress will settle this question to everyone's satisfaction.' Liebknecht's contribution to the discussion, as given in the police report, contains a concrete compromise proposal which does not, however, go much beyond the point of view of the majority of the Executive.[19]

How did the French respond to Haase's letter? We know little about their reaction. The letter was not circulated. But it surely accounts for the change in attitude on the part of Vaillant and Jaurès. Everything seems to indicate that they regarded the letter as a compromise proposal and examined it in that light. Jaurès, who understood the nature of the disagreement, took it upon himself to find a solution. He drew up a compromise text designed to satisfy both Vaillant and the Germans.

We should mention in this connection that recently historians have wondered why and how it should have happened that at the extraordinary congress in Paris in July 1914 Jaurès, 'the moderate, the mediator, suddenly joined the left wing of his party; as the radicals renounced the possibility of insurrection he became the most determined advocate of the general strike'.[20] Is this really the way to put the question? Was there an irreconcilable contradiction between Jaurès's attitude at the Paris Congress and his behaviour in the decisive week of 26–31 July 1914 (as 'Jaurès's writings and actions hardly permit the assumption that the politician remembered the text which he had put to the vote ten days previously')? Does not the answer

[19] Liebknecht said :'We must leave no doubt that we are whole-heartedly opposed to militarism and that we are not prepared ever to make concessions to it either in peace or in war. Therefore we must jointly, on the basis of the present amendment, search for a solution that will be fair in its tactics to all countries while committing them to use every means to prevent war.' According to the police report 'a resolution was adopted', but it is not spelt out in the report.

[20] Cf. Annie Kriegel, 'Jaurès en juillet 1914', *Le Mouvement social* 49 (1964), 67.

to this contradiction lie in an 'explanation of the whole Jaurès phenomenon'?[21]

In the first place Jaurès did not suddenly become an advocate of the general strike.[22] His behaviour was determined by the guiding principle of his political ideas: to make the struggle for peace more effective. In June and July 1914 Jaurès adopted the line which he had defended at Stuttgart in 1907, namely that it was imperative to decide on effective measures in the struggle for peace, 'from intervention in parliament and agitation to the general strike and insurrection'.

At the same time he remained moderate and conciliatory. The purpose of the proposal which he wanted to draft, and on which he wanted his party congress to vote, was to prevent a Franco-German clash in Vienna by narrowing the gap between the respective points of view. Having learnt from past experience—preparing for the Congress at Stuttgart—and being a clever politician who knew the International inside out, Jaurès realized that a compromise could only be reached after a test of strength and provided the whole weight of the French party was thrown into the scales. The party had at any rate gained considerably in standing because of its successes in the general election of the spring of 1914.

In June and early July Jaurès was content to follow as an observer the dispute between the opponents and the advocates of the Vaillant–Keir Hardie proposal in France. Dominated by Guesde, the Fédération du Nord at its congress in June 1914 rejected the proposal on the grounds that it conflicted with the resolutions adopted at Stuttgart.[23] The congress of the Fédération de la Seine, on the other hand, on 5 July 1914, by a large majority approved a report by Albert Thomas expressing sup-

[21] Annie Kriegel, 'Jaurès en juillet 1914'. *Le Mouvement social* 49 (1964), 68.

[22] Vandervelde said in this connection in his memoirs: 'Those who had the privilege of knowing Jaurès, of receiving his confidences at various moments in his life know that with him it was never a case of the flash of lightning on the road to Damascus. The modifications which he made to his doctrine or to his attitude were always the result of a slow development, of a long and thought-out internal evolution' (Émile Vandervelde, *Souvenirs d'un militant socialiste* (Paris, Denoël, 1939), 158).   [23] A. Rosmer, *Le Mouvement ouvrier*, vol. i, 45.

port for the Vaillant–Keir Hardie amendment. Jaurès did not give his opinion. But there was good reason for his silence. He knew that if on the eve of the Congrès National there was growing support for the amendment, the opponents of the proposal in the International would be compelled to demand a new formulation to prevent the SFIO, as a section of the International, from making the proposal its own. That would be the moment for him to intervene officially. This calculation proved correct. On 14 July 1914 Victor Adler, one of the most determined opponents of the Vaillant–Keir Hardie proposal, wrote to Kautsky: 'One might have a word with the French . . . or at any rate with Vandervelde and Huysmans . . . about the Keir Hardie–Vaillant amendment. The French are increasingly set on it, and for us (and probably for the Germans) it is less acceptable than ever. It must be re-worded.'[24] Therefore he asked Kautsky, who was going to Brussels to attend a conference on the unification of Russian social democracy, to start negotiations with the French delegates with this end in view. But the French did not attend the meeting. They were all at the extraordinary SFIO congress, the debates of which were a kind of dress rehearsal for the forthcoming congress in Vienna. Against the opposition of the Guesdists, who put forward all the arguments from the arsenal of the SPD leadership, Jaurès made himself the advocate of the general strike.

But instead of defending the Vaillant–Keir Hardie proposal he submitted a new text:

[The Congress] considers a simultaneous and internationally organized workers' general strike in all participating countries, combined with anti-war propaganda among the masses, the most workable of all means to prevent war and to force upon governments the international arbitration of the dispute.[25]

After lengthy debates Jaurès had his way: his proposal was approved by 1,690 votes in favour and 1,174 against.[26]

[24] *Victor Adler-Briefwechsel*, 595.
[25] For the English text of the resolution, see Walling, 202.
[26] See the reports on the session of the extraordinary congress which appeared in *L'Humanité* of 17 July 1914; cf. also A. Rosmer, op. cit. 46–7; and J. J. Fichter,

Since the general strike as envisaged in this proposal presupposed internationally co-ordinated action, and since the plan could not be implemented without German co-operation, one may justifiably ask whether Jaurès really proposed to stand up for the resolution at the Vienna Congress. What new arguments would he advance to make the opponents of the resolution change their minds?

A detailed examination of the new text as formulated by Jaurès shows that there was more to it than a change of form or a rewording to provide a less 'radical' draft. The general strike is seen in a wider context and becomes one of the weapons in the battle plan for peace. Jaurès saw the general strike as coupled with an international arbitration Court, thereby coming closer to the German point of view. His reasoning was twofold: the general strike could be an effective means of pushing through an international arbitration Court; and once the arbitration had been recognized by the great powers the decisions could be enforced by means of a general strike if governments refused to accept the Court's rulings. The proposal as formulated by Jaurès was basically designed to link the effectiveness of diplomatic solutions with what he called 'the means of action produced by the creative spirit of the working class'. On 18 July 1914 he replied in *L'Humanité* to the attacks of the contemporary press on the resolution:

Why does *Le Temps* in its diatribe forget that the most important aim of the general strike is to substitute arbitration for warfare? The motion provides that a general strike as a preventive measure against the threat of war shall be 'organized simultaneously in all countries' for two reasons: to increase the chances of peace and to save the most generous nations, and the most fearless human beings, from unplanned and unilateral action that might undermine their means of defence . . .

Elucidating his proposal in the course of the discussions at the SFIO congress and in his articles Jaurès took up Haase's most

Le socialisme français de l'affaire Dreyfus à la Grande Guerre (Geneva, Droz, 1965), 196 ff.

important objection: the general strike, as provided for in his resolution, should be called before and not after the declaration of war. He was in complete agreement with the German social democrats when he said: 'Once war has broken out we can take no further action.' The same point of view is found in his reply to Guesde who treated Jaurès's proposal as an act of 'high treason' against socialism:[27] 'As our strength grows, so our responsibility grows also; not when the storm has broken and when the nations, half defeated, are no longer capable of action but before then must they use all the means at their disposal, the most effective of which is the general strike directed against war.'[28] To sum up, with the general strike socialism merely displayed its true role, supplying its arsenal with an effective anti-war weapon which would strengthen the workers' confidence in their powers and translate into action their desire for peace.

Finally he advanced an argument which the International simply could not resist. If it recognized the principle of the general strike as a potential anti-war weapon, it could help the French workers' movement to unite the socialist parties and the trade unions. The <i>rapprochement</i> with the CGT in July 1914 was not a tactical manœuvre but the realization of an idea constantly in Jaurès's mind.[29] The unification argument was particularly effective because after the Amsterdam Congress Jaurès came to be regarded as the advocate of socialist unity, and after Basle as the champion of international peace.

Did Jaurès really believe that the German socialists would accept his text? After the Paris Congress he expressed himself

[27] At the Paris Congress Guesde said angrily: 'Even if a general strike were to break out, how and with what means could the ISB organize a movement everywhere simultaneously? Nor would it be enough if the Socialist Bureau could set off this general strike simultaneously in all countries. Inequalities in the organization of the workers and the socialists would continue to exist in the participating countries, resulting in the defeat of the best organized country. And this is an act of high treason against socialism' (J. J. Fichter, op. cit. 198).

[28] <i>L'Humanité</i> (17 July 1914).

[29] On Jaurès's efforts to mediate between the party and the CGT see Annie Kriegel, 'Jaurès, le Parti Socialiste et la CGT à la fin de juillet 1914', in <i>Bulletin de a Société d'Études jaurèsiennes</i> 7 (1962), 5–10.

optimistically on the subject, for example in the following statement of 19 July:

It is true that [the German socialist party] is basically opposed to
adventures and revolutionary slogans. But it is also true that it is
increasingly aware of the need for energetic action. The idea of the
mass strike which it rejected barely fifteen years ago as an anarchistic aberration, is now considered seriously, and recognized as a
weapon.[30]

Was this comment merely made to set people's minds at rest, or
does it show a misunderstanding of the true position of German
social democracy? Does it reflect the exchange of views between
Jaurès and Karl Liebknecht on 13 and 14 July 1914 in Paris,
when Liebknecht told Jaurès that his party leadership had
adopted a conciliatory attitude towards the general strike as an
anti-war weapon?[31] Or does it simply reveal Jaurès's honest
conviction that the Vienna Congress was bound to accept his
new formulation because German social democracy could now
have few objections, its basic distrust excepted? This last explanation sounds plausible and is confirmed by Jaurès's con-
temporaries. Pierre Renaudel in his evidence at the Vilain trial
said: 'The purpose [of adopting the proposal submitted to the
SFIO congress by Jaurès] was to force the German and Austrian
socialists to take the same road . . .' And he added that Jaurès
had been

the only man whose word could at that moment reach across the
frontiers and the first trenches and appeal to the common sense and
the conscience of the Germans. He alone could do this not only
because he enjoyed the standing in parliament and in his own country
to which I have already referred, but because of his immense international repute.[32]

[30] *L'Humanité* (19 July 1914), 1.
[31] Cf. Georges Haupt, 'Une rencontre : Jaurès — Karl Liebknecht en juillet 1914',
n *Bull. Soc. d'Ét. jaur.* 19 (1965), 3–7. Liebknecht had also had a meeting with Jean
Longuet; cf. the letter from Longuet to Kautsky of 26 July 1914, Kautsky archives,
Amsterdam, IISG.
[32] Cf. *Le procès de l'assassin de Jaurès (24–29 mars 1919)* (Paris, Éditions de
l'Humanité, 1919).

A police report said that the resolution 'was formulated so vaguely as to border on twaddle' and regarded this vagueness as intentional because 'for Jaurès's supporters it was of interest only as a means of forcing through the acceptance of the general strike at the Socialist Congress [in Vienna]'.[33] These testimonies must necessarily be viewed with reservations. Jaurès did not put forward his resolution as a tactical manœuvre and it is wrong to accuse him of hiding his intentions behind vague formulations. He did not mean to content himself with forcing the German socialists to act according to his ideas, and to exploit the result of the Paris negotiations to that end. His speech at the Congress, the explanations which he gave subsequently in his articles, are evidence of his desire not to put any pressure on the Germans and not to let any ambiguity of interpretation arise but, on the contrary, to reassure them, to convince them by explaining his intentions and ideas. It was feared, in fact,

that the Germans and Austrians would refuse to accept the amendment and so its adoption would have created a dangerous split in the international movement between those very groups where the split was to be most avoided . . . It was for this reason that Jaurès publicly declared, a few days before his death, that he did not intend to force the issue in Vienna . . .[34]

It was in this spirit that Charles Rappoport outlined the deliberations of the party congress in *Neue Zeit*:

Opinions on our French friends' resolution may be divided. But we must recognize that in view of the great political role which our red hundred [102 deputies] and their leader, Jaurès, play in parliament, this resolution represents both a daring step and an act of great political significance . . . It is not lightheartedly, but in full awareness of their responsibility to the people and to the International, that our French comrades have decided on this important step.

[33] Quoted by A. Kriegel, art. cit. 5. This hypothesis seems confirmed by a memorandum of the *Sûreté générale* of 23 June 1914: 'The CAP thinks that since the disappearance of Bebel the German socialists have decided to use the general strike as a means of pressing their claims. In these circumstances there is no doubt that they will agree to the [French] proposal' (A. Kriegel, *Aux origines du communisme français*, vol. i, 51).
[34] Cf. Walling, 43.

In the same article Charles Rappoport, who presented the CAP's point of view, described the place of this amendment among the other resolutions taken by the International: 'The resolution adopted in Paris seems to be supplementary to the Stuttgart resolution.'[35]

Unfortunately we do not have the report which Jaurès was to have submitted to the congress in Vienna, because, in spite of frequent reminders by Huysmans, he failed to write it.[36] The excuse which the secretary of the SFIO, Dubreuilh, gave to the Executive of the ISB appears inadequate. He maintained that Jaurès, overburdened with work and committed to many important tasks, had found no time to prepare his paper.[37] But there seem to have been other reasons. Above all Jaurès was waiting for the majority of his party to come over to his side. He also preferred not to make a written report because he had no wish to be tied to a final text before the international congress. He wanted to explain and defend his point of view orally to the commission because he was aware of the power and appeal of his word and because as an experienced parliamentarian he also knew that in the cut and thrust of discussion he could adapt his arguments to the situation and to his opponents.

Although the historian is thereby deprived of an important document, he can find the basic ideas which Jaurès intended to develop at the Vienna Congress in a letter written on 25 July 1914 by Louis Dubreuilh to Camille Huysmans. He said:

As regards the report on imperialism Citizen Jaurès tells me that his most important ideas are summarized in the resolution which he has submitted to our national congress and which has been adopted by its majority. As these ideas are therefore known to all sections of the International he does not think it necessary to put them into a report.[38]

[35] Cf. Charles Rappoport, 'Der außerordentliche französische sozialistische Kongreß', *NZ* xxii. 2 (1914), 744–6. Longuet wrote to Kautsky: 'In his excellent article for *Neue Zeit* Rappoport has given you a clear statement of our point of view' (letter from Longuet to Kautsky of 26 July 1914, Kautsky archives, Amsterdam, IISG).
[36] ISB archives.   [37] Ibid.   [38] Ibid.

The letter confirms that in Vienna Jaurès intended to defend the proposal which he had advocated at the extraordinary congress of his party. Jaurès's reply can certainly not be dismissed as an excuse, invented to calm the persistent secretary of the International, who as the congress approached urged Jaurès to produce the report that was vital to this congress. Four days later at the meeting of the ISB Jaurès confirmed his decision; in such critical circumstances he flatly opposed all last-minute attempts to use the seriousness of the hour as a pretext to delete this thorny resolution from the agenda of the international congress.

The congress in Vienna might have worked out a compromise or it might even have made Jaurès's formula its own. But its stamp of approval would not have made the resolution enforceable; on the contrary such a solution, a Pyrrhic victory, would probably have resulted in deepening the split with the trade union leaders by making it public. The French had long viewed with distrust their German counterparts who had repeatedly refused the French proposal for joint and concerted pacifist action. Nor is it pure speculation to suggest that the German trade union leaders would have rejected any such resolution approved in Vienna. During the preparatory work for the congress they demonstrated their bitter opposition to the motion and showed awareness of their importance: 'Without the trade unions whom the politicians purely and simply like to dismiss as inferior the optimistic advocates of the general strike cannot implement their plan,' Legien said.[39] Paradoxically he based his argument on the French example: 'In France the state of hypnosis produced by the pro-general strike propaganda has weakened the trade union organisations.' He thought moreover that the French trade union movement accepted his analysis: 'The strongest French unions, for example the printers' union, are opposed to general strike tactics and favour the idea of trade

---

[39] See the report of the meeting between the SPD executive committee and the general committee of the German trade unions on 11 Dec. 1913 (cf. Ch. 8, p. 164, n. 6).

union and political activity as pursued by us in Germany up to now.' The example which Legien cited was accurate but it was taken out of its context. The CGT certainly had no illusions, it no longer accepted the idea of the general strike except on an international scale. Only a reformist minority adopted a categorically negative stand. The CGT always avoided comment on the possible use of this weapon in case of a defensive war and isolation at international level.[40]

In the last resort it was the stand taken by the French and the Germans that determined the form and application of resolutions which depended on their good will. Dušan Popović, the Serbian socialist leader, explained the situation in a memorandum to the ISB in 1912:

In reply to the question whether it is possible to prevent a war and by what means—an issue of international importance—we think that the correct socialist answer can be given, not by the parties with the most eminent leaders or the greatest revolutionaries, but primarily by the parties which by virtue of their organisation and number present a powerful factor in international politics. The most accurate solution to this problem can be found, not by those who have the greatest genius or the biggest heart, but by those with *the greatest power*.[41]

We must not exaggerate the significance of the Franco-German compromise on anti-militarist measures which seemed to be emerging. Vaillant, the optimist, felt hopeful. But the discussion remained purely theoretical without leading to any commitments. No one thought then that the problem of concrete measures might become of importance in the immediate future.

[40] Cf. Jacques Julliard, 'La CGT devant la guerre (1910–1914)', *Le Mouvement social* 49 (Oct.–Dec. 1964), 61—2.
[41] Memorandum quoted by D. Popović, ISB archives (Popović's italics).

PART III

The Collapse

9

The ISB in July 1914

THE assassination at Sarajevo on 28 June 1914 caused little stir among socialists.[1] Their reaction did not differ from the reaction of public opinion in general. A historian of the International, Julius Braunthal, who lived through these events, says:

To the socialist parties—as to the whole world—it seemed incomprehensible that over Austria's quarrel with Serbia Germany would risk the leap into the darkness of a war against Russia, France, and Britain. They did not think that there would be a European war, they did not think that any war at all could come out of the Sarajevo incident.[2]

The socialist organs were inclined to view the assassination of Archduke Franz Ferdinand and his wife as just another episode in the Balkan tragedy which had been a topic of discussion for many years. Jaurès saw in this murder '[one more] rivulet [joining] the stream of blood that has flown in vain on the Balkan peninsula', in that eastern part of Europe that 'will remain a slaughter-house'.[3]

In Germany the SPD executive met the day after the assassination to discuss whether the consequences of this event[4] could endanger the international congress in Vienna. The party chairman, Hugo Haase, feared that 'not only will relations between Austria and Serbia deteriorate and the nations will again be threatened by war' but that the mood in Austria would prevent

---

[1] Cf. J. Joll, *The Second International*, 158–9. For France, cf. Annie Kriegel and Jean-Jacques Becker, *La Guerre et le mouvement ouvrier français* (Paris, Colin, 1964; coll. 'Kiosque'). For Germany, cf. K. Schön, *Der Vorwärts und die Kriegserklärung, vom Fürstenmord in Sarajevo bis zur Marneschlacht, 1914* (Berlin, 1929).

[2] J. Braunthal, *Geschichte der Internationale*, vol. i, 355.

[3] *L'Humanité* (30 June 1914), 1.

[4] A police report of this meeting was published by Jürgen Kuczynski in *Der Ausbruch des ersten Weltkrieges und die deutsche Sozialdemokratie, Chronik und Analyse* (Berlin, Akademie Verlag, 1957), 187–8.

8271840   N

the socialists gathered in the monarchy's capital from openly dis-
cussing the most important items before the congress, imperialism and the International's attitude to war. Ebert disagreed
with this analysis. He did not think 'that the assassination will
have international repercussions and result in greater tension
between Austria and Serbia'. After an exchange of views Molkenbuhr was authorized to ask the Executive Committee in
Brussels to convene a plenary meeting of the ISB so that the
Austrian delegates could give their opinion on the need to
change the arrangements for the congress. It was the first time
that the SPD took the initiative of convening the Bureau. Huysmans hastened to pass on the proposal to Friedrich Adler, the
secretary of the Austrian party. Adler reassured him. He regarded the fears of the Germans as unjustified.[5] In short the
Balkan vicissitudes barely affected the socialists whose attention
was focused on the forthcoming congress.

Vienna thus continued to be the venue for the congress, the
preparations for which were almost complete. The Austrian
organizing committee had arranged a very varied programme
for the delegates and had solved the accommodation problem.
This was certainly not easy because all affiliated parties had accepted with alacrity the official invitation to the congress issued
by the ISB in March 1914, and proposed to send even more
delegates than to previous congresses. Countries which had
never previously been represented announced their intention to
participate. Representatives were expected from China, Persia,
and from several Latin American countries.

All that remained to be settled were a few technical details.
For example, there was the choice of foreign speakers for the
great rallies planned to take place after the congress in all
Austro-Hungarian cities. The speaker most in demand was
Jaurès who declared his readiness to go with Huysmans, or with
Dubreuilh, to Brno and to Prague to address meetings.[6]

[5] The correspondence between Huysmans and Friedrich Adler is in the ISB
archives and the Friedrich Adler archives (IISG, Amsterdam).
[6] ISB archives.

The ISB secretariat needed all its energy to settle the differences within some of its national sections so as to restore unity among them before the Vienna Congress. In December 1913, the ISB Executive Committee was authorized by the ISB to exert its influence as a mediator also with the warring factions of the Russian and Polish social democrats, an undertaking that proved very difficult because of the repeated refusal of the Bolsheviks to take part in any such discussions. In January 1914 the secretary of the ISB succeeded during a short stay by Lenin in Brussels[7] in persuading the Bolshevik leader to change his negative attitude to the idea of a conference which would bring together the representatives of all Russian factions under the aegis of the ISB. In June and during the first weeks of July, the secretariat's effort consisted in solving the disagreements within the ranks of Polish and Russian social democracy. Finally, the much discussed Unification Conference was held on 16 and 17 July in Brussels.[8] This meeting ended with partial success: the Executive Committee managed to form the 'Brussels bloc'—a revival of the 'August bloc'. The Bolsheviks maintained their position and went on to reject the basis for unification proposed by the ISB. In spite of the open hostility of Lenin, the Executive Committee was satisfied with the results obtained and expected from the Vienna Congress a decisive pronouncement on the question of Russian unity. On 21 July 1914 Huysmans wrote to Friedrich Adler: 'The Russo-Polish conference went off well. I hope that in Vienna we can impose *unification*. The Bureau will then have to decide definitively on the Polish inner conflicts. We count on your father [Victor Adler].'[9]

The atmosphere of that summer of 1914, which promised to be neither more quiet nor more eventful than the year before, has often been described. The political and diplomatic world was on holiday or preparing to go on holiday. Like the heads of state many leading personalities of the International were taking

---

[7] Cf. *Correspondance entre Lénine et Huysmans*, 128 and *passim*.
[8] Cf. O. Hess Gankin and H. H. Fisher, *The Bolsheviks and the World War*, 127–31.
[9] ISB archives.

their summer holidays in the middle of July: Kautsky was preparing to visit Rome, Bernstein was in Switzerland, Ebert on the island of Rügen, Scheidemann was climbing in the Alps, and Victor Adler was relaxing at Bad Nauheim.

An air of calm pervaded the International. Neither in the Bureau's correspondence nor in the debates of the various socialist parties at the conference held in preparation for the Vienna Congress was there any mention of the international situation or any sign of preoccupation with the conflict between Austria and Serbia.

It was not until 21 July that Friedrich Adler, the secretary of the social democratic party of Austria began to doubt the possibility of holding the International's congress in Vienna. A press censorship was already in operation. In the report on the extraordinary congress of the French socialist party published in the *Arbeiter Zeitung*, all references to the Vaillant–Keir Hardie proposal had been deleted. There was no member of the party executive in Vienna with whom Friedrich Adler could have discussed the alarming news. Because they were all on holiday it was not until 23 July that he succeeded in arranging a meeting to discuss his suggestion to transfer the international congress to another country. Adler reported that in spite of the unanimous acceptance of the proposal 'the vast majority of comrades, and above all Dr. Renner, . . . absolutely refused to believe in the possibility of war'.[10]

Three hours after the meeting Austria issued its ultimatum to Serbia. Friedrich Adler immediately sent a report to the ISB stating officially that in these circumstances it would be difficult to hold the international congress in Vienna.[11] But even before receiving the message Huysmans, on the basis of press reports, had taken it upon himself to make the necessary arrangements to transfer the congress to Switzerland.[12] Nevertheless, the inter-

---

[10] Friedrich Adler, *Vor dem Ausnahmegericht* (Jena, 1923), 197.

[11] The text of this letter is reprinted in Haupt, *Le Congrès manqué*, 272 ff.

[12] He addressed himself in particular to Hermann Greulich and asked him to take the necessary steps to ensure that the international congress could meet at

national situation did not appear universally threatening. What people anticipated was a more local conflict.

The Austrian ultimatum reverberated, to use Stendhal's expression, like 'the sound of a gun fired at a concert'. 'The ultimatum was a great surprise to me,' Kautsky wrote to Victor Adler. 'It came quite unexpectedly. I thought that old Franz Josef and the young one wanted to be "left in peace". Now we suddenly have a declaration of war because that is precisely what the ultimatum is. It is war, local war between Austria and Serbia.'[13]

But on 24 and 25 July the situation still seemed very confused and people adopted an attitude of wait-and-see. Nevertheless, Huysmans decided on 24 July to convene an urgent plenary meeting of the ISB because of the critical situation in central Europe. He telegraphed to the members of the Executive Committee: 'War expected. Must I convoke Bureau.' Anseele replied the same day from Ghent: 'Am agreed; however do not convene the Bureau until tomorrow when you will have more precise news from the countries concerned. The comrades from Vienna might be able to suggest what we should do. Send them a telegram.' The telegraphic reply from Vandervelde who was resting at Shenley arrived only the following morning.[14] 'If Adler agrees, yes. Can come to Brussels if presence necessary.' Thereupon Huysmans sent the following telegram to Jaurès, Vaillant, Victor Adler, and Molkenbuhr: 'Do you consider meeting of Bureau necessary?'

Jaurès received the telegram at Lyons where he was due to speak that evening at an election meeting in the suburb of Vaise. He replied immediately at 5.30 p.m.: 'Urgently convene Bureau.' Adler's telegraphic reply came shortly afterwards: 'Convening of Bureau almost inevitable to sanction change of

Berne. The socialist party of Switzerland was prepared to make the necessary arrangements (ISB archives).

[13] Cf. *Victor Adler Briefwechsel*, 593. P. Scheidemann reacted in the same way: 'This is war, it is clear that they want war' (P. Scheidemann, *Memoiren eines Sozialdemokraten*, vol. ii, 71).

[14] All the unpublished documents, the entire exchange of letters and telegrams relating to the ISB session of 29 and 30 July are in the ISB archives.

congress venue; but wait until tomorrow for situation to clarify.'
Had Adler just had word that diplomatic relations between
Austria and Serbia had been broken off? We do not know.
Jaurès heard the news half an hour before his speech at Vaise.
At that moment he became aware of the threat. In a brilliant
speech, the last he ever made in France, he sounded a sombre
note: 'Citizens, I want to tell you tonight that we, that Europe
has never in forty years been in a more dangerous and a more
tragic situation than that in which we find ourselves at this
hour, when it is my responsibility to address you.'[15] Though
worried he remained confident.

On the morning of 26 July Huysmans telegraphically called
the delegates of the ISB to a meeting in Brussels on Wednesday,
29 July. If on this occasion the wheels moved fast, it was more
because of the organizational experience gained than because of
the seriousness of the hour. The calm exhibited by the great
majority of the International's leading personalities was indicative of the prevailing mood. On this occasion, interestingly
enough, roles were reversed. For the first time in fifteen years
the SPD party executive realized the seriousness of the situation
and reacted more quickly than the rest.[16] As early as 24 July
Kautsky was convinced that after the ultimatum the outbreak
of a war with Serbia could not be doubted. The next day, 25
July, the German party executive published a radically orien-
tated manifesto:[17] 'A serious hour has struck, the most serious
for decades. Danger approaches. We are threatened by general
war.' In the name of 'the German proletariat', in the name of
'humanity and civilization', the party executive made an 'impassioned protest against the warmongers' criminal intrigues'.
In spite of the alarming tone of this proclamation the German
party leaders were convinced that the conflict would remain
localized. Most members of the party executive ruled out the

---

[15] The text of this speech is reprinted in many works. Most recently it has been
published in Jean Jaurès's *L'Esprit du socialisme* (Paris, Gonthier, 1964), 175–9.

[16] Cf. Kautsky to Victor Adler, 15 July 1914, in *Victor Adler Briefwechsel*, 595–7.

[17] The manifesto was reprinted in *L'Humanité*; the German text is found in
Grünberg, 51.

possibility of war between Austria and Serbia and thought that Kautsky was too pessimistic.

On the same day, 25 July, an appeal by the Austrian social-ists emphasized the consequences of an armed conflict for the peoples of the monarchy. But the appeal stressed the local character of the conflict and made no reference to its effects on the rest of Europe. Nor did it make any mention of the Austrian socialists' willingness or ability to resist the threat of war.[18]

What echoes did these two manifestos have? How did the working masses respond to their appeals? The socialist press pub-lished reports of anti-war rallies in many Austrian and German towns.[19] But it seems that these demonstrations were the result of the excitement created by the situation and not of any real disquiet. In a letter to Victor Adler of 25 July 1914 Kautsky refers to the passivity and indifference of the masses. He speaks of the ultimatum and continues:

There is no doubt [about] a war with Serbia [after] the ultimatum. This state of affairs probably means the end of the Keir Hardie–Vaillant amendment. Now would really be the moment for an anti-war protest in Austria with a mass strike. But there is not the slightest sign of any protest campaign by the masses. We must be content to preserve the unity of the parties in the circumstances. Our Polish friends in particular will make this difficult for us.[20]

Between 25 and 27 July there was therefore no repetition of the excitement and waves of workers' protest that had swept across Europe in November and December of 1912. In France it was the CGT alone that drew attention to the imminent threat and invited the Paris workers to anti-war demonstrations.[21] During these days neither the CAP nor the French delegates to the ISB were anything like as apprehensive as during the Agadir

[18] Ibid. 89.
[19] On the attitude and activity of the SPD during the July crisis see Camille Bloch's study 'Les socialistes allemands pendant la crise de juillet 1914', *Revue d'Histoire de la Guerre mondiale* (Oct. 1933). Extensive quotations are given in the German socialist press and reports on these rallies are found in J. Kuczynski, op. cit. 70–7. Cf. also F. Klein, ed., *Deutschland im Ersten Weltkrieg*, vol. i, 262 ff.
[20] *Victor Adler Briefwechsel*, 596.
[21] A. Kriegel and J.-J. Becker, op. cit. 63 and *passim*.

crisis or the Balkan wars. Although the CAP regarded the
ultimatum as a last warning it did not really believe that it was
irrevocably so. A new international crisis was certainly expected, but Jaurès still thought that Austria and Serbia would
come to terms. Although aware of the seriousness of the situation, he too on 26 July was not unduly perturbed. The other
French delegates, Vaillant, Guesde, and Sembat, believed that
the conflict would remain localized; they too remembered the
false alarm of December 1912. Fully convinced that the French
Government really wanted to preserve the peace, they thought
that on this occasion it was the duty of the socialist parties of
Austria and Germany to take the initiative and to act. Therefore
the French delegates had no intention of asking first for a meeting of the ISB.

Nevertheless, Dubreuilh said in his letter of 25 July 1914 to
Huysmans:

Several federations have today asked us telegraphically to call an
extraordinary meeting of the ISB. Although our Party Bureau has
yet come to no decision on this matter it has asked to convene the
CAP for a general discussion of the request, and of the serious
international situation created by Austria's ultimatum to Serbia.
This meeting will take place on Monday, 27 July, at five p.m. and
if necessary I shall immediately inform you of the outcome.[22]

The reaction of most sections of the International was the
same as that of the CAP. Although on 25 July the International's
Chairman, Vandervelde, in Britain on holiday, found the news
'very disturbing', he refused to believe in war, even in a localized war between Austria and Serbia. He was of the opinion
that the period of international *detente* was over and that the
world faced 'another period of crisis and conflicts'.[23]

Was the reason for this relative calm that the socialists were
awaiting the outcome of the ISB meeting, that the leaders of the
French party and the other sections first wanted to achieve
'international co-ordination of the whole socialist movement of
Europe'? Or did they in the last resort take an optimistic view

[22] Dubreuilh to Huysmans, 25 July 1914, ISB archives.
[23] Vandervelde to Huysmans, 25 July 1914, ISB archives.

of a confused situation and were they therefore anxious, in view of past experience, not to dramatize the international situation prematurely? There is no support from published or unpublished sources for the first hypothesis. The issues which the meeting discussed and the work which it accomplished show what really was at stake and allow us to give a positive reply to the alternative explanation. Let us first examine the attitude of the leaders of the International on the eve of this meeting and see what the gathering hoped to achieve.

After 1913 the socialist world, like the French section, was anxious to believe in peace in Europe—however precarious—'so as to obliterate the very memory of the political vicissitudes of the past years'.[24] The various crises that had shaken Europe had led the socialists to conclude that regional conflicts, such as the one in the Balkans, would not lead to a European clash and that they could be settled by diplomacy. This view was not based on political short-sightedness nor on a lack of realism. Professor Renouvin observes that 'the Balkan conflict of 1914 was in principle very similar to that of 1909; a Russo-Austrian conflict which threatened to involve Germany and France because of the alliances game'.[25] It was therefore logical that most of the delegates to the ISB, and Jaurès more than the rest, firmly believed in the possibility of a diplomatic solution, particularly as the prevailing confusion led them to misjudge the situation. More than ever, even the socialist leaderships had to rely on contradictory press reports as their only source of information. They failed to unravel the mysteries of the diplomatic situation and to divine the rulers' intentions which changed from hour to hour. On 27 July Jaurès noted bitterly that 'tumultuous events overwhelm a confused and helpless world'.

[24] *La Bataille syndicaliste* (25 July 1914), 1: 'Let us conceal nothing. The peace in Europe in which—precarious though it was—we tried to believe so as to obliterate the very memory of the political vicissitudes of the past years . . .' (quoted in A. Kriegel and J.-J. Becker, op. cit. 63).

[25] Cf. Pierre Renouvin, *Les Origines immédiates de la guerre (28 juin–4 août 1914)* (Paris, Costes, 279 pp.); and same author's *Histoire des relations internationales* (Paris, Hachette, 1955, vol. vi, 376 pp.).

In contrast to November 1912 the International was this time overtaken and fooled by events. Both its left and right wings actually saw the situation in the same light. Thus one of the central figures of the German radical Left, Julian Karski (Marchlewski), examining the stock exchange prices of 23 July 1914, came to the conclusion that 'there is at present no serious danger of war'.[26] Only after Austria's ultimatum to Serbia did the Left radicals begin to show signs of slight unease.

It was not until 27 July, after Berlin had rejected Sir Edward Grey's proposed mediation, that the socialist leaders gradually became aware of the seriousness of the situation. 'War [between Austria and Serbia] has become inevitable,' wrote Rosa Luxemburg to Huysmans on the same day.[27] In Italy on that day the socialist members of parliament and the leaders of the socialist party met, and afterwards published a strongly pacifist declaration which demanded Italy's neutrality. Also on 27 July at 5 p.m. the CAP met in Paris. After a discussion of the latest news Jaurès drafted a manifesto which appeared in *L'Humanité* the next morning. He warned public opinion against a policy of force which 'can at any monent produce a catastrophe in Europe such as there has never been'. But the CAP continued to believe in a diplomatic solution and expressed its confidence in the French Government which was thought to be wanting peace and to be working effectively towards that end.

The socialists, the workers of France, make an appeal to the whole country to gather all efforts for the maintenance of peace. They know that in the present crisis the French Government is most sincerely anxious to avert or to diminish the risks of conflict. It is asked to apply itself to securing a policy of conciliation and mediation rendered all the easier by the readiness of Serbia to accede to the major portion of the Austrian demands. It is asked to influence its ally, Russia, in order that she shall not seek a pretext for aggressive

[26] 'Börse und Politik', *Sozialdemokratische Korrespondenz* (23 July 1914) (quoted in J. Kuczynski, op. cit., 32).
[27] Rosa Luxemburg to Camille Huysmans, in G. Haupt, 'Quelques lettres inédites de Rosa Luxemburg (1908–1914)', *Partisans*, 45 (Dec.–Jan. 1969), 10.

operations under cover of defending the interests of the Slavs. Their efforts thus correspond with those of the German social democrats in demanding that Germany shall exercise a moderating influence on her ally, Austria. Both at their posts of action have the same work and the same end.[28]

According to this manifesto the principal objective of the ISB meeting due to be held the following day in Brussels was 'to express with the utmost force and unanimity the joint determination of the European proletariat to maintain peace' and 'to agree on vigorous joint action' against the threat of war. A statement issued on 27 July by the leaders of the Italian socialist party shows that they hoped for the same result from the ISB meeting.

In reality such statements expressed a wish rather than the true intentions of the Bureau. When Huysmans decided to call a meeting he was thinking primarily of the international congress and wanted to give the leading European socialists an opportunity to hear a report on the situation from the Austrians, the delegates of the country directly affected by the crisis. The letters which the secretary of the ISB wrote and received between 25 and 28 July concerning this meeting refer exclusively to these two points. At first Vandervelde thought only of an enlarged meeting of the Executive Committee attended by delegates of the countries immediately concerned, Austria, France, Great Britain, and Germany. In his reply of 26 July to Huysmans's telegram Vaillant emphasized:

If I were to give way to my feelings I would say that it is important for the ISB to meet, at any rate to examine the possibilities. But it is a matter for the Serbian and the Austrian sections, *above all the Austrians*, to take the appropriate decisions and to translate them into action. Our friends from Vienna, particularly Adler, are especially well placed to ask for our advice and to decide what can be done for peace, because with their knowledge of the situation they are in a better position to do so than all the others.[29]

Vaillant's letter is at the same time revealing and explicit. It

[28] English text taken from Walling, 174.
[29] Vaillant to Huysmans, 26 July 1914, ISB archives.

was in this spirit that the socialist leaders went to Brussels.[30] But their haste betrayed a certain degree of anxiety. Were they aware of the gravity of the situation? Did they come with precise ideas on what action to take? Or did they gather in Brussels solely for consultation? The records of the meeting provide some answers to these questions.

[30] In his memoirs 'Une vie révolutionnaire', Charles Rappoport gives the following account of the mood of the French delegation: in the train on the way to Brussels on the evening of 28 July 'the conversation was animated and varied. There was no mention of war' (quoted MS., 199). Not only the socialists leaders but also the militant revolutionary syndicalists felt relieved. For example, Rosmer, who on 27 July was of the view that the 'threat of war' had never been closer, wrote the next morning: 'We are a little more relaxed this morning; the situation seems less serious. On Saturday evening and Sunday it seemed truly frightening. Austria appeared to be on the point of attacking and automatically a European war would have begun. But this plan did not materialise, there was talk of mediation and it seemed as though the general conflagration could be avoided' (*Archives Monatte*, 19).

10

The Last Session of the ISB: Optimism or Blindness?

T H E session opened on the morning of 29 July 1914 in the offices of the Centre for Workers' Education on the sixth floor of the Maison du Peuple[1] in an international atmosphere that was growing more tense every hour. The news of Austria's declaration of war on Serbia and the pro-war demonstrations in Paris and Berlin formed the background to the first meeting. A large number of highly reputed delegates had come from all over Europe. Most of the leaders of the socialist parties were present. But the absence of three delegates caused comment. The Serbian delegate, whose report on the situation had been expected with great interest by the Bureau, did not appear, neither did Ebert of the German delegation,[2] nor the delegate of the Bolsheviks, Litvinov (who was to have come in place of Lenin, who was at Cracow).[3] For the historian it is the latter's absence in particular that is regrettable because a viewpoint was thereby lost that might have significantly affected the post-1914 controversy about the collapse of the Second International.

Until recently historians of socialism have known little about the last session of the International Bureau in Brussels. The press was not admitted, the meetings were held in camera, and the official records of the session have never been published. The historian was therefore forced to fall back on accounts subsequently written by participants. These reports must be treated with considerable reserve. As they were written long after the

---

[1] Cf. Henri de Man, *Cavalier seul* (Geneva, Éditions du Cheval ailé, 1948), 80.
[2] Ebert had also been invited in the telegram which Huysmans sent to the party executive on 28 July 1914 (ISB archives).
[3] Cf. *Correspondance entre Lénine et Huysmans*, 114.

event, they tend to be incomplete and inaccurate, and above all describe the session with the hindsight of the great shake-up that took place after 1914. While Émile Vandervelde, for instance, emphasizes the International's determination to oppose the war, Angelica Balabanoff, who became a follower of Zimmerwald and the Third International, stresses in her memoirs the impotence of the Second International.

The official record of the session, compiled by the secretary of the Bureau, shows what really happened. Although the minutes were hastily prepared—the debates are reported in an abbreviated form, in a sort of telegraphese, and important details are frequently omitted or garbled—they constitute the only authentic account of the session.[4]

The discussion centred on two questions. The first concerned the international situation, the second the forthcoming international congress.

Neither the record of the debates nor the reports of the delegates of the major countries affected by the July crisis point to any loss of nerve or dramatization of the situation. Only the Austrian party leader, Victor Adler, seemed crushed. Already seriously ill at the time, he seemed to age visibly in those critical days. He was only a shadow of the man whom Kautsky, after the death of Bebel, had seen as the intellectual and moral

---

[4] There are only a few participants' accounts of the session and they vary in value. Historians have mostly used Angelica Balabanoff's *My Life as a Rebel* (London, 1938), 114 and *passim*. But Balabanoff's memoirs are misleading, her recollections of this session are sometimes inexact and tendentious. Even the dates she gives for the conference (27 and 28 July) are wrong. Several other personalities who took part in the meeting have subsequently related some episodes of this debate. Cf. Émile Vandervelde, 'Victor Adler und die Internationale', *Der Kampf* xxii (1929); Fr. Adler, *Vor dem Ausnahmegericht*, 198 and *passim*. The most valuable account comes from the Spanish delegate A. Fabra-Ribas, in *La Vie socialiste* (1 Aug. 1931), 11–13. On this occasion he did not confine himself to his recollections but published long extracts from his report on the session, transmitted in August 1914 to the executive of the Spanish Socialist Party. This account was again published under the title 'Jean Jaurès à Bruxelles', *Bulletin de la Société d'études jaurésiennes*, 28 (1968), 1–8. See another exceedingly valuable source: the notes taken by the Swiss delegate Robert Grimm during the session (Grimm archives, Amsterdam, IISG). The basic document, the official report written in French by the ISB secretary, which I discovered in the ISB archives, is published in full, below, pp. 250–65.

leader of the International. His son Friedrich, who accompanied him to Brussels, later said that Victor Adler had come to the session 'convinced that it was impossible to do anything against the war'.[5] The session began with Victor Adler's account of the situation in Austria–Hungary. He painted a sombre picture and admitted openly that his party was powerless to prevent war against Serbia. There was no question of anti-war activity in Austria because the party was incapable of action. Therefore the Bureau should not count on the proletariat of the monarchy. The only suggestion Victor Adler made in the circumstances was to save the existing workers' organization and above all his own party.

This dramatic and at the same time completely passive view was shared only by the Czech delegate, Nemec. 'After these disappointing and pathetic statements the gathering was seized by a certain discomfiture', commented Louis Bertrand in his memoirs.[6] The delegates who heard Adler found his statement 'exaggeratedly pessimistic' and above all 'out of place in these tragic hours'. His observation that he could do nothing was all the more disheartening because delegates valued the far-sightedness and extraordinary political judgement of the Austrian socialist leader. Even Adler's son, Friedrich, was for the first time 'opposed to the policy of his father'[7] for whom he had a very high regard. The atmosphere of that first morning meeting on 29 July is described in the report which the Spanish delegate, Fabra-Ribas, sent to his party leadership a month later:

Adler's speech not only made a poor impression but created profound dissatisfaction. Haase was particularly annoyed and Rosa Luxemburg outraged. While Henri de Man translated the Austrian delegate's statement into French, Rosa Luxemburg came

---

[5] Fr. Adler, *Vor dem Ausnahmegericht*, 198.

[6] Louis Bertrand, *Souvenirs d'un meneur socialiste* (Brussels, vol. ii), 224.

[7] Cf. Max Ermers, *Victor Adler, Aufstieg und Größe einer sozialistischen Partei* (Vienna, 1932), 317. See also Julius Braunthal, *Victor und Friedrich Adler, Zwei Generationen Arbeiterbewegung* (Vienna, Wiener Volksbuchhandlung, 1965), 211 ff.

up to Michael Corrales and myself and said in a state of great agitation: 'The session cannot go on in this sort of atmosphere. We must answer Adler with energetic speeches and with facts which speak louder than words; Morgari and Axelrod must report on the anti-war campaigns of our Italian and Russian friends. And you must tell us what happened in Spain in July 1909.' Haase who listened to this conversation agreed with Rosa Luxemburg and seemed ready—as he had been once before—to use language different from Adler's.

This happened at the first meeting which took place in the morning. At lunch Adler's speech—Nemec's had been less important —was the sole topic of conversation among delegates. Because time was getting on several of our friends asked Jaurès whether he, like most comrades, agreed that Rosa Luxemburg's suggestion should not be put into effect until the end of the evening meeting.[8]

Jaurès agreed. The afternoon meeting passed off as planned. But out of consideration for the aged Austrian party leader there were no polemics or personal attacks. According to the Spanish delegate, the great respect which Adler's personality inspired 'prevented the disapproval from being expressed too strongly'. Haase alone, because of the close links between his party and the Austrian party, could afford to say tactfully that 'the Austrians are wrong in their passivity and resignation' and to imply that 'he had expected "something different" from the Austrian comrades'.[9]

After a discussion on the date and agenda of the international congress, the meeting proceeded to consider the political situation. In an attempt to dispel any pessimism, the Russian, British, German, and Italian delegates sought to convince the assembled company of the possibility and necessity of an effective intervention against any threat of war.

The Social Revolutionary Rubanovich and the Menshevik social democrat Axelrod attempted to imbue the ISB with new

[8] There is no mention of the role which Rosa Luxemburg played at this session in the very extensive biography by J. P. Nettl, who merely quotes Angelica Balabanoff's recollections. Cf. J. P. Nettl, *Rosa Luxemburg*, vol. ii, 601–4.

[9] Cf. A. Fabra-Ribas, art. cit.

optimism and confidence by replying positively to the question of whether the Russian proletariat was determined to oppose war. Axelrod asserted 'that revolution would break out in Russia if there is a war'. The British delegate, Bruce Glasier, spoke even more movingly and stated emphatically that the British proletariat was ready to obey the International's instructions down to the last detail, and said that he was convinced that the red flag of the socialists and the trade unionists would be held high.

In his report on the situation Hugo Haase used the German social democrats' familiar arguments to reaffirm their view that the governing classes, and above all German industry, did not want war. Only a Russian attack could make Germany intervene. About his party's actions Haase's conscience was clear, although he had few illusions about the chances of preventing Germany going to war should the government decide to do so. 'We shall do our duty', the SPD chairman assured the ISB, without committing himself in detail. Jaurès emphasized the role which his party, the SFIO, would have to play in a country whose government wanted peace.

'Jaurès was admirable although afflicted by terrible migraine,' reported Fabra-Ribas.

He did not answer Adler directly, but very skilfully expressed his satisfaction with the firm attitude of the German comrades, and emphasized that they were thereby helping the French socialists and those of the countries directly affected by the conflict to show their governments that the socialist party is a force to be taken into consideration.

The ISB's view of the international situation found expression in the final resolution of the meeting. Although most delegates regarded the situation as critical they believed that there was time to hold the international congress and then decide on joint action. Indeed the only concrete decision taken was to advance the date of the congress. It was called for 9 August in Paris and the first item on the agenda was 'The proletariat and the war'. The decision was taken at the suggestion of Haase and Jaurès. They saw this congress as playing a great political and psychological role and wanted it to become the starting-point of a new peace offensive, similar to that initiated by the Basle Congress. Therefore Jaurès protested vehemently against Angelica Balabanoff's suggestion to postpone the congress and let the ISB take the necessary decisions. In the circumstances 'we need the congress,' Jaurès replied. 'Its deliberations and resolutions will give the proletariat confidence. The cancellation of the congress would be a disappointment to the proletariat.' According to Jaurès any decision taken by the ISB alone would make no impact whatsoever. The national parties must participate unanimously in joint action because they felt that they should do so and not because of any decision taken by the Executive, which had no means of ensuring that its directives would be obeyed. This could only happen after a congress of the International.

Like Jaurès, most of the delegates present in Brussels looked to the congress as a powerful means of exerting pressure on the governments and therefore wanted to make any decision on the prevention and limitation of war, or any agreement on related and simultaneous action, dependent on the resolutions of the forthcoming sessions of the International. Hence there was no discussion in detail on how to apply the preventive strategy advocated by the International and above all the French socialists' suggested general strike. Angelica Balabanoff says in her memoirs that at this ISB meeting she referred to previous discussions on the feasibility of a general strike, but that her observations met only with surprise and hostility.[10] But no reference to any such remark is found in the official record of the session in the notes of the Swiss delegate, Grimm, or in Fabra-Ribas's report.

The matter was certainly discussed in the course of the session but in a different context: should the question of the general strike remain on the agenda of the international congress or not? To Victor Adler's intervention that all 'questions on which there is disagreement' should be deleted from the agenda of the International's session convened in Paris, Jaurès replied

[10] A. Balabanoff, op. cit. 114–15.

curtly: 'Dealing with problems on which there is disagreement is a matter of tact. It is not possible to ignore the question of the general strike. And this, we never have done, not even at Basle. Yet agreement was reached.'[11] It was not Balabanoff but the other delegate from Italy, Morgari, who in his report on the situation in his country touched on the question of the general strike.

We must note, however, that in the official record of the session his remarks are reproduced in garbled form. Morgari is supposed to have said: 'As far as the attitude of the Italian proletariat towards the general strike etc. goes it is impossible to make predictions. The Italians understand the Austrians' difficulties.' But the notes of both the Spanish and the Swiss delegates show that Morgari said exactly the opposite. Fabra-Ribas reports:

Morgari: 'We have already told our government that we shall not allow it to support Austria. If it refuses to listen, that is if it does not observe neutrality, the strictest neutrality, we shall immediately call a general strike. We do not know whether this will have the desired result but we shall do our utmost to make it a success.[12]

According to Grimm's notes Morgari said:

Italy is not as good [an] ally as is thought. [The] parliamentary group met the day before yesterday. [It] demanded that Parliament should be called. Demonstrations are being held everywhere and it is thought that if war breaks out there will be a general strike in Italy.

The fact that these two participants, who wrote their accounts independently of one another, agree in the essentials on what was said makes their version plausible. All the more so because Grimm paid particular attention to the statement of the delegate of a neighbouring country which itself had organizations in Switzerland (the Italian socialist party of Switzerland), whereas the clerk, whose duty it was to keep the records for the ISB secretariat, was exhausted after a long day of discussions and failed to give the last speech of the meeting his full attention.

---

[11] Cf. above. [12] A. Fabra-Ribas ,art. cit.

It was not solely because the international congress was due to meet a few days later that the most determined advocates of the general strike present at the meeting, Vaillant and Keir Hardie, did not raise this issue; they did not regard the situation as serious enough to justify the use of this last resort. As a matter of fact the only concrete proposal put forward at the ISB meeting came from Vaillant, who repeated the suggestion made during the crisis of December 1912 that 'the socialists of the small countries (Belgium, Switzerland, Holland, Norway, Denmark, and Sweden) should advise their governments to propose the establishment of a court of arbitration for the settlement of international conflicts'.[13] The suggestion was accepted in principle and the Bureau decided that the countries mentioned should be 'free to choose whatever means they regard as best suited to gain the ear of their governments'.

After spending all day at the ISB meeting the delegates of the major countries, on the evening of 29 July, addressed a big international peace rally at the Cirque Royal in Brussels.[14] All of them—and Haase first of all—delivered impassioned speeches full of confidence in the International and in the proletariat which, as Jaurès put it, 'is feeling its power' and through its delegates 'in Paris will express its demand for justice and peace'. Jaurès's moving speech 'roused the audience'[15] of this memorable meeting—vividly described by Roger Martin du Gard in *L'Été 1914*[16]—to 'paroxysms'. Charles Rappoport says in his memoirs:

Never before was the great socialist orator as great, as eloquent, as persuasive or as moving. These final public words of his were truly sublime. This man whom the vicious reactionaries and some so-called radicals have calumniated as *the advocate of Germany*, whose assassination is dreamt of in certain society salons, and whom Mr. Charles Maurras has publicly condemned to death, began at

[13] A. Fabra-Ribas, art. cit.
[14] On this meeting, see Jean Steingers, 'Le dernier discours de Jaurès', in *Jaurès et la Nation*, 85–9; and J. Joll, *The Second International*, 164–5.
[15] A. Fabra-Ribas, art. cit.
[16] Cf. Schlobach, '*L'Été 1914*: Roger Martin du Gard, historien et romancier', *Le Mouvement social*, 49 (1964), 119–41.

this tragic moment in history by insisting on the innocence of France which had done everything to preserve the peace.[17]

The raving enthusiasm of thousands of citizens of Brussels turned people's heads and made them mistake their dreams for realities. On the evening of 29 July 1914,[18] the delegates to the ISB, although exhausted, were highly satisfied with the results achieved. The meeting of the Bureau which had been held in camera and which had begun with an admission of impotence and defeat not only took a positive turn but reached its climax with the public affirmation of the International's power and determination to fight for peace.

The meeting on the following morning was short. A communiqué submitted by Haase (but according to Angelica Balabanoff drafted by Jaurès) was adopted.[19] The text, published by the press on the same day, contained nothing new in relation to the earlier statements by the national sections. Emphasis was put on the proletariat's growing anxiety as the international situation deteriorated. The communiqué stressed that it was a matter of emergency to hold more anti-war demonstrations and to insist on solving the Austro-Serbian conflict by means of arbitration; it announced that it had been decided to convene the international congress urgently in Paris, 'which will give powerful expression to the determination of the proletariat of the world to preserve the peace'.[20] The possibility of a world-wide clash was not being considered at all.

The ISB had thus concluded its session without reaching a decision; because in the opinion of the delegates of the national sections only 'the International Socialist Parliament' could decide on joint socialist action. It never occurred to them that the

[17] Cf. Ch. Rappoport, 'Une vie révolutionnaire', quoted MS.

[18] This applies particularly to Jaurès and Rosa Luxemburg. See Camille Huysmans's letter to Benedikt Kautsky of 11 Mar. 1949, in Rosa Luxemburg, *Briefe an Freunde* (Hamburg, 1950), 116, n. 2. Indisposition caused by exhaustion prevented Rosa Luxemburg from speaking at the Cirque Royal meeting.

[19] This fact is confirmed by de Man who wrote in his memoirs: 'I also see Hugo Haase with his arm around Jaurès's shoulder helping him to draft a last appeal' (Henri de Man, op. cit. 80).

[20] See the ISB circular of 31 July 1914. Printed in French, German, and English, ISB archives.

congress might not take place because a sudden storm seemed improbable. Vandervelde quotes the following words which Jaurès is supposed to have said to him a few hours before his departure for Paris: 'This is going to be another Agadir, we shall have ups and downs. But this crisis will be resolved like the others.'[21]

The mood at the end of the session was therefore one of confidence and it was in this spirit that the ISB delegates left Brussels. The Bureau did not fear an imminent European war and had no doubt that peace between Austria and Serbia would soon be re-established. The leaders present in Brussels, above all Haase and Jaurès, thought that the 'localization policy' had a chance of success and were firmly convinced not only of the International's ability to intervene effectively but also of its sections' determination to act. Angelica Balabanoff was left with this impression of the session: 'Very few of those present, Jaurès and Rosa Luxemburg among them, seemed aware of what was in store for the working class, but even the most far-sighted had no conception of the dimension or the proximity of the catastrophe.'[22] And in her memoirs she said that when the news of partial Russian mobilization was announced at the afternoon meeting of 29 July, nobody, least of all the Russian delegates, Rubanovich and Axelrod, was prepared to believe it. According to Vandervelde's recollections, 'Even when we stood in the shadow of war, optimism continued to prevail. . .'.[23] Was it optimism or blindness? The mentality of a generation of socialists whose pacifism corresponded to their deep humanitarian feelings explains why both elements should have been present. In spite of the repeated prediction that mankind was threatened by a catastrophe, they could not believe, as Jaurès put it, 'that the humane men of all countries' would allow

[21] Vandervelde, *Souvenirs d'un militant socialiste*, 171. On the last day which Jaurès spent in Brussels see also Camille Huysmans's memoirs in *ABC*, 39 (Antwerp, 26 Sept. 1959), 4.

[22] A. Balabanoff, op. cit. 114.

[23] Cf. Vandervelde in *Histoire de l'Internationale socialiste* (Brussels, L'Églantine 1924), 26.

themselves to be dragged into a catastrophe and that men conscious of the responsibility of governing their countries would let themselves be pushed to the brink of the abyss. According to Rappoport's recollections, Jaurès 'believed until the last minute in the triumph of reason and good sense', while Haase, 'as a Marxist, was less susceptible to pacifist illusions'.[24] In spite of this difference in attitude neither Haase nor the other Marxists foresaw on 30 July 1914 that the Austro-Serbian conflict would develop into a world war. In the confusion of July 1914 the vicissitudes of the crisis encouraged a similar analysis in all socialist circles. Rosmer wrote on 30 July: 'At any rate the threat of a European war is no longer imminent as in the first days. As the situation is developing now the crisis might last days or even weeks.'[25]

We may well ask what political factors there were to justify socialist confidence in a peaceful solution of the crisis of 29 and 30 July 1914. Firstly, the leading socialists of the great countries, with the exception of Russia, were convinced of the pacifist intentions of their governments. Bruce Glasier said at the ISB meeting that in Britain 'the whole of the Cabinet wanted peace'. Jaurès was even more explicit. He believed that the French Government was pursuing an active peace policy. In fact he thought that in France only small groups of war profiteers and militarists were in favour of an aggressive policy. At the decisive moment he therefore trusted the French Government. In Brussels at the meeting of the Bureau and in his speech at the Cirque Royal, on 29 July, he confirmed clearly and unequivocally the determination of France and of his government to preserve the peace:[26]

[24] Ch. Rappoport, 'Une vie révolutionnaire', quoted MS., 202. The testimony of the British delegate contradicts these claims: 'None of those present in Brussels, the German delegates included, counted on a European war' (Bruce Glasier, 'The Last Watch of the International. Jean Jaurès's "Good Bye" ', *Labour Leader* (6 Aug. 1914), 1).

[25] Cf. *Archives Monatte*, 21.

[26] The English text is found in Walling, 127–8. In his memoirs Rappoport tells of a conversation with Jaurès on the morning of 30 July: 'When I was having coffee with Jaurès I asked him *à propos* of a phrase in his article in *L'Humanité* in

As for us French socialists, our duty is simple: we do not need to impose on our government a policy of peace. Our government practices peace . . . I have the right to say that at the present moment the French Government wants peace and is striving to maintain peace . . . As for ourselves, it is our duty to insist that the government should speak forcibly enough to Russia to make her keep her hands off.

This task seemed simplified by the domestic problems facing the Tsarist regime, which was forced to move cautiously after the big strikes which had just ended in St. Petersburg.

Germany's leading socialists, Haase no less than Rosa Luxemburg, were equally convinced of the peaceful intentions of Wilhelm II and his government: it seemed impossible to them that Berlin and Vienna could be playing the same game.[27] Haase was strengthened in this conviction following an interview with the German Chancellor who had summoned him on 26 July 1914.[28]

On the day that she left for Brussels, Rosa Luxemburg gave the Kaiser a 'pacifist reference': 'If you ask whether the German Government is ready for war there is every reason to reply in the negative,' she wrote on 28 July:

which he had asserted that the French cabinet was working for peace: "Are you sure about Poincaré?" He replied: "I am referring to the cabinet" ' ('Une vie révolutionnaire', quoted MS.).

[27] Rubanovich, one of the Russian delegates who was at the meeting, relates an exchange of views between Jaurès and Haase, which took place on 29 July after the SPD chairman had given his account of the present position of affairs: 'At around six in the evening, during the meeting of the International Socialist Bureau, Jaurès, turning to Comrades Kautsky and Haase, asked them the question: "Are you absolutely sure, as you have just said in your analysis of the situation, that your government and your emperor especially, knew nothing of the Austrian ultimatum to Serbia?" Haase replied: "I am absolutely convinced that our government has had no part in the quarrel." Jaurès shook his head and expressed his doubts. Among other facts, he cited the case of an influential German journalist who, when leaving Paris a few days before, had said quite openly that within a few days "one would hear a resounding blow on our Kaiser's table" ' (*Le Populaire du Centre* (21 Oct. 1914) (quoted by H. Goldberg, *Life of Jean Jaurès*, 567, n. 38)).

[28] As Ebert, Scheidemann, and Molkenbuhr were not in Berlin Haase was accompanied by Otto Braun. See *Protokoll der Reichskonferenz der Sozialdemokratie Deutschlands vom 21., 22., 23. September 1916* (Berlin, 1916), 60; E. Haase, *Hugo Haase*, 25; F. Klein, ed., *Deutschland im Ersten Weltkrieg*, vol. i, 269.

One can honestly agree with the panic-stricken makers of German policy that at this moment any prospect looks brighter to them than that of shouldering the terror and risk of a war with Russia and France, and in the last resort even with Britain, all for the sake of a Habsburg whim.[29]

The belief that the German Government did not want war was generally accepted by the SPD.[30] Its leaders subsequently admitted in an attempt to justify themselves that they did not know the exact facts, that they had been misled by their government which had done everything to cause confusion. Kautsky, for example, attributed the SPD's failure to this lack of information.[31] In fact the inexorable speed of the mechanical development of events escaped everyone, including the French socialists. They did not think that anyone would jeopardize the peace on account of Serbia. Their opinion was not based merely on a misinterpretation of the political constellation in July 1914 or on a lack of information about what was happening behind the governmental scenes. It is explained by their general view of basic motives. To the socialists it was inconceivable that the governments' immediate plans, which could—as in fact happened—make events move with a terrifying speed, should be immune to the 'logic' that was allegedly the basis of the interests of capitalism.

The published and unpublished documents reveal yet another aspect: the psychological prerequisites for the capitulation of 4 August, the *Union sacrée* mentality, which was there even at the session in Brussels. The question of who was responsible for the international crisis, and consequently for any possible aggression, was indirectly asked on that occasion and the various

[29] *Sozialdemokratische Korrespondenz* (28 July 1914), quoted by J. Kuczynski, *Der Ausbruch des Ersten Weltkrieges* . . . , 53. Generally Austria alone was held responsible and thereby the extent of the crisis was minimized. In this the socialist press of France and Germany agreed. On 30 July Rosmer had the impression that 'Austria has been authorized to make a military demonstration in Serbia to restore its prestige there' (*Archives Monatte*, 21).

[30] Cf. J. Kuczynski, op. cit. 61.

[31] Cf. Karl Kautsky, *Wie der Weltkrieg entstand* (Berlin, 1914), 78.

viewpoints were stated. The French delegates disagreed with the Germans. At the ISB meeting on 29 July, and again on the same evening at the Cirque Royal, Jaurès publicly attacked German diplomacy (which he had accused for years of 'being wily and brutal') and condemned in particular the calculating and alarming manœuvres of the Imperial Government. In spite of *Vorwärts*'s assurances, Vaillant had formed a firm opinion about Germany's peaceful intentions when he wrote to Huysmans on 26 July 1914: 'If Germany made an oral promise to Austria when the latter sent its ultimatum to Serbia, then this was done for the sake of war, and war we shall have. If not, there remains every prospect of an improvement in the situation.'[32] After the end of July France's leading socialists and French public opinion, rightly or wrongly, could only conceive of 'a defensive war for which they bore no responsibility'.[33]

The SPD leadership, on the other hand—for example, Haase—while conscious of the fact that the German Government had an important contribution to make to the peaceful solution of the July crisis, did not reject the possibility of Germany being forced into a defensive war. In his speech at the afternoon meeting of the ISB on 29 July Haase said: 'We know that Germany wants peace but if Russia intervenes Germany must also intervene.' At lunch he said explicitly to Rappoport: 'If France alone were involved our attitude would be simple. But there are the Russians. What the Prussian boot means to you the Russian knout means to us.'[34]

There was no one at the ISB meeting who was not aware of the Russophobia which prevailed in the circles of German social democracy. That the participants were impressed by Haase's words is attested by Bruce Glasier's statement at the Labour Party Congress of 1917: 'At the last meeting of the Bureau before the war the then leaders of the German Social

[32] ISB archives.
[33] J. Julliard, 'La C. G. T. devant la guerre', 49.
[34] Ch. Rappoport, "Une vie révolutionnaire", quoted MS.

Democratic Party declared frankly that if there were the least danger of Germany being invaded by Russia, they could not, and would not, even if they could, resist mobilization.'[35] But the atmosphere at the Brussels meeting of 29 July 1914 was such that no one paid any attention to such nuances. A further element contributing to the optimism of the International's leading figures was the conviction that, in spite of having been let down by the Austrian socialists, the parties of all the other countries, and in particular the French and German parties, would act in accordance with the resolutions adopted jointly in the past. Fabra-Ribas reported: 'After the session of the Bureau and after the great rally at the Cirque Royal, the socialist delegates left Brussels convinced that come what may the International would do its duty.'

The optimistic leading article which Jaurès wrote for *L'Humanité* on 29 July confirms this view: 'The exchange of ideas and information which the International Bureau has just concluded has shown that socialists everywhere are aware of their duty. The great demonstrations of the German socialists are a wonderful answer to those who condemn our German comrades' alleged inactivity.'[36] Like most of the delegates in Brussels Jaurès preferred to listen to Haase's assurances, that the German proletariat was determined to use its strength to prevent war, rather than to the ultimately far-sighted pessimism of Adler, who said openly at the session that his party could not take action in such circumstances. All the participants were confident that the German social democrats were determined to resist their government's manœuvres.

But such a statement raises certain questions:

Was Jaurès's confidence in German social democracy not to some extent assumed? Did the man who, during his famous controversy with Bebel some years previously, had very much doubted whether behind its impressive façade this social democracy was

[35] *Report of the 16th Annual Conference of the Labour Party* (Manchester, 1917), 125.
[36] *L'Humanité* (30 July 1914), 1.

in fact reliable, and whether this vast army was prepared for the struggle—did this man on the eve of 1914 really believe what he said?[37]

Although this problem cannot be solved without a thorough examination of Jaurès's attitude towards the SPD,[38] it is possible in our present state of knowledge to make some tentative suggestions.

We know that in the critical days of 1914 most of the SPD leaders were in fact little inclined to oppose war by the use of carefully considered measures and by mobilizing their party's powerful machinery. It is doubtful, however, whether at the time anyone, Jaurès included, could have foreseen the events of 4 August. On the one hand there were in July 1914 only few signs which could have made Jaurès suspicious, while on the other there was good reason for his illusions. All the German party leaders with whom he came into contact during these eventful weeks were convinced internationalists who also underestimated the influence and power of the right wing of their party.

Characteristic of this situation was the discussion which Jaurès had on 14 July 1914 in Paris with Karl Liebknecht, a determined anti-militarist who had full confidence in the internationalism of the German working class. And in Brussels, at the ISB session, Jaurès's contact was Haase, who belonged to the Centre Left which was opposed to the emergence of nationalistic and militaristic trends. It must be said, however, that the activities of the pacifist left never went beyond the limits of the traditional measures which even the German Government did not regard as dangerous.

But in Brussels Haase adopted a very radical and very confident attitude: on the day that he left Berlin the workers of the capital had held big anti-war demonstrations. The next day at the meeting Haase was handed a telegram from Braun reporting

---

[37] Jacques Julliard, 'Le mystère Jaurès', *France-Observateur* (4 June 1964), 12.
[38] There are many references to this in Maurice Lair's *Jaurès et l'Allemagne* Paris, Perrin, 1934), 294 pp.

anti-war protests by 100,000 demonstrators in Unter den Linden. Did this piece of news determine his appraisal of the situation? Was he so impressed by this news or was he carried away by the atmosphere of the great rally in Brussels when he said: 'Austria seems to count on Germany but the German socialists declare that secret treaties do not commit the proletariat to anything. The German proletariat says that Germany must not intervene even if Russia does.'

Haase's sincerity cannot be doubted. But an examination of his speech at the ISB session reveals ambiguities and contradictions; a number of questions remain. For example, during the afternoon meeting of 29 July, commenting on a *Temps* dispatch which had just been received, Haase said: 'The story about the conversation which I am supposed to have had with the Chancellor is a complete fabrication. The government has made no attempt to influence the social democrats who were notified by a representative of the government.' The records of the session do not show whether Haase was answering a participant's question or a statement made in the *Temps* dispatch. The reference was obviously to the discussion which he had had with Bethmann-Hollweg three days previously.

Rappoport recalled that 'Without my taking the initiative Haase began to talk about the attitude of social democracy towards the war, which after his conversation with the Chancellor, of which he had told me during the morning, he probably knew to be imminent'.[39] However, we know that in Haase's absence Südekum, after an interview with the Chancellor, Bethmann-Hollweg, wrote on 29 July 1914 a letter the text of which leaves no doubt about the attitude of the majority of the party leadership. Südekum reported that in his conversation with Ebert, Braun, Müller, Bartels, and Fischer, the assurance, which he himself had given to the Chancellor on the

---

[39] Cf. Ch. Rappoport, 'Une vie révolutionnaire', quoted MS., 201. Rappoport was only making a guess here, because with reference to a conversation which he had had the same morning with Haase, he says '[Haase] told me that he was summoned by Chancellor Bethmann-Hollweg. I did not ask him for details' (ibid. 200).

same day, was confirmed: 'That—because of the wish to serve the cause of peace—no action whatsoever (general strike or partial strike, sabotage or anything similar) was planned or need be feared.'[40]

Had Haase been told of Südekum's step? It is difficult to answer this question because a number of facts are obscure. Above all we do not know whether Südekum had one or two discussions with the Chancellor. There is a reference in Grotjahn's memoirs to the interview which Südekum had with the Chancellor presumably on 28 July, at which the international situation and the intentions of the German Government were discussed.[41] The interview lasted from 2 p.m. until 3.30 p.m. when Haase was still in Berlin. In his letter to Bethmann-Hollweg of 29 July 1914, Südekum mentioned the discussion which they had had the morning of the same day and added: 'Herr Haase is still in Brussels but is expected back tomorrow.' If the chairman of the SPD was not informed of Südekum's step, then there must have been a real 'plot'. Two days later, when the SPD executive was convened to listen to Haase's account of the ISB session, the game was over.

The Südekum episode, seems to confirm the view that the active support given by the SPD to preparations for war was the result of the 'machinations' that led to the victory of the

[40] This document was published by Dieter Fricke and Hans Radandt, 'Neue Dokumente über die Rolle Albert Südekums', in *Zeitschrift für Geschichtswissenschaft* (1956, vol. iv), 757–8. On this interview between Südekum and the Chancellor, see also Ludwig Bergsträsser, *Die preußische Wahlrechtsfrage im Kriege und die Entstehung der Osterbotschaft 1917* (Tübingen, 1929), 3.

[41] A. Grotjahn, *Erlebtes und Erstrebtes* (Berlin, 1932), 150: 'Thursday, 29 July, 1914. Zehlendorf, in the morning.—Südekum, obviously disturbed, came with me to the station. He told me that he had been asked by phone to call on the Reich Chancellor, Bethmann-Hollweg. The interview had lasted from 2 p.m. till 3.30 p.m. According to the Chancellor, the threat of war is more and more imminent; he is doing his best to prevent the war but one of our parties is in favour of it. Then, talking about the leading personalities among the foreign ministers: Sasonov, in Petersburg, is an over-excited man prone to take over-hasty decisions which might unleash the whole process. Vienna, on the other hand, is under the sway of passion rather than led by reason. Then, the man one can still rely upon is Grey, but he is "compelled" to deal with English—not German—policy. Südekum is convinced that the Chancellor does not want a war.'

right wing, which controlled the key positions in the party.[42] But some historians question this interpretation; they see the SPD vote for the war credits on 4 August not as a victory of the right wing but as a failure of the Marxist centre.[43] To them the explanation lies in the development of German social democracy and especially of the Marxist centre which—while continuing to use revolutionary terminology—had in practice long before 1914 taken the road of reformism and compromise which ended in the *Burgfrieden*, the party truce.

This is not the place to examine these apparently contradictory interpretations. In fact they seem not to contradict but to complement each other, relating as they do to different spheres. We must not forget that the paradox of the situation within the SPD became apparent only during the testing period and afterwards. At the end of July 1914, when the socialists concentrated their activities on demonstrating their opposition to the war, it is true to say that the left wing had the upper hand; what the position really was became clear only when the war became a reality. For various reasons German social democracy appeared to be unanimously pacifist at the time of the ISB session. But its opposition to war was restricted to encouraging the German Government in its pacifist attitude, which the leading social democrats did not question. The SPD's pacifism was active so long as it was confined to approved activities, to rallies and protest movements. In other words, while war seemed avoidable the attitude of the German delegates in Brussels was the same as that of the majority of their party.

The situation changed fundamentally when preventive strategy failed. It now became evident how wide the gulf was that separated the helpless and divided left wing from the active right, which was prepared for this eventuality. In the critical days at the end of July 1914 only the right wing of the SPD considered war as a possibility and consequently resolved to give

---

[42] Cf. e.g. William Maehl, 'The Triumph of Nationalism in the German Socialist Party on the Eve of the First World War', *Journal of Modern History* xxiv (March 1952), 27–41.

[43] Cf. Schorske, 242 ff.

the government its active support. While the left wing continued to mistake its pacifist illusions for reality, the right wing of the party looked towards the future with a clear-sightedness that bordered on cynicism. To this group belonged the socialist union leader, Carl Legien, who two days before the ISB session, on 27 July 1914, spoke his mind during a discussion with Jouhaux and other leading CGT personalities.[44] From this brief encounter at the Belgian Trade Union Congress in Brussels many French historians have deduced that 'German social democracy refused to co-operate with the French socialists and trade unionists in preparing joint opposition by the European proletariat to a possible war'.[45]

But this interpretation is unconvincing. The German trade union leaders certainly showed little enthusiasm for action, and Legien, who had always been an opponent of a general strike, went so far as to say openly that in the case of war there was only one thing to do: 'We shall defend ourselves.'[46] But one must not mistake the attitude of the general committee of the German trade unions, which belonged to the right wing of the German workers' movement, for the attitude of the SPD. Because not even at the end of July 1914 can it be said that the German social democrats adopted a negative attitude; their estimate of the situation and of the prospects for the future was shared by the majority of the International.

The International's whole plan of campaign was—as appears from the discussion at the ISB session of 29 and 30 July—linked up with the forthcoming congress.

The lack of proportion between the number of delegates who attended and the results achieved or hoped for was

[44] The reports on this encounter which took place on the occasion of the Belgian Trade Union Congress in Brussels are confused, brief, and contradictory. There seems to have been no more than an unofficial exchange of views over a meal. On the meeting see A. Kriegel, *Aux origines du communisme français*, vol. i, 55–6, n. 3; Drachkovitch, 148; A. Rosmer, *Mouvement ouvrier*, 135 ff.; and especially *Archives Monatte*, 20–1.

[45] Cf. e.g. Camille Bloch, 'Les socialistes allemands pendant la crise de juillet 1914', *Revue d'Histoire de la Guerre mondiale* (Oct. 1933).

[46] Heinz Josef Varain, *Freie Gewerkschaften, Sozialdemokratie und Staat* (Düsseldorf, Droste Verlag, 1956), 71.

striking.[47] The ISB knew how to get its own way when it was a question of supporting the action of one of its sections. But it was powerless when it came to grappling promptly with events and deciding on a common line of action. The vast majority of delegates seemed content to resign themselves to the inevitable and to rely on collective moral pressure rather than on action by the individual parties.

Two days after the meeting events began to move fast, defying the predictions of socialist headquarters. This was no longer the moment to ask why they had been more deceived than the rest of the world, to question the lack of information and foresight. The time had come for swift decisions which could be translated into immediate action, an eventuality never foreseen for a second by the Brussels meeting. The time had come for concerted international action. Historic moments cannot be timed with a stop-watch. During those three important and dramatic days events moved so fast that every minute was crucial. But on 1 August, with the failure of its preventive strategy and in the absence of any alternative, the International collapsed before it had realized what had happened, before socialist opinion had become aware of the situation.

---

[47] 'And thus it also became clear that the International was powerless to prevent armed conflicts between nations . . . Nothing positive emerged from this meeting, the general sense of disillusion was profound,' wrote L. Bertrand, *Souvenirs d'un meneur socialiste*, vol. ii, 224.

11   War or Revolution?

The reversal of workers' policy in August 1914 . . . raises considerable problems. This is why it has remained the object of an ideological controversy which in the course of forty years has lost none of its virulence. If it is the historian's first duty . . . to decide scrupulously what happened and when, he will ultimately have to give his views on 'how' and 'why'.[1]

THE comment is apposite but it fails to emphasize the paradoxes. The 'why' and the 'how' have often been treated as a secondary issue by the historians who have dealt with the question. 'The International and the war' has remained a fertile field for hasty generalizations and for brilliant explanations, which have in fact systematized this complex problem and perpetuated partisan myths.

Trying to understand the mechanism of the failure, the 'how', leads to fathoming the 'why', not only in the realm of ideology, but also of history. Thus, time must be divided and stages defined.

Taking as one's point of reference 4 August—the day on which the SPD in the Reichstag voted for the war credits and on which the *Union sacrée* was proclaimed—means confusing two distinct moments and problems: the 'failure' of the International, that is its inability to avoid war between the nations, and the 'collapse' of either the International or internationalism, the fact that the war was accepted and actively supported by the majority of socialists.[2]

[1] A. Kriegel, *Aux origines du communisme français*, vol. i, 61–2.

[2] 'Hence the socialists were powerless to prevent war, the International cannot be condemned on this count and its break-up must not be ascribed to its inability to prevent the outbreak of war. Nevertheless, the International was forced in August 1914, to discard the revolutionary mask that it had been wearing, and this action seemed tantamount to its own dissolution' (A. Rosenberg, *A History of Bolshevism from Marx to the First Five Years' Plan* (London, OUP, 1937), and Anchor Books, 1967, 73).

In the over-all picture, 4 August is an important point, but neither of arrival nor of departure. The *Union sacrée* was not the result of a simple change of line, a sudden conversion, or a definite choice. The three vital days that followed the collapse of the International acted as a catalyst in the long chain of events which was reaching its logical conclusion.

In fact the ISB meeting of 29–30 July 1914 marked the end of the International. Hardly had the delegates arrived back home when the pace of events quickened, giving the lie to their predictions. After Jaurès's assassination, particularly on the following day, the morning of 1 August, when Germany and France ordered general mobilization, it became apparent that the International could no longer act either as an institution or as a collective force. On the same day, before leaving for Paris with Müller, the SPD representative, Huysmans, the secretary of the ISB, sent a short circular, the last, to the affiliated parties: 'In view of the latest developments the congress in Paris has been postponed until further notice.'[3]

The International thereby admitted that it was powerless to influence events. Without directives, without joint and co-ordinated tactics, the national sections were left to act as their leaders thought best.

Fatalistic resignation prevailed. War was seen as a *fait accompli*. The manifesto prepared by Südekum[4] during the afternoon of 31 July, in reply to the government's ban on all demonstrations and published by the SPD leadership on 1 August, accepts both defeat and the impossibility of action without the smallest note of protest. The SPD handed itself and the International a certificate of good conduct; the proletariat

[3] The purpose of the mission of Hermann Müller, the secretary of the SPD, to Brussels on 31 July 1914 and to Paris on 1 Aug. 1914 remains unexplained. We are in fact dealing here with an episode that was pushed to the fore during the war so as to divert attention and to prevent people from facing their actual responsibilities. See Merle Fainsod, *International Socialism and the World War* (Cambridge, Harvard U.P., 1935), 40 ff.; A. Rosmer, *Mouvement ouvrier*, 312 ff.; J. Joll, *The Second International*, 171 ff.

[4] *Das Kriegstagebuch des Reichstagsabgeordneten Eduard David, 1914–1918*, ed. by Susanne Miller with the co-operation of Erich Matthias (Düsseldorf, Droste Verlag, 1966), 4.

had done its duty to the end, but the pressure of events had been too strong for labour's pacifist determination.

1 August therefore opened up a new chapter in the story of 'The International and the War'. It was felt as a tremendous defeat by the whole of the workers' movement, whereas the SPD's vote in favour of the war credits and the *Union sacrée* were seen as betrayals only by a minority. On 1 August, who could have discerned the dividing lines that were to emerge three days later? At the end of July and the beginning of August, the majority and the revolutionary minority, whose viewpoint on imperialism differed, both made the same predictions about the outcome of the international crisis, the same observations on the gravity of the situation and on the possibility of a peaceful solution. The surprise effect of the war was therefore universal. But there the agreement ended. And dissension started again on the question of what socialist action should be once war had broken out; after 1 August the majority adopted an attitude of resignation, whereas the minority, who did not know what to do or how to do it, was convinced of the need to do something.

Annie Kriegel says that 'we must be careful not to use cross-section data in time-series analysis',[5] provided—I must add—we keep to the realm of history and do not perpetuate myths. But for fifty years the historical approach has oscillated between two types of explanation, which are alternatively propped up with some shift of emphasis. The first is that of the *betrayal* by the leaders, who were 'eaten up by opportunism' and had abjured the oaths sworn at the International's great gatherings.[6] The very term *betrayal*, which stems from the realm of polemics, is not a historical concept but an ethical one, constituting a judgement which rationalizes the subsequent feelings of the

[5] Annie Kriegel, 'Août 1914. Nationalisme et internationalisme ouvrier', *Preuves*, 193 (Mar. 1967), 28.

[6] This type of explanation is found in the works of Soviet historians as, for example, in the important and recent collective history of the Second International, prepared under the direction of Professor L. B. Zubok, *Istorija Vtorogo Internacionala* (Moscow, 'Nauka', 1965–6, 2 vols.).

generation of 4 August but does not stand up in the face of obvious contradictions. Why did these same leaders who 'betrayed' their followers in August 1914 keep their promises in November 1912 in circumstances no less dramatic? Under pressure from the demonstrating masses whom they had themselves mobilized? But why did the same movement fail in July 1914? Why did these same masses succumb to a war psychosis? Why had they surrendered to nationalism?

It was the flaws and contradictions in this line of argument that provided grounds for the second type of explanation which is no less polemical and ideological. The argument runs that at the end of July and the beginning of August 1914, the dilemma confronting the leaders of the International was whether to defend their countries and abandon the revolution, or to save their party and give up their internationalist *raison d'être*. Faced suddenly with an event that left no room for ambiguities, they were compelled to choose between internationalism and patriotism.[7] Starting from concrete premises the advocates of this hypothesis then encountered imaginary problems.

International socialism was in fact motivated by conflicting impulses and its policy was characterized by ambiguities which socialists at the time preferred to ignore. They found refuge in short-term solutions and compromises, thereby avoiding the issues that would have forced them to take a stand. 'The International's total inability to oppose the war'[8] had its roots in the organization's many contradictions, in the foundations and in the theoretical weaknesses of a preventive strategy that determined the concrete forms of socialist attitudes and policies. Based on the majority's view of imperialism, on an interpretation which the facts belied, the International's pacifist strategy was characterized by marked contradictions: an awareness of new

[7] The most brilliant advocate of this thesis is undoubtedly Annie Kriegel. In a series of studies she puts forward new ideas and documents, takes up and enlarges this idea but also sets out the arguments against it.

[8] Cf. Madeleine Rebérioux's comments in 'L'historien devant notre temps. La deuxième Internationale à la veille de 1914. Progrès et perspectives de recherches', *Démocratie nouvelle* 2 (1966), 34–6; cf. also *Annales, ESC* 2 (May–June 1967), 697–701.

stages in the evolution of capitalism; an appreciation of the immediacy of the threat and a basic optimism as to the outcome of the crisis that ignored the possibility of a universal clash.[9] The International's activities on the world scene were therefore adventitious and dictated by the seriousness of the crises. Neither the equation 'war = revolution' nor the alternative 'war *or* revolution' was in the minds of the leaders of the International.

In July 1914 the workers' movement did not consider the possibility of war. The ISB meeting of 29–30 July showed that the socialist leaders were convinced that war was impossible and that the crisis would be resolved peacefully. Six years later Kautsky wrote: 'It is surprising that none of those present at the meeting thought of raising the question of what to do if war were to break out before the international congress that was due to meet in Vienna in August 1914, or which attitude the socialist parties should adopt in this war.'[10] To this confession by Kautsky, on the morrow of a disaster which he had not foreseen, let us add a more general observation on the connection between ideology and reality—a confusingly complex reality which contrasted with theory, and ironically invalidated the predictions of one of the most brilliant analysts of the time, who was among those who, after the Basle Congress, formulated the International's new doctrine on the assumption that imperialism would now move in a pacifist direction. 'The German social democrats, the "brain of the International", who had talked so much about the danger of imperialism and devoted so much attention to anti-war propaganda, never seriously thought about the position of social democracy if war were to break out after all.'[11] In making this observation in 1916 Friedrich Adler revealed the blockage which was caused by the weakness of the

9 For an analysis of this view of imperialism, cf. above, Ch. 7.

10 Cf. Karl Kautsky, *Vergangenheit und Zukunft der Internationale* (Vienna, 1920), 12.

11 Friedrich Adler, *Die Erneuerung der Internationale. Aufsätze aus der Kriegszeit* (Vienna, 1918), 12. Pannekoek's statements confirm Adler's: 'The question of *how* to resist the war was not properly put, since no firm *yes* had yet been heard on the question of whether the war was, or was not, to be resisted' (S. Bricianer, *Pannekoek et les conseils ouvriers*, 127).

ultra-imperialist theory and which, at the same time, provided an excuse for the lack of any alternative to preventive strategy.

In the theory of imperialism, as formulated by Kautsky and Bauer, there was no longer a place for revolution—though, of course, as part of the propaganda arsenal and as a permanent threat to governments, there was the warning expressed by Jaurès: 'War will be the starting point of the international revolution.' Intoxicated by words, the socialist leaders remained vague about the concept and form of this 'revolution' to which, at the height of the crisis, public reference was made at the Cirque Royal rally in Brussels on 29 July 1914 by both Jaurès and Haase. 'Let our enemies beware. It may well be that, angered by so much misery and oppression, the people will awaken at last and make socialist society a reality.'[12]

It is impossible to say whether the leaders of the International were the captives of their own myths or whether their reaction was the classical manifestation of that characteristic trait of the Second International: reformist practice screened behind verbal radicalism. It is clear, to quote Max Adler, that

the rapid growth of social democracy in the last ten years before the war did not in any way produce a strengthening of its revolutionary character. On the contrary, behind its two main spheres of activity there was a disquieting lowering of standards and an adaptation to the social order of capitalism.[13]

But if the majority had relegated the plan for a revolution to the distant future, or more precisely, as Otto Bauer says, if 'present reformist practices were allied to future revolutionary principles', a number of socialist leaders were convinced that, because the middle classes felt increasingly threatened by the workers' movement, their fear of revolution constituted an important stabilizing factor. But as Georges Sorel remarked, speaking of the metamorphosis of socialism at the beginning of the twentieth century: 'A social policy which is based on middle

[12] The whole speech was collected by J. Steingers, 'Le dernier discours de Jaurès', 85–106.

[13] Max Adler, *Démocratie et conseils ouvriers*, ed. by Yvon Bourdet (Paris, Maspero, 1967), 80.

class cowardice and consists of always giving way to the threat
of violence must create the idea that the bourgeoisie is doomed
and that its disappearance is only a matter of time.'[14]

Were not the socialists themselves bound to become victims
of the dilemma in which they sought to enmesh the bourgeoisie?
Did this conviction not encourage the illusion of a false dialectic?
Uneasiness and fear grew. Critical voices were raised. In 1911
Harry Quelch criticized Kautsky's theories and maintained
that 'war and armaments, instead of bringing about the Revolution, are more likely to stave it off'.[15] Otto Bauer, who in 1908
had claimed that 'the future imperialist war will bring the Revolution, [that] the world-wide imperialist catastrophe will in-
fallibly mark the beginning of the world-wide socialist Revolution', in 1912 uttered the following warning: 'The proletarian
revolution is never less feasible than at the start of a war when
the concentrated might of the state and the power of nationalist
passion are against it.'[16]

As for Jaurès, who kept reiterating the warning all along,
he was more aware than anyone else of the equivocal meaning
of the formula. His own prognosis, more subtle, was more
lucid too:

From a European war a revolution might surge up and the ruling
classes would do well to consider this. But it may also result, and for
a long period, in crises of counter-revolution, of furious reactions,
of exasperated nationalism, of stifling dictatorship, of monstrous
militarism, a long chain of retrograde violence . . .[17]

Only the extreme Left thought in terms of a strategy of revolution in which war would act as a catalyst.[18] But none of

[14] Georges Sorel, *Réflexions sur la violence* (Paris, Rivière, 1937), 55.
[15] Cf. Harry Quelch, 'The Folly of War and the Possibilities of Peace', *The Social-Democrat* (15 Aug. 1911), 338. In his work, *The Road to Power*, Kautsky asks whether revolution could be due to war. After listing three possibilities, he comes to the following conclusion: 'If revolution considered as the result of war is but one eventuality out of many, then revolution as the result of class struggle is a "sheer necessity".'
[16] Quoted after N. Leser, *Zwischen Reformismus und Bolschewismus*, 267.
[17] *Œuvres de Jaurès*, vol. ii, 247.
[18] Cf. U. Ratz, art. cit. 219 ff.

this argumentation was produced in the imbroglio of July 1914. Nor can any reference be found in the correspondence or the records of the private discussions of the socialist leaders to the alternative of war or revolution.

This state of affairs cannot be blamed solely on the reformism or the opportunism in which the International was enmeshed, and which Lenin singled out for condemnation in August 1914. He himself was to say eight years later, in his directives to the Soviet delegation to the conference at The Hague:

> On the question of combating the threat of war . . . I think that the greatest difficulty lies in overcoming the conception that this is a simple, comparatively easy problem. 'We shall retaliate for war with strike or revolution'—that is what all prominent reformist leaders are constantly telling the working class. And very often the apparent radicalism of the proposed measures pacifies the workers, co-operators, and peasants. Perhaps the best method would be to start with the sharpest refutation of this view; to declare that particularly now, after the recent war, only the most foolish or utterly dishonest people can maintain that this answer to the problem of how to combat war is of any use; to declare that it is impossible to 'retaliate' against war with revolution in the simple and literal sense of these words.[19]

What then was the problem that obsessed the International's leading brains at the end of July 1914? The handling of a situation that had become dangerous but that would not necessarily result in a general conflagration.

As for the feeling of helplessness that spread after 1 August, Victor Adler—the representative of a country already involved in the war and of a party that had been the first to capitulate—had already sensed it on 29 July. On the eve of the last ISB session a few socialist leaders realized in a moment of despair, or of lucidity, that the International was in no way prepared for a major crisis. What action should then be taken? What means of pressure used? On 26 July Vaillant commented in a letter to Huysmans: 'At the moment the situation, serious as it is, may deteriorate still further and the International is not

---

[19] Lénine, *Œuvres*, vol. xxxiii, 460.

prepared for active and effective intervention . . .'[20] On the following day Ebert, expressing himself in favour of convening the ISB, wondered what his party and the International could do other than issue manifestos: 'What shall we do now? Have we prepared more far-reaching measures? There can after all be no repetition of Basle.'[21]

'There can after all be no repetition of Basle'—this phrase provides the clue to the problem. Let us briefly restate the facts. In November 1912 at the height of a profound crisis the bells of Basle rang out the warning that Europe was on 'the brink of the abyss'. It was not the impressive gathering of socialist delegates from all over Europe, their unanimity and their impassioned speeches, that raised the alarm, but the workers' anti-war movement which had begun the previous year, the growing pressure of which put a stop to any widespread attempts at aggression. By July 1914 even the cinders of this pacifist fire had ceased to glow. Since 1913, with the easing of international tension, the International, on the basis of an optimistic view of the direction in which imperialism was moving, had quickly undertaken a radical revision of its position.[22]

But was the ebbing of the workers' emotions the result of the demobilization tactics of the social democrats? Here the answer extends beyond the limited circle of the leaders of the International. Two 'unknown quantities' come in: the behaviour of the working masses and the calculations of the governments.

Whereas in November 1912 the socialists had behaved as makers of history, at the eve of the Great War their role had turned into a passive one. In November 1912 they had placed themselves at the head of an offensive movement and their attitude had had a distinct bearing on their governments' decisions; in July 1914 they were caught short by events and, deprived of the dynamism of labour's protests, pushed on to the

[20] Vaillant to Huysmans, 26 July 1914, ISB archives.
[21] Friedrich Ebert, *Schriften, Aufzeichnungen, Reden. Mit unveröffentlichten Erinnerungen aus dem Nachlaß* (Dresden, 1929, vol. i), 309.
[22] Cf. above, Ch. 7.

defensive, into a position of disorientated spectators, finally to be submerged by the wave of nationalism. The socialist masses' reversal of attitude remains a crucial point. Why should militant socialists, who only the day before had been opposed to a hypothetical war, rush to defend their country once war had broken out? Why was organized labour seized with patriotic fervour and why did ' "class man" allow himself to be easily integrated into the nation'?[23]

There is no shortage of interpretations and theories.[24] Most of them are based on the two types of explanation referred to above. One of the traditional views, touched up but not basically altered by Soviet historians, derives from Lenin's statements: disorientated by the betrayal of their leaders, the working masses could not demonstrate their internationalism. Diametrically opposed to that view, there is another explanation which has equally ideological roots. It stresses 'the extraordinary climate of national unity . . . on the eve of mobilization, the irresistible upsurge of patriotic fervour which swept aside all ideologies',[25] that is to say the shift in attitude of the masses, whose nationalist enthusiasm worked on party leaders. In other words, in abandoning its principles social democracy did not betray the working masses but remained their authentic political expression. Even historians who reject these two types of explanation agree that the change of line was extremely sudden and stress the surprise effect of this reversal on the socialist leaders of all shades including the revolutionaries. About German social democracy in July 1914 Abendroth says that nobody had foreseen 'the possibility of

[23] The expression is that of E. Labrousse.
[24] For a critical survey, cf. H. Haag, 'La social-démocratie allemande . . .', in *Comité international . . . Stockholm 1960.*
[25] Historians who witnessed these events dispute this unanimity. André Latreille, for example, recalls 'the emotion of a horror-stricken working class crowd, the silent sadness of peasants used to disaster, confronted with a war which they were sure that France had not wanted, which they tried to persuade themselves would not be long but which the older generation was afraid might take the same turn as "in the seventies" ' (André Latreille, '1914: réflexions sur un anniversaire', *Le Monde* (31 Dec. 1964), 7).

reverting to apparently "national" feelings against all reason with such an eruption of violence. Nobody had believed that the rational thought of an entire population could vanish if people were persuaded that the "nation" . . . was directly threatened'.[26] But the facts belie this analysis.

Were the masses led astray by their leaders or were the leaders deserted by the masses? By putting the problem in those terms, the historian limits the scope of his analysis to a purely abstract and speculative level.

Let us try to restate the data that will enable us to suggest some lines of research.

There is no doubt that the International needed the support of the masses in resorting to preventive strategy. On 22 July 1914 Jaurès, explaining why he viewed the situation with apprehension albeit without fear, listed the three factors that were in favour of peace: (1) The growing expenditure on armaments heightened popular discontent. (2) Public opinion showed an increasing desire to solve conflicts not by aggression but by peaceful means, by arbitration. (3) The organized workers' movement was expanding and becoming more radical, as was demonstrated by the general strike in Belgium in 1913 and the growing social unrest in Britain (and also by the mass campaign fought in France against the three-year conscription law).

But Jaurès emphasized repeatedly that the pacifist determination of the masses would cease to be an element of resistance once war was there: 'Having watched the storm clouds gather, the people . . . cannot act when they have been struck by lightning.'[27]

The socialist leaders of all shades were always explicit about the devastating psychological effect on the working masses of the outbreak of a war and about the fact that no internationalist education could withstand the onslaught of nationalism.

[26] Wolfgang Abendroth, *Aufstieg und Krise der deutschen Sozialdemokratie* (Frankfurt am M., Stimme Verlag, 1963), 46.
[27] Summary record of the extraordinary congress of the SFIO, 14–16 July, *L'Humanité* (17 July 1914).

How accurately did Engels in his letter to Bebel of 22 December 1882 foresee the situation of August 1914:

I regard a European war as a misfortune; this time it would be frightfully serious; chauvinism would be unleashed for years to come because each nation would be fighting for its existence. The work of the revolutionaries in Russia who are on the brink of victory would be rendered null and void and our party in Germany would at once be submerged by a wave of chauvinism and destroyed; exactly the same would happen in France.[28]

He voiced the same idea, the same warning in September 1886:

There is no doubt that war will make our movement fall back everywhere in Europe, destroy it completely in many countries, stir up chauvinism and nationalist hatred and among many uncertain prospects offer us only this one *with certainty*: that after the war we shall have to start again at the beginning but under far less favourable conditions than those which prevail today.[29]

Twenty-five years later Kautsky expressed the same fears:

If the people can be persuaded to blame the war not on their own government but on the villainy of their neighbour . . . the whole population will be imbued with a burning desire to safeguard its frontiers against the vile enemy, to protect itself against his invasion. Everyone will become a patriot first and foremost, even the internationalists . . .[30]

In his report on imperialism, prepared in July 1914 for the Vienna Congress that never met, the Dutch socialist leader, Vliegen, while demonstrating reassuringly that a European war was impossible, refers to the possible intervention of factors that might disturb his idyllic picture. He is under no illusion regarding the strength and depth of the workers' pacifist and internationalist ideas, nor regarding the activities of the International, which can only be of a preventive nature, and whose effectiveness—in case the warring factions succeed in unleashing a European war—is questionable.

It is possible [Vliegen wrote] to be optimistic about the ever growing strength of the socialist parties and their ability to prevent

[28] Friedrich Engels, *Briefe an Bebel* (Berlin, Dietz, 1958), 71.
[29] Ibid. 140. [30] K. Kautsky, 'Krieg und Frieden', 104.

war even if the government has decided on war. In this respect I am not one of the optimists. Once war has been declared it is no longer the voice of common sense but guns that speak. As a rule national feeling is stronger than anything else and the spirit of belligerency spreads rapidly, a spirit which the working class has not, unfortunately, managed to shed.[31]

Lenin came to the same conclusions as the revisionist Vliegen when he assessed the lessons of the First World War. In the brief which he prepared for the Soviet delegation to the conference at The Hague he said:

We must explain the real situation to the people, show them that war is hatched in the greatest secrecy, and that the ordinary workers' organizations, even if they call themselves revolutionary organizations, are utterly helpless in the face of an actually impending war.

We must explain to the people again and again in the most concrete manner possible how matters stood in the last war, and why they could not have been otherwise.

We must take special pains to explain that the question of 'defence of the fatherland' will inevitably arise, and that the overwhelming majority of the working people will inevitably decide it in favour of their bourgeoisie.[32]

Was this a sudden collective shift of attitude caused by a swift reversal of the situation? Should we retain as the basis of our explanation the sociologically flavoured hypothesis about the complex relationship between nationalism and internationalism in the workers' movement, determined by the long process of the 'sub-culture's' integration into a *global* society? Or should we seek the explanation in a change in the attitude of the working class, in the less visible activity of the grass roots militants, echoes of which reached the surface only in muffled

[31] G. Haupt, *Le Congrès manqué*, 215–16.
[32] Lénine, *Œuvres*, vol. xxxiii, 461. This was, for example, also Trotsky's view throughout: 'Once the mobilization was announced,' he wrote a number of weeks after the outbreak of the war, 'Social-Democracy found itself face to face with the concentrated governmental power, which, supported by a powerful military apparatus, was prepared to overcome all obstacles in its path with the collaboration of all bourgeois parties and institutions . . . In such circumstances there can be no talk of revolutionary activity from the party . . .' (L. N. Trotsky, *Der Krieg und die Internationale* (Zürich, 1914), 41–2).

form? Here social psychology might serve as our instrument[33]— not in the formal use of psycho-analytical vocabulary and the rigid application of its concepts, but in its suggestive directions of research. The historian faces some difficulties as regards both method and sources. Lucien Febvre has tried to define what line should be taken: 'The anonymous masses? Their case lends itself to psychological approach based on a study of the masses actually at hand, a study the results of which can without effort (or so one assumes) be applied to the masses of yesterday, to the historic masses.'[34] This idea of 'the masses at hand' called for some remarkable comments at the time. Thus, analysing in 1916 the theoretical and practical weaknesses of German social democracy, Friedrich Adler concluded: 'The political effectiveness of the day-to-day struggle was achieved at the expense of clear working-class principles. Numbers of workers even had the illusion that the "possibilities without limit" were unrelated to time and that social democracy was always in a position to prevent war.'[35]

The view advanced by Lenin in 1922 agrees with that of Friedrich Adler: the whole of socialist propaganda, the manifesto of Basle included, had presented the war problem in such a way as to raise hopes among organized labour. 'To admit in theory that war is a crime, that war is inadmissible for a socialist, etc., is idle talk because there is nothing concrete in putting the question thus. It does not bring home to the masses how war can become imminent and start.' The bourgeois press was aware of this failure and exploited it to condition the masses psychologically.

These sophistries are perhaps the principal means by which the bourgeois press rallies the masses in support of war [wrote Lenin];

[33] In a letter to Monatte written as early as 14 Oct. 1914, F. Brupbacher suggested the need for psychological studies to understand the great change that had affected class conscience: 'From a pedagogical point of view, it would be interesting to analyse psychologically to what extent the difference between the ideas held before the war and those which exist now were already subconsciously there before the war' (*Archives Monatte*, 34).

[34] Cf. Lucien Febvre, *Combats pour l'histoire* (Paris, Colin, 1959), 208 (coll. 'Histoire et Psychologie').   [35] Fr. Adler, *Vor dem Ausnahmegericht*, 12.

and the main reason why we are so impotent in the face of war is either that we do not expose these sophistries beforehand, or still more, that we wave them aside with cheap, boastful and entirely empty phrases.[36]

The news that war had broken out had a traumatic effect on a sub-culture in which socialist propaganda had fostered an atmosphere of calm and confidence. Propped up by a whole ritual, a language, and an imagery that created the satisfactory feeling of having powerful organizations and of making great progress numerically and geographically, the diffuse internationalism of the workers' movement could not combat the upsurge from deeper strata of sensibility, as, for instance, Jacobin patriotism or 'visceral' Russophobia. In 1915 another observant and able contemporary, the Dutch left-wing socialist Henriette Roland Holst, expressed a similar view:

The present world war has shown not only that internationalism was not anchored as deeply in the proletariat as we thought ten or twelve years ago but above all that like every other principle this one is helpless in the face of sentiments, trends, inclinations, and emotions that surge up irresistibly from the subconscious even if the principle is clearly worth supporting.[37]

Friedrich Adler advanced yet another hypothesis: 'The awakening amidst the harsh reality of the month of August created in numbers of workers the surprising state of mind that might in the language of the new psychiatric school of Vienna be described as pro-war enthusiasm corresponding to some overcompensation for insurrectional desires'.[38]

Should we therefore conclude that it is necessary to proceed to an analysis of socialist mentality, by focusing upon the evolution of such notions as internationalism, war, etc., upon their extension and their adoption by the labour? Several well-documented monographs[39] have shown up the ambiguity of social democracy's theoretical bases, the limits of its inter-

---

[36] Lénine, *Œuvres*, vol. xxxiii, 461–2.

[37] Quoted after *Archiv für die Geschichte des Sozialismus und der Arbeiterbewegung* (1916, vol. vi), 316.

[38] Fr. Adler, op. cit. 12.   [39] Cf. e.g. Drachkovitch; Jemnitz, op. cit.

national engagements, and the growth in this environment of nationalist sentiment,[40] in the light of which the reversal of August 1914 does not appear as a surprise. Interesting and useful though these political or ideological explanations are, they do not suffice when it comes to the study of the social factors involved; they reveal only symptoms, buried roots, and premises. As elements in the analysis of a global phenomenon, they, like social psychology, must be added to other factors which together will enable us to understand the impetus that sprang from the very depths of the social movements. Nationalism and internationalism are not dichotomic concepts nor abstract sentiments. The real problem is to know under what social and political conditions the workers' movement was most receptive to the one or to the other. Jean Bouvier's methodological study on 'The workers' movement and economic circumstances'[41] opens up a productive line of thought by revealing the dialectic in the fluctuations of the workers' movement and the swings of an economic nature. Without succumbing to the 'sin of the century . . . the desire to explain everything in terms of economic phenomena', Bouvier presents the problem in these terms:

The sociology of the trade union movement and of the working masses, the size and structure of the concerns, the role of the ideologies, the degree of maturity of the trade union organization, the degree of *tension in the social situation* and the political connections directly influence—the backcloth of economic flux being given— *the ups and downs of the workers' movement.*

Along this line of thought one could suggest that it is the dynamism of mass mobilization in a period of social tension that renders the workers' movement, or more precisely the workers in motion, more susceptible to ideological considerations; the prevailing view of internationalism is translated into militant pacifism. It is indeed important to stress the correlation between the growing intensity of the economic and social struggles and

---

[40] Cf. e.g. W. Maehl, 'The Triumph of Nationalism . . .', 30–41; Dieter Groh, 'The "Unpatriotic" Socialists and the State', *Journal of Contemporary History*, 4 (1966), 151–78.   [41] Cf. *Le Mouvement social*, 48 (1964), 3–30.

the support of mobilized labour to the socialists' internationalist slogans like 'war on war'. In 1910 and 1912 the major European countries in their phase of economic expansion experienced a tidal wave of social unrest which expressed itself in violent demonstrations against the rising cost of living and in frequent mass strikes. Does not the explanation for the scale of the anti-war militancy (which reached its climax at the time of the extraordinary Congress of Basle)[42] lie in this connection between pacifist agitation and profound economic and social unrest with a background of labour protests against the high cost of living? There is a correlation between the curve of social tensions, the increasingly radical demands of the workers, and the ideological, anti-capitalist option which was discernible from the intensity of the pacifist struggles.

The example of 1912 suggests two comments:

1. The crystallization of collective feeling on the slogan 'war on war' is more noticeable in the actual movement than in the commentaries of the press whose objective was to mould public opinion.

2. This crystallization is a short-term adventitious phenomenon which explains the rapid fluctuations in labour's attitude. An examination of the course of these fluctuations between 1910 and 1914 would show the concomitance of the pressure of social agitation and ideological choice. Social tensions had visibly diminished by the eve of August 1914. Otto Bauer's report to the Vienna Congress that never met highlighted the recovery of the capitalist economy, which had led also to an improvement of the workers' position. Moreover, the strike statistics from 1909 to 1914 show a declining curve after 1913. Besides, after 1913, pacifist propaganda was relegated to second place in socialist activity. A close study of the correlation and interaction of these two phenomena would bring us somewhat nearer to an understanding of the collapse of 1914.

Although in July 1914 the working masses were less receptive to anti-militaristic slogans than in the past, it would be a

[42] See above, Ch. 4.

mistake to conclude that they were ready to fall an easy prey to
patriotism and to regard their state of mind as one of the factors
that influenced the socialist leaders and made them react too
late to 'stem the tide'. After 25 July Kautsky justified the leadership's lack of activity by reference to this 'state of mind of the
masses'.[43] We cannot judge the validity of this defence without
considering the mechanics of mass mobilization and the role of
avant-gardists and political guides assumed by the social democratic parties. Spontaneity is not the critical characteristic of
large-scale pacifist movements whose elements are both spontaneous and directed, aware and driven on. It was for the leadership of the workers' organizations to initiate and direct these
movements. But in July this mobilization of labour was only
timidly pursued.

There were several workers' demonstrations against the
war from 27 July onwards, in France and in Germany. Sixty
thousand people took part in an impressive rally in Berlin on
27 July, and demonstrations followed in the great industrial
centres of Germany.[44] These activities favourably impressed the
French revolutionary syndicalists who disapproved of the Germans' reluctance to take action. On 30 July Rosmer wrote to
Monatte: 'Nevertheless they have moved, they have had good
meetings and a street demonstration. We have done no more
ourselves.'[45] There was part hope and part exaggeration in his
remark—a frame of mind which was not exclusive to him. The
resolution passed at the German rallies in turn referred to the
example of the French comrades. Moreover, in a general way
the revolutionary elements expected extensive mass movements
and liked to interpret the facts in a reassuring light. The strikes
in St. Petersburg were to them part of a general pacifist movement. 'After the recent strikes', Rosmer wrote to Monatte on
30 July 1914, 'the Tsar cannot feel too happy. There is even
talk of serious labour troubles in Poland. But strict censorship

[43] *Victor Adler Briefwechsel*, 596.
[44] Much information on this subject is found in J. Kuczynski, *Der Ausbruch des Weltkrieges* . . . .
[45] *Archives Monatte*, 21.

makes it impossible to get anything but snippets of information.'

In fact, these demonstrations which were initiated by the local organizations (without much conviction) did not herald a great workers' counter-offensive, nor did they form part of any plan of campaign. The socialist leadership continued to advise caution. However, for Jaurès, the real safeguard, the only guarantee, 'what is more important than anything else, is the continuity of the campaign, the perpetual awakening of the minds and consciences of the workers'. Was it not possible to mobilize the masses or was there a lack of determination to do so? In fact the fear of being too hasty, of starting off premature campaigns presented the leaders of the major socialist parties with a dilemma: to keep their sang-froid or to be overtaken by events. Caught up in this vicious circle, they succumbed to a feeling of impotence. Even Jaurès began to doubt whether the International could act if it came to the point. A threatening danger hung over the socialists' designs—the part played by secret diplomacy which Jaurès had always feared.

The idea of caution that won unanimity among the socialist leaderships, was diversely motivated. The Germans were afraid of compromising the future of the party by committing it too hastily to large-scale ventures. Jaurès, who insisted as much on 'the heroism of patience' as on that of action, found it 'essential to preserve the working class from panic and confusion; premature action could have serious consequences of a kind diametrically opposed to the desired effect'. 'The greatest threat at present comes not . . . from the actual will of the people but from increasing nervous tension, from growing uneasiness, from sudden impulses produced by fear, from great uncertainty and prolonged anxiety. It is possible that the masses will surrender to this mad panic and it is not certain that the governments will not surrender to it,' he said on 31 July in his leader in *L'Humanite*.

In this context the leaders of the workers' movements were genuinely worried by the size of the nationalist movements with their shock troops of pugnacious students. It was with that anxiety in mind that Rosmer wrote to Monatte on 28 July 1914 about the rally organized on 27 July at Paris by the CGT, a demonstration which completely satisfied the revolutionary syndicalists: 'It was non-violent but it was well attended and no attempt was made to reply with nationalism or chauvinism.'[46]

The socialist leaders adopted a policy of wait-and-see and confusion also prevailed among the radical Left. What should be done, what steps should be taken? Neither the German nor the French Left could give an answer. In Germany on 27 July the radicals merely asked the leadership to mobilize the masses without, however, realizing that such action was urgently required.[47] On the situation in France Rosmer passed on to Monatte the impression of Bakunin's friend James Guillaume who was struck by the 'confusion prevailing among the revolutionaries. Everybody was saying that they must act but nobody produced a precise proposal'. Two days later Rosmer himself confirmed this impression: 'There is much good will here but no leading idea.'

This disarray inevitably grew when no action was taken on 1 August and deteriorated into demoralization after the traumatic experience of 4 August—'a betrayal of the most elementary principles of international socialism, of the vital interests of the working class', according to Rosa Luxemburg.[48]

When we come to examine the frame of mind of the masses should we not pay as much attention to this demoralization as to the working-class capitulation to nationalism, the extent of which has been assumed rather than proved? 'The fact that in August 1914, popular opinion, the working masses, the organized movements of socialists and workers were on the side of what in France was called the *Union Sacrée* and had originated in a blaze of patriotism'[49] is not evidence.

---

[46] *Archives Monatte*, 21.

[47] J. Kuczynski, op. cit.; Jemnitz, op. cit.; J. P. Nettl, *Rosa Luxemburg*, ii, 601–7.

[48] Cf. G. Badia, 'L'attitude de la gauche social-démocrate allemande dans les premiers mois de la guerre, août 1914 — avril 1915', *Le Mouvement social*, 49 (Oct.–Dec. 1964), 102.   [49] A. Kriegel, art. cit. (*Preuves*), 26.

In this period of 'ebbing' the working masses were indeed
more susceptible to nationalistic propaganda than in periods
of growing radicalism. But in this connection another question
arises. When exactly did this 'extraordinary climate' of patriotic fervour develop, before or after 1 August? The wish to
follow chronological order and to clarify the course of events is
neither futile nor dictated by a taste for pure description. Such
an approach enables us to set out the data, whereas the
explanations that are usually advanced confuse cause and effect,
the workers' reaction before and after mobilization. It is a
mistake to attach equal importance to the attitude of the masses
towards the war in the last days of July and in the first days of
August. The evidence is contradictory depending on which
camp the witness eventually joined after 1914. As regards the
minority internationalists this phenomenon is observable from
1 August onwards. 'If the socialist party, crushed by the tragic
death of Jaurès, deprived suddenly of this farsighted genius and
dominating personality had not allowed itself to be swept along
by the nationalist current it could certainly have played an
important role.' It is thus that R. Nicod describes the situation
in France in a letter to Monatte, dated 24 November 1914.
He adds that it was on 1 August that 'we completely lost
our heads . . .'[50] There is no shortage of examples from the
same quarters. The evidence of Merrheim or Frossard, on
the other hand, seems to contradict this view. They speak
of 31 July 1914 as the moment when nationalistic currents
swept across the country, paralysing the leadership of the
socialists and the trade unions and thwarting all attempts at
resistance.

Do not these assertions, made as they were four years after
the event when public opinion was acutely aware that the
workers' movement shared in the responsibility for the failure
and the capitulation in the face of the war, antedate, consciously
or otherwise, the facts to which they refer? Maybe, one ought
to reverse the statement of the problem, and regarding the

[50] *Archives Monatte*, 31–2.

datum 'wave of nationalism' not as the cause but as the consequence of the breakdown of the socialist parties. In other terms, the socialists' hopes and expectations collapsed on 1 August in the face of their inability to deal with the *fait accompli*, the mobilization. Thereafter aggressive passions ran riot.

With this 'chronological' clarification in mind we can examine the second 'unknown' referred to above—the calculations of the governments.

Obviously one of the factors that any government must bear in mind before accepting the risk of a war is public opinion in general, and in particular that of the sectors that have for years displayed militant pacifism. As a key-point, social democracy and the workers' movement had great weight in the governments' decisions.[51] Was it sheer gambling, or were those decisions based on a serious estimate of the strength and weakness of social democracy?

Little research has been pursued on the attitudes and reactions of European governments towards the socialist movement during the critical phase before the mobilization and after the outbreak of hostilities. At one stage the governments aimed at neutralizing the workers' movement; then they tried to associate it with their venture. Although the mechanics, the means, differed from country to country, the similarities and parallels are striking. The police archives show that both the German and the French governments were perfectly informed on the state of mind, the discussions, and the decisions at all levels of the workers' organizations.[52] By the end of July 1914, the authorities were fully aware of the flaws in the International and in the socialist parties of their respective countries, and of the weaknesses of the pacifist strategy. Fritz Sternberg has observed that the governments had long ago ceased to believe in the socialist threat that

---

[51] Cf. Wolfgang J. Mommsen, 'Die Regierung Bethmann-Hollweg und die öffentliche Meinung, 1914–1917', *Vierteljahreshefte für Zeitgeschichte*, 2 (1969), 119–21.

[52] To quote one example: the summary records of the meetings of the SPD leadership or those of their joint meetings with the trade union general Executive, the parliamentary group, etc., are found in the archives of the police praesidium in Berlin, Section VII–4.

war in Europe would bring revolution in its wake.[53] Did they appreciate that behind the flights of rhetoric and the expressions of confidence there was impotence? In any case they were sufficiently well informed to know whether the socialists would translate their resolution into action, whether the masses were ready to follow them, and whether it was worth taking risks. Above all they knew in the light of the experience of 1911–12 that in translating words into pacifist deeds the International was hampered by the vital time factor. In order to mobilize 'the army of the proletariat', in order to bring up the individual conscience to the level of the collective psychology, lengthy preparations were required on the part of the socialist leadership. In July 1914 the governments realized that the brakes which had been put on the socialist anti-war struggle could not be taken off in a matter of days, that even if the socialists mobilized or demonstrated they could not stand up to the rising tide of patriotism and chauvinism. Taken unawares by events the International failed to master them. 'We have been taken in tow by the government and by Sir Edward Grey and that is the way we are going,' Rosmer noted with sorrow at the end of July 1914.[54] The governments inevitably noted this confusion and profited from it. But the socialists were not totally immobile. In July in the country that was to take the initiative in starting hostilities on a general scale, Germany, they demonstrated their determination to resist war and this protest remained unanimous as long as it was tolerated. The conservative elements, the Kaiser, and the military watched these demonstrations with some apprehension. On 29 July Wilhelm II wrote in the margin of a telegram from Nicholas II: 'The socialists are out in the streets campaigning against the war; this must not be allowed, above all *not now*. If these troubles recur I shall proclaim a state of emergency and have the leaders arrested, the lot of them. At the present time we can permit no

53 Fritz Sternberg, *Capitalism and Socialism on Trial* (London, Victor Gollancz, 1951), 142–3.
54 *Archives Monatte*, 21.

socialist propaganda of any kind.'[55] After all the anti-war opposition could flare up again suddenly and violently if no steps were taken to nip it in the bud. On 24 July 1914, when a state of emergency was proclaimed in Germany, the general staff thought of employing the 'plan for internal mobilization' and of arresting anyone likely to cause difficulties: the leaders of the national minorities and the socialists. Hans von Delbrück, Secretary of State for the Interior and Vice-Chancellor, showed more political finesse or prudence. He and Bethmann-Hollweg believed that the use of terror on the eve of a war was a crass mistake which would yield no dividend. They must temporize, manœuvre, and not allow the political parties and the social democrats in particular an opportunity of coming out in open hostility to the government. The two men thought that it was better to gain the socialists' confidence and avoid the threat of having to face a strong internal opposition if war broke out. In its dealings with the party leadership and its supporters the German government proved ambivalent, using their language and arguments to rally them to the cause it wanted them to adopt.

It was necessary for the German Government to establish direct contacts with the SPD executive if it wanted to discover the party's real intentions and gain its active support. On 24 or 25 July Delbrück approached Südekum whom he knew personally and who suggested that the Chancellor should invite Haase and Ebert to call on him.[56] This move did not yield the expected result. Haase apparently failed to understand Bethmann-Hollweg's reference to the threat of war and his reply was unequivocal. The socialists would not allow Germany to support Austria if the latter was threatened because of the monarchy's greed in the Balkans.[57] However, the Chancellor received confirmation that the social democrats believed in the

[55] *Die deutschen Dokumente zum Kriegsausbruch 1914*, herausgegeben im Auftrag des Auswärtigen Amtes (Berlin, 1927, vol. ii), 48 (Doc. no. 332).

[56] Clemens von Delbrück, *Die wirtschaftliche Mobilmachung in Deutschland*, aus dem Nachlaß herausgegeben, eingeleitet und ergänzt von Joachim von Delbrück (Munich, 1924), 100–5. [57] Cf. E. Haase, op. cit. 25.

government's pacifist intentions and the point was that they should not be disillusioned. Bethmann-Hollweg would not change the directives which he issued concerning the SPD. 'They could be won over if we could assure ourselves of their viewpoints, negotiate with them directly, and get the military's guarantee to restrain their stupid *Socialistien-fresser*.'[58] When, for example, *Berliner Lokal Anzeiger* on 30 July announced German mobilization, the government hurriedly confiscated all copies of the paper and denied the news with such success that the SPD believed it to have been a provocation on the part of warmongering elements.[59]

The confidential conversation which Bethmann-Hollweg had had with Südekum twenty-four hours previously had dispelled any fears that the Chancellor might still have harboured. The interview had enabled him to reassure himself about the social democrats' frame of mind and to gauge the extent of their determination. Südekum's news was important. The government now knew that the SPD would remain an active but loyal opposition and that there was no reason to fear its resistance if a general mobilization was proclaimed. With his letter of 29 July 1914 to the Chancellor, Südekum at one blow destroyed the socialists' most important psychological weapon: their threat, repeated only a few days previously, to reply with force to any form of warmongering.

The objective was not to neutralize the SPD, but to include them in a future national unity; to make certain of their loyalty it was necessary to make Russia responsible for the coming conflict.[60]

Haase, the party chairman, said that he was summoned on 26 July by the Chancellor to promise that his party would take no steps that might give the Russians an excuse to carry out

---

[58] Cf. Eberhard Pikart, 'Der deutsche Reichstag und der Ausbruch des ersten Weltkrieges', *Der Staat*. Zeitschrift für Staatslehre, öffentliches Recht und Verfaßungsgeschichte (1966), no. 1, 59.

[59] Cf. Egmont Zechlin, 'Bethmann-Hollweg, Kriegsrisiko und SPD, 1914', *Der Monat*, 208 (Jan. 1966), 27.

[60] Cf. Fritz Fischer, *Der Krieg der Illusionin*, 699.

their aggressive intentions.[61] Bethmann-Hollweg referred to this threat, aware of the need to present the war as self-defence so that the nation would consider it legitimate when it broke out. He knew that 'a policy that risked war by demonstrating its power as a preventive measure would be unacceptable to the public opinion of Europe and of international pacifism as it appeared in the doctrine of German social democracy'.[62] On the other hand, the SPD was certain to support a war in which the aggressor appeared to be the much-hated Russian Tsarism. Bethmann-Hollweg was familiar with the ins and outs of this Russophobia which had existed for years among the party leadership and among organized labour, in spite of the view of the marxist Left that Russia was not only the stronghold of reaction but also the home of the revolution. Although the German Government's trump card against social democracy was the faith which people had in it, there was another factor which enabled it to adopt a stick and carrot policy in its dealings with the social democrats. From 1910 onwards the party and the trade unions feared the destruction of their organizations. In July 1914 in particular they fully expected this to happen. Their main concern was therefore to save them. At the ISB meeting at Brussels much time and energy was devoted to this, mainly on the part of the Austrian and Czech delegates, Victor Adler and Anton Nemec. Several years later, de Man recalled his impressions of the meeting:

It was curious to learn from hearing them talk that the main reason for their nervousness was their apprehension regarding the threat to their organization. As experienced socialists and as men of considerable intelligence they no doubt also remembered the other physical and moral disasters that might result from the war; but they spoke above all about the organization being threatened by dissolution, the party offices being closed, the press being muzzled, and the delivery vans of the party paper being requisitioned by the army.[63]

On 1 August many SPD officials were ready to depart, to

[61] Cf. *Protokoll der Reichskonferenz . . .*, op. cit. 60.
[62] Cf. E. Zechlin, art. cit. 24.
[63] Cf. Hendrik de Man, *Zur Psychologie des Sozialismus* (Jena, 1927), 223; cf. also Robert Michels, *Political Parties* (New York, Dover, 1959), 394.

renew the experience of the period of the emergency laws. The trade unions on their part refused to take action that might 'lead to the working class struggling defencelessly in want and misery'.[64] The German Government was aware of this fear and knew how to exploit it.

In France the police were equally well informed about the difficulties that stood in the way of implementing the agreement between the SFIO and the trade unions.[65] Jaurès needed all his authority and idealism to make this joint action and pacifist action in general a reality. One of the organic weaknesses of the anti-war campaign in France arose from the fact that everything centred on one man, Jaurès, so that when the news of his assassination spread in France and abroad, the socialist party leaders and militants immediately concluded: 'This means war.'[66] As Romain Rolland wrote to Charles Rappoport, it 'has been the biggest defeat of this war, a defeat for the whole world'.[67]

Shortly afterwards, on the evening of 31 July, the confederal committee of the CGT decided 'to drop the principles', that is to say to renounce the general strike. It seems that the Minister of the Interior, Malvy, was at once informed of this decision. On 1 August at 1.0 a.m. he sent a telegram to the prefects instructing them not to arrest any of the persons listed in the famous *Carnets B*.[68] The instruction was unequivocal. It began with the following clause: 'As we have every cause to think that

---

[64] Cf. Sitzungsprotokoll über eine gemeinsame Sitzung des Parteivorstands und der Generalkommission der Gewerkschaften am 11. Dezember 1913; angefertigt von Diener, 15. Dez. 1913. St. A. Potsdam, Pr. Br. Rep. 30, Berlin C, Polizeipräsidium, Tit. 95, Sekt. 7, Lit. J., no. 2, vol. 3.

[65] Cf. e.g. A. Kriegel, art. cit. (*Bull. Soc. Ét. jaur.*), 1–11.

[66] Many telegrams which reached the ISB give witness to this reaction. Trotsky, on his part, gives evidence of the psychological shock due to the spread of the news: 'When I heard that he had been assassinated I was still in Vienna and had to leave hurriedly; the news affected me as deeply as the first rumbles of the great turmoil' (L. Trockij, *Voina i revoljucsija* (Moscow–Petrograd, ii), 207).

[67] Letter from Geneva, 30 June 1915, Rappoport archives, Amsterdam, IISG.

[68] It consists of a list of 3,000–4,000 militant workers, which was set up by the government on the basis of information from the prefects; in case of general mobilization, all the people whose names were mentioned on the list were to be arrested.

all the persons listed for political reasons in the *Carnets B* can be relied upon . . .'[69] The difference between Malvy's confidence and that given by Bethmann-Hollweg on 30 July to a meeting of the Prussian cabinet was one of expression only: 'Nothing much need be feared' from the SPD if war broke out.[70]

In spite of the threat that the response to a great European war would be a revolution, 'in July 1914 the government was not unduly worried about a social revolution, uprisings, refusals of military service, or mass strikes', says the German historian Egmont Zechlin.[71] In July 1914 this was certainly so. But would this confidence have been justified beyond the immediate future if the war had not broken out? Here we pass from the realm of certainty to that of hypothesis.

The hypothesis suggested by several historians (É. Halévy, A. Rosenberg, A. Mayer) can be formulated as follows: it became one of the functions of the First World War by the use of force to nip in the bud a threatening revolution. The war takes its real significance not only in relation to the rivalry of the great powers and to the system of alliances, but in relation to the potential revolution.[72]

[69] Annie Kriegel, 'Patrie ou révolution: le mouvement ouvrier français devant la guerre (juillet–août 1914)', *Revue d'Histoire économique et sociale* 3 (1965), 379.

[70] *Die deutschen Dokumente zum Kriegsausbruch* (1927, vol. ii), 178.

[71] E. Zechlin, art. cit. 26.

[72] This thesis was first set forth, though admittedly in a nuanced and prudent fashion, by Élie Halévy in his Rhodes Memorial Lectures (1929). (These lectures were published in 1930 with the title *The World Crisis, 1914–1918: an Interpretation*, by the Clarendon Press.) Some thirty-five years later, in his postscript to a new edition of Halévy's essays on socialism and war, Fritz Stern remarked: 'It is likely indeed that this conscious or, far more likely, unconscious, fear of revolution played a considerable role in the pre-war conduct of foreign policy everywhere in Europe, and it seems incredible that questions of this sort have rarely even been asked by historians since Halévy' (in Élie Halévy, *The Era of Tyrannies* (New York, 1965), 321–2). This observation is no longer relevant, for Arno J. Mayer, in his *Wilson vs. Lenin: Political Origins of the New Diplomacy, 1917–1918* (New York, World Publ. Co., 1964), has placed this consideration at the very heart of his interpretation of the origins of World War I. In a more recent article, in which he clearly set out his conceptual framework for this question, Mayer stated that '. . . in their bid to recover greater internal control, embattled governments tend to flaunt the spectre of external dangers with the calculation that international tensions short of war can help to foster domestic cohesion' (Arno J. Mayer, 'Internal Causes and Purposes of War in Europe, 1870–1956; a research Assignment', *Journal of Modern History*, xxxxi, no. 3 (Sept. 1969), 291–303).

Whether out of suspicion or by dint of hint, as early as the
pre-1914 period, this idea spread among several socialist circles.
Indeed, it had nothing in common with overstatements, such as
those by of Gustave Hervé, who asserted in 1907, that it was
a conspiracy of the ruling classes of the various capitalist countries so as to prevent the advent of socialism—and this at the
cost of war.[73] We shall rather refer to a set of analyses which,
in contrast to the view prevailing at the time, did not exclude
the probability of a war. At the beginning of 1913, for instance,
Charles Rappoport added to his book on the social revolution a
final chapter entitled 'War and Revolution'. For him the ruling
classes were torn between two conflicting trends: 'Fear of the
revolution is both a stimulant to the supporters of war and an
obstacle in the way of the achievement of their criminal design.'
The war could breed revolution or it could be the great anti-
revolutionary force, 'the greatest enemy of the proletariat'.
Rappoport develops his idea in these terms:

In vain do we gather millions of followers, in vain do we increase our
war funds because war only sets proletarian against proletarian.
Public liberties are suppressed and our war funds are dissipated.
What an admirable method for the ruling classes to rid themselves
of their opponents, to decimate them better and more effectively
than with prisons and gallows which make a lot of noise without
doing much work. Faced with the growth of the working class and
with a constantly rising tide of socialism the ruling classes are
tempted to stake their all.[74]

Charles Rappoport was one of the spokesmen of marxist dialectics, according to which: 'War must be . . . the supreme
attempt of the capitalism of any particular country to avoid
revolution by appealing to national unity against an outside
enemy . . .'[75]

The terms in which Rappoport presents this argument are
no doubt over-simplified. If we wish to examine this question

[73] F. Stackelberg, *Mystification patriotique et solidarité prolétarienne* (Paris, Ed. de
la Guerre sociale, 1907).
[74] Cf. Charles Rappoport, *La Révolution sociale* (Paris, Quillet, 1913), 490–1.
[75] Cf. Leo Valiani, *Histoire du socialisme au XXᵉᵐᵉ siècle* (Paris, Nagel, 1948), 41–2.

in all its complexity we must diagnose the state of Europe's health at the beginning of the twentieth century. Did the Continent suffer from a disease the symptom of which was that its inhabitants faced the alternative of revolution or emigration, as Marc Ferro has put it?[76] If the answer is in the affirmative, then which were the social and geographical sectors particularly affected? If we look upon 'revolution as both a reality that develops spontaneously and an idea that grows in the minds of the most perceptive individuals',[77] we must not rest satisfied with a diagnosis of the disease but look at its carriers and the regions where it breeds.

Firstly, the social sectors must be examined, starting with the infinitely complex environment of the workers' movement. Although the social democratic parties made constant reference to the diseased state of capitalist society, they abstained from prescribing the radical remedy. On the contrary, as organized bodies they found themselves on the side of order, and on the eve of war the socialist leaders' energy was concentrated on the struggle with their increasingly militant radical minority. This fact helps us to understand why the majority of the International's leaders agreed to the *Union sacrée* or the *Burgfrieden*. In the case of the SPD, beyond the seduction of patriotism, the devotion to the national state, and the mentality of a 'loyal' opposition, the party's morbid fear of its own left wing plays its part. Ebert, the party's second chairman, set the tone. On 27 July 1914 he wrote to the executive that in the event of a catastrophe 'We shall also have difficulties inside our party. The war and the powerful revival of the workers' movement in Russia will give Rosa's followers new ideas . . .'[78] In 1913 and 1914, this obsession with 'Rosa's men' preoccupied Kautsky as well. The explanation cannot be sought only in the radicalism and aggressiveness of the active minority, which though defeated at the congress of Jena had not surrendered. Maybe,

[76] Cf. Marc Ferro, *La Grande Guerre, 1914–1918* (Paris, Gallimard, 1969), 17–18.
[77] Cf. Maurice Merleau-Ponty, *Sens et non-sens* (Paris, Nagel, 1963), 314.
[78] Fr. Ebert, op. cit. 309.

some investigations ought to be pursued as regards the connections between such fears and the deeper currents that were
stirring up the labour movement, the fermentation and radicalism produced by the rising cost of living. These reactions often
exceeded the party directives.

In September 1917, Otto Bauer described the situation in
the years 1911–14 in these terms:

The increasing cost of living and the development of employers'
associations had considerably reinforced class antagonism. The
growth of German social democracy, the monstrous wave of strikes
in England, the awakening of the Russian proletariat announced
gigantic class struggles.

Everywhere, the reformists' illusions appeared to have been left
behind: in France, 'ministerialism' seemed to be abolished; in Italy
the working class had expelled the reformists from the party; in Austria,
the majority at the Vienna Congress in 1913 had risen with seeming
resoluteness against the reformists' illusions which had proliferated
as a result of the electoral victory.

Everywhere, the working class seemed to be determined to follow
in Marx's steps. The mighty development of cartels and trusts,
the rapid process of subordination of world economics to financial
capital, the renewed antagonism between the great imperialist
powers foreshadowed the era of the decisive clash between Capital
and Labour.[79]

When this blaze died down at the eve of the war the European
movement was affected by a profound malaise as stressed by
Kautsky in a letter to Adler of October 1913, in which he
insisted on the European nature of the phenomenon. '. . . if the
misery continues to grow during the winter we may see manifestations of despair, savage strikes and revolts in the streets;
this could lead to a political crisis, to severer measures against
us but also to a crisis in the party.'[80] For Kautsky it was all due
to a stagnation of the European labour movement, whereas the
left wing of the German party saw it as a move towards greater
radicalism and reproached the leadership for its lack of action.

This malaise with its uncertainties strongly affected other

[79] Preface by Heinrich Weber [Otto Bauer] to Gustav Eckstein, *Der Marxismus
in der Praxis* (Vienna, 1918), 3–4.   [80] *Victor Adler Briefwechsel*, 582–5.

social sectors. It took hold of the young generation who were in latent rebellion against adult society and who demanded, as Ernst Fischer has put it, more 'poetry' in life.[81] The romantic revolt affected the young of the middle classes as much as working-class youth. The former were absorbed in deviant movements which provided them with 'a means to eschew direct conflict with fatherly forces', while the working-class youth were attracted to a militant body, the International Organization of Socialist Youth, which stood on the extreme left in the socialist movement. But even the offspring of the bourgeoisie were 'dissatisfied with the age and hate of their parents' world: revolution or war, they want[ed] to escape from this well-ordered pigsty'.[82] Like Ernst Fischer, Marc Ferro, a French historian, saw the First World War as the great 'liberator' of energy: 'By going to war the soldiers of 1914 found a new ideal which to some extent took the place of revolutionary aspirations.'[83] Such observations were frequent even among contemporary observers. Brupbacher wrote to Monatte on 19 October 1914: 'Even our dear James Guillaume sees the war as a continuation and a development of the great revolution.'[84] But we must eschew hasty generalizations. The war did not represent a satisfactory alternative to socialist youth as a whole. On the contrary it made them more radical more quickly and strengthened the internationalist leanings of their organizations. The war seemed to widen the gulf between the two trends— patriotism and revolutionism—in the youth movement. But the split was temporary, and four years later the two came together in the revolutionary wave of 1918–19.

The process of radicalization within the workers' movement, the revolt of the young generation against hypocrisy, as well as the rebellion of the intellectual fringe 'against the banality of the bourgeois world' aggravated the malaise. We know the

[81] Ernst Fischer, *Probleme der jungen Generation* (Vienna, Europa Verlag, 1963), 38 ff. Cf. also Walter Z. Laqueur, *Young Germany; a History of the German Youth Movement* (New York, Basic Books, 1962).

[82] E. Fisher, *Probleme . . .*, op. cit. 43.

[83] M. Ferro, op. cit. 21.

[84] *Archives Monatte*, 34.

literary side of the intellectual avant-garde movement: expressionism and futurism mingled with the weariness expressed by Georg Heym, Vladimir Mayakovsky's revolutionary impulse, Marinetti's violence. The intellectual history of Europe seen from this angle remains to be explored.[85]

But it is not enough to take note of these symptoms among various social groups. Further analysis will be needed to localize the malaise within the period's specific contradictions. Which were the sensitive areas, the centres of fermentation? Can we accept the assertion that there was an explosive zone on the threshold of revolution or in the throes of a profound crisis an area stretching from the Rhine to the borders of Europe with the tension mounting as we move eastwards or southeastwards? The examples generally quoted, that of the rising revolutionary wave in Russia which culminated in big strikes in the capital on the eve of the war,[86] or that of the 'red week' from 7 to 14 June 1914 when Italy experienced its strongest upsurge of insurrectionary fever since 1870 (according to the testimony of Angelica Balabanoff)[87] still need to be proved.

It is legitimate for historians to ask whether the war broke the rhythm of the revolutionary crises only to make them more violent in 1918 or whether it affected their development, directing it towards a nationalist solution in Austria-Hungary, distorting it into a fascist revolution in Italy, and

[85] Cf. e.g. Madeleine Rebérioux, 'Critique littéraire et socialisme au tournant du siècle', *Le Mouvement social* 59 (1967), 3–28. On expressionism as a means of social protest against bourgeois society cf. Walter H. Sokel, *The Writer in Extremis: Expressionism in Twentieth Century German Literature* (Stanford U.P., 1959). On this war generation of intellectuals who doubted the wisdom of their elders and who searched widely for a faith and ideals, and whose cultural rebellion turned into a political crusade during World War I, see the reflections of H. Stuart Hughes, *Consciousness and Society: the Reorientation of European Social Thought, 1890–1930* (New York, Knopf, 1958), 338.

[86] For Rosa Luxemburg the function of the war was to retard 'what we have felt welling up for years: the resurgence of the Russian revolution. The Russian proletariat which after 1911 had managed to raise up the leaden weight of the counter revolutionary period . . . did not permit the war to disorganize it or the dictatorship of the sword to muzzle it or nationalism to lead it astray except for two and a half years.' (Rosa Luxemburg, *Œuvres*, II: *Écrits politiques, 1917–1919* (Paris, Maspero, 1969)).

[87] A. Balabanoff, op. cit. 128–9.

aborting it in Germany in bitter defeat? In this context, the revolutions of 1917–19 would not appear as an incident inserted artificially into the history of the Great War or as a violent catastrophe interrupting long-term developments, but as a process in which the war acted as a delaying or a deviating force and not as a catalyst. We may say that the war crystallized the long-enduring resignation towards the real prospect of revolution, and enmeshed the International in the maze of its own contradictions thus driving it to deadlock and inevitable collapse.

Appendix

Because of the critical international situation and the threat of war between Serbia and Austria the members of the International Socialist Bureau were summoned on 26 July by telegram to a session of the Bureau held on 29 and 30 July 1914 in the Maison du Peuple at Brussels.

Wednesday morning, 29 July

Chairman: Comrade Émile Vandervelde.

Members of the Executive Committee present:

Great Britain	James Keir Hardie, Bruce Glasier, Dan Irving
Germany	Hugo Haase, Karl Kautsky
Austria	Dr. Victor Adler, Dr. Friedrich Adler
Bohemia	Edmond Burian, Anton Nemec
France	Jean Jaurès, Édouard Vaillant, Jules Guesde, Marcel Sembat, Jean Longuet
Italy	Angelica Balabanoff, Morgari
Spain	Fabra-Ribas, Corralès
Russia	Ilya Rubanovich, Pavel Axelrod
Latvia	P. Winter, Otto Braun
Poland	Rosa Luxemburg, Walecki
Denmark	Stauning
Holland	Troelstra
Belgium	Émile Vandervelde, Édouard Anseele, Louis Bertrand, Camille Huysmans
Switzerland	Karl Moor, Robert Grimm.

Comrade Henri de Man acted as interpreter.

A private record of the proceedings was kept in German by the Swiss delegate Grimm (IISG). Where his account differs from the official French text (ISB archives) it is referred to in the notes as 'Grimm's version'.

The first item to be discussed was whether the press should be allowed to be present.

Vaillant: At the last session of the Bureau the press was not admitted. Only members of the Bureau were allowed to be present. The same procedure might be adopted on this occasion.

Vandervelde agreed. It could be dangerous to admit the press. A communiqué could be issued. (*Adopted*)

Huysmans anxious to avoid difficulties criticized the presence of Comrade Rappoport.[1]

Vaillant: Rappoport was present in London.

Huysmans: The Argentinian party had sent us a letter saying that Rappoport represented them at the London meeting, no more. If we admit him to this session we risk a complaint from the Argentinian party.

Rappoport: My nomination appeared in the party's official paper. My mandate has not been withdrawn. I merely wish to keep Argentina informed on this session of the Bureau.

Vandervelde: This is against the regulations. Let us have the views of the Bureau.

(*The majority is against admitting Rappoport*)

Vandervelde proposed that the representatives of the countries involved in the conflict should report on the situation.

Guesde: Let the delegates of the national sections present be given the floor.

Jaurès: Let us proceed in the order of events. Let us first hear Austria, Bohemia and Serbia, then Russia, France, Germany, and so on. (*Adopted*)

Victor Adler: I shall not tell you the things that you all know. But let me say that Austria's provocative note came as much of a surprise to us as to everyone else. We were of course forewarned by the various diplomatic moves. But we did not expect war. Although Serbia has accepted the principal points of the Austrian ultimatum, a few points excepted, war is with us.

The party is defenceless. To say anything else would mean deceiving the Bureau. One must not be misled by the news. We now see the result of years of class agitation and demagogy. Demonstrations in support of the war are taking place in the streets. There will be a new situation in our country which is full of

---

[1] Charles Rappoport was a French socialist who originated from Russia. He took part in the Russian revolutionary movement and joined the Russian social democratic workers party in 1902. In France he became a well-known marxist journalist and political writer. At the thirteenth session of the ISB, held in London in 1913, he represented the socialist party of Argentina.

national problems and contrasts.[2] What this new situation will be
nobody knows. The south Slav question, Serb agitation in Bosnia,
all this has naturally had a detrimental effect on Serbia. With us
hostility towards Serbia is almost natural. I personally do not
believe that there will be a general war. In Austria people want to
finish Serbia. Let us look at the situation as it affects the party.
We cannot ward off the threat. Demonstrations have become
impossible. One risks one's life in the process and must expect to be
imprisoned. That we may have been through before. But our whole
organization and our press are at risk. We run the danger of
destroying thirty years' work without any political result. Is it not
dangerous to encourage Serbia inside our own country? Are we not
taking on a great responsibility by wanting to make the Serbs
believe that Austria is threatened by revolution? We must protect
the proletariat against such an infection.[3] We must protect our
institutions. Ideas of striking, etc., are mere fantasies. The matter
is very serious and our only hope is that we alone will be the victims,
that the war will not spread. Even if it remains localized the party
is in a very sad position. Our enemies will be fortified and encouraged
by their successes. We have had the pleasure of being allowed to
organize the international congress in our country. We made
careful preparations for it. The Austrian proletariat without
distinction of nationality has looked forward impatiently to this
congress. It is sad but there is nothing to be done about it. We hope
that the Bureau believes us when we say that we could not have
acted differently. We want to save the party.[4] What the Bureau can
do and we together with it is to condemn the guilty and to attempt
to localize the conflict.

Our industry is likely to be militarized; every refusal to work will
be dealt with under martial law.

In spite of everything we hope that the great war will be avoided.
To believe this may mean believing in a miracle but we hope
nevertheless.

Haase: I want to make a very important announcement. People
ask what the proletariat is doing at this critical moment. If the
bourgeois press is to be believed the proletariat remains chauvinistic.
But the following telegram which I have just received from Berlin
clearly proves the contrary.

    [2] *Adler*: In the nationalities struggles war appears as a kind of delivery, a hope
that something different will come . . . In addition there is the feeling that Serbia
is creating unrest. (*Grimm's* version.)
    [3] To preserve workers from chauvinistic infection . . . (*Grimm's* version.)
    [4] . . . and thus also the party enterprises. (*Grimm's* version.)

Haase then read the text of a telegram signed by Braun saying
that in Berlin on the previous day thousands of workers had
demonstrated against the war and for peace at twenty-seven
crowded meetings and in the streets.[5]

Nemec[6] described the situation in Bohemia where there had been
pro-war demonstrations by the bourgeoisie. The bourgeoisie regarded the war as the result of the policy of recent years. But one
must not forget that the steps which the Austrian Government had
taken against Serbia had made the situation more critical still.
In his view the Serb socialists were in favour of union with Austria.
The bourgeoisie regarded war as a means of reducing the influence
of social democracy. Together with the German socialists of Austria
his comrades had considered the possibility of a general strike. Both
parties had come to the same conclusion; their organizations were
at stake.

Victor Adler hoped that the Bureau would not make any fatal decisions
although the Bureau's decision would tip the scales. The Austrian
party would see what measure of responsibility it could shoulder.[7]

Jaurès wanted information about prospects in Bosnia-Herzegovina and among the Croats. What did the Hungarians expect
from the war?

Victor Adler: The Croats are Catholic. The Serbs are Orthodox.
The Croats are very loyal to the dynasty. The Serb element does
not predominate in Bosnia. There are Croats and Mohammedans.
It was the Croats who organized a pogrom against the Catholic
clergy.[8] As regards Hungary the Magyars are against the Slavs,
particularly against the Rumanians.

[5] The telegram read out by Haase refers to: Processions by ten thousand people
in *Unter den Linden*. Clashes with the police . . . Chauvinists attempt counter-
demonstration in *Unter den Linden*. Hilferding expelled from Berlin. (*Grimm's*
version.)

[6] *Nemec*: Never before such a mobilization in Austria. After suppressing Serbia
economically Austria proposes to strangle it. Preventive censorship has been
introduced. Three hours to begin with, with prolongation. Most important is that
the proletariat should not be seized by the intoxication of war. There can be no
question of a general strike. The authorities would use this as the occasion to
dissolve and destroy the party. There will anyway be hunger revolts in Austria.
Secrecy of correspondence has been abolished. The co-operative mill has been
confiscated. The party car has been confiscated. The International must not take
any decisions which will adversely affect the Austrian workers. (*Grimm's* version.)

[7] *Adler*: The Bureau must not restrict its decisions because of consideration
towards Austria. The Bureau cannot make any such allowances. (*Grimm's* version.)

[8] Croats are fanatical Austrians for confessional reasons, because the Serbs are
Orthodox. The position in Hungary is even more (complicated), contrast between
Magyars and all Slavs very great. Serbia is not only a threat to Austrian imperialism

Who governs Austria at present? The Emperor is like a prisoner. Policy is made by Berchtold and Tisza. In Hungary the situation is very confused. It is certain that part of the working class has been carried away by militant ideas. From the point of view of Austria's interest one must also bear in mind Serbia's demands concerning Bosnia.

Haase: It was difficult for us to leave our respective countries at this moment. We must return immediately and therefore, if possible, conclude the session this evening.

Vandervelde: We are counting on several of you for the meeting this evening.[9] Your absence would cause great disappointment.

Keir Hardie: Why finish today? It would be a mistake to conclude this session in too much of a hurry.

Vaillant: How can we stop now. Come what may we must not go our various ways until we have finished, this afternoon or tomorrow morning.

Huysmans: Vaillant thinks that we shall achieve nothing today. That means that we must meet again tomorrow morning.

Rosa Luxemburg: We must act quickly and with determination. Let us issue no manifesto but decide on the congress. Let us then try to finish today.

Hasse thought that a manifesto was required. If it was necessary for them to stay they would stay. Diplomats always acted quickly. Let them do the same.

Nemec: Adler maintains that the Serb element does not predominate in Bosnia. The opposite is true. The majority in Bosnia consists of Serbs. We in Prague are not afraid of the struggle, we are only afraid of the destruction of our party.[10]

Wednesday afternoon, 29 July

The meeting opened at 3.15 p.m.

Haase: I propose that the International shall assemble for the congress at Paris not later than the end of next week. It is for the

but also to the shape of present-day Austria. From our present-day point of view we cannot allow Austria to attack the autonomy of other nations.

The peoples of Austria are not only oppressed by the government, they oppress each other. If Bosnia and Hercegovina became part of Serbia there would be a conflict in these provinces with the other nations. Today these questions are decided solely by the relative position of strength. (*Grimm's* version.)

[9] He is referring to the big international rally which was held that evening at the Cirque Royal. Vandervelde, Haase, Morgari, Keir Hardie, Rubanovich, Troelstra, and Jaurès spoke. Their speeches were published in *Le Peuple* of 30 August 1914.

[10] *Nemec* protests that the Bureau pays no consideration to Austrian organizations. (*Grimm's* version.)

International to prove that it is alive. This congress must make an impression on the workers of all countries, on the political situation in all countries. We must prove that the International is not a negligible quantity. Let us use what influence we have. If at Paris Russians, Austrians, Frenchmen, Germans, Italians, and so on jointly raise their voice in protest we can have the satisfaction of having done our duty. We do not know whether we shall be successful but we must do our duty.

Vaillant: This congress will not be an extraordinary congress but an ordinary congress. The French will be very happy to act as your hosts. You can start today taking the necessary steps to open on Sunday week at Paris the congress that should have taken place at Vienna.

Irving regretted both proposals. It was understandable that the congress should be transferred to another place. But the British were unhappy about the change of date. The number of delegates would be very different from that expected in Vienna.

Huysmans: Let us be precise. We shall organize this congress on the lines of the one at Basle. We cannot make France bear the entire costs of the congress. Let us delete alcoholism, unemployment, and the increase in the cost of living from the agenda and retain only imperialism and immediate political issues, such as the deportation of our South African comrades. We must accept the proposed date. Some of the Africans[11] are already in Europe. It is possible to wire to America. The duration of the congress will be limited and there will be no commissions.

Vandervelde: Let us take the points one by one. First the place, then the date, then the costs and finally the organizational details. First the place: does anybody propose any city other than Paris?

Keir Hardie: Paris was not proposed. London would also be suitable.

(Paris was agreed upon)

Angelica Balabanoff: Vaillant says that the congress will not be an extraordinary one. But if we meet now it will be an extraordinary congress. Can the Bureau not take an immediate decision? In my opinion it would be better to postpone the congress and not to meet. We must not turn the congress into nothing but a demonstration. We must decide on action.

Jaurès: The International Socialist Bureau will agree upon the form of the anti-war demonstration and the sovereign congress will

[11] Meaning the South African delegates.

take the final decision. It will adopt whatever agenda and resolution it wants to adopt. The decisions of the congress cannot be made conditional on the present session. We need the congress. Its deliberations and its resolutions will give the proletariat confidence. The cancellation of the congress would be a big disappointment to the proletariat. To hold it at Vienna has become impossible; but that is not enough reason to cancel it. We must convene the congress as soon as possible at Paris. If it could be done tomorrow then we should do it tomorrow. The congress can open on Sunday 9 August with a big demonstration. A vast mass of people will be present. Thereby we shall all have contributed to the work for peace.

Bruce Glasier: The British reject the proposal to change the date of the congress. They would have no objection if it was possible to prevent the war by any form of direct action. But the socialists in the countries concerned are impotent. We all esteem our Austrian comrades but we think that they should have said: let us sacrifice our property to do our duty. As regards the congress we think that it will be attended by only a few delegates. No trade union delegates will be able to come.

Haase asked the British to bear in mind that extraordinary circumstances demand extraordinary measures. It had been impossible to foresee the congress. It was equally difficult for all to attend. If Germany and France were embroiled in a conflict the congress could not take place. Therefore it was very difficult to arrange things. When Jaurès spoke of the sovereignty of the congress, of hearing all views, there was agreement that it was the duty of the International Socialist Bureau to take measures that would prove the usefulness of the congress. They must be united at the congress. Therefore they must avoid all disputed questions, for example that of the general strike in the case of war and similar issues. Let the International Socialist Bureau act accordingly.

Victor Adler: Haase's proposal offers a solution. The congress must meet as soon as possible. There have been doubts about the location. We could have chosen a city in Switzerland but big demonstrations would have been impossible there. If even so the congress should happen too late it will not be because of us. I am in favour of Haase's date. To reply to Bruce Glasier: I do not know how I could have reported differently. It is my responsibility to report without worrying about what people think. Let our English colleagues believe us when we say that our position is very difficult, much more difficult than theirs and they see difficulties even in sending delegates two weeks earlier to a congress. It is not a question of property; it is a question of our arms which we do not want to lay down before we have taken action on behalf of the International. I did not think that at a moment such as this it was necessary to sing our own praises. But if that is what is wanted from us I apologize for not having done so and ask you to despise us no longer.

Irving: If we have spoken of difficulties they concern not only Britain but also the other nations.

Keir Hardie: If the only argument in favour of advancing the date of the congress is to hold an anti-war demonstration I cannot support the proposal. This is not a sufficient reason. We must keep the agenda. The items on it are of lasting interest whereas the war may pass. Keeping the agenda means not changing the date of the congress. Let us first discuss the agenda. The discussion will show whether or not to keep to the old date.

Vandervelde: Let us take a vote because a discussion will take too long. If it would take the powers as long to organize the war as it takes us to organize the war on war we could sleep in peace.

I therefore put to the vote: 9 August or the original date.

(9 August is adopted with the British and the Italians voting against.)

Agenda

Troelstra: This congress cannot be considered as extraordinary. We cannot turn it into a second Basle Congress. This would suggest that the Basle Congress had had no result. Consequently it would be a contradiction not to discuss the other points. If we debate imperialism we must also debate the general strike, the behaviour of the bourgeoisie in times of peace, and so on.[12] Let us move the congress but let us not alter the agenda.

Vaillant: We have changed the place and date of the congress. Let us keep the agenda. If that means that the congress is not an extraordinary congress it will nevertheless be one because of the circumstances. This we must take into consideration. What worries the international proletariat most at present is the threat of war. How can the war be avoided, limited, or prevented? Therefore we must place the question of war at the top of the agenda. How can we discuss the question of the rising cost of living if there is a famine as a result of the war? How can we discuss imperialism if war is there. Let us therefore put at the top, above imperialism, the steps

---

[12] *Troelstra*: How can we discuss imperialism when the Dutch have already raised the question of collaborating in the bourgeois peace movement? (*Grimm's* version.)

to be taken against the war and let us keep the original agenda. Thereby we shall satisfy the proletariat and the public and do our duty.[13]

Vandervelde: The question of the war certainly overshadows everything. If the threat is removed we shall have our congress.

Rosa Luxemburg[14] considered that the procedure adopted at Paris should be the same as at Basle. The question of the war overshadowed everything and therefore they must above all focus on that point. The other items would suffer as a result. They would be dealt with quickly and without the necessary interest.

Rubanovich: Today we must take steps against the war which we shall not prevent once it is there. In this respect we have never entered into an obligation *vis-à-vis* the proletariat. We must hold the congress. That is certain. We are conscious of the seriousness of the moment and agree with Troelstra's proposal to adhere to the agenda for which we have prepared ourselves. But in view of the situation let us begin with the question of imperialism and the steps to oppose the war.

Sembat agreed with Vandervelde that it was possible to combine the proposals of Vaillant and Troelstra. If necessary the other items could be deleted from the agenda of the congress. If not, the congress would be a conference and an anti-war demonstration.

Keir Hardie proposed that imperialism and the war on war should not be dealt with under the same agenda item. It was necessary to distinguish and to discuss two very different problems: the present situation and imperialism—the future.

Kautsky did not think that in ten days there would be universal peace. In those circumstances it would be impossible for his delegation to travel to Paris to discuss questions which could be discussed later. At present they could not stay long abroad. Therefore there should be no discussion of the possibility of future wars. He thought that future wars would be prevented if the present war was averted.[15]

Jaurès: The situation is critical. The French accept both suggestions. At the beginning they thought that the agenda should be adhered to. The Germans propose that nothing but the war should be discussed. Perhaps the best solution is the one suggested

[13] *Vandervelde*: There is no difference of opinion between Vaillant and Troelstra. (*Grimm's* version.)

[14] *Luxemburg*: Given the circumstances there can be no repetition of the Basle demonstration in Paris . . . (*Grimm's* version.)

[15] *Kautsky*: We shall not have the time nor the peace of mind to talk about alcoholism etc. Let us not discuss imperialism at Paris. Luxemburg's proposal is the most appropriate. (*Grimm's* version).

by Vandervelde. Another difficult question is how there can be any discussion at Paris. If I have understood Adler correctly questions on which there is no agreement should be avoided. Our comrades, like Haase, know that one can say what items should be put on the agenda but not what will be said. The French have received clear instructions. They must speak. To discuss problems on which there is no agreement is a matter of tact. It is impossible to avoid the question of the general strike. This always happened, even at Basle. Nevertheless agreement was reached. Let the discussions in the commissions be related to the work of plenaries. Let us prove that we have enough tact to know how to organize.[16]

Sembat proposed to close the discussion on that item.

Haase proposed to put everything on the Paris agenda but to add as a first item: the war and the proletariat. The first item would thus have a bearing on the present situation. The congress had the right to change the agenda if it thought that this was desirable.

Keir Hardie: The present situation and the future must be dealt with separately. There will be a misunderstanding.

(Haase's proposal was adopted)

Vandervelde: The costs must be borne jointly, as at Basle. *(Adopted)*

Walecki inquired about the duration of the congress.

Vandervelde: It is impossible to decide that point. We must see what the situation will be at the time [of the congress].

Kautsky: It is not certain that we shall be able to meet at Paris; therefore let us take precautions.

Vandervelde proposed that in that case the Executive Committee should be permitted to decide. *(Adopted)*

Jaurès asked that the decisions of the session should be remembered.

Vandervelde: Let us examine the political situation; but let us be brief.

Victor Adler: What will the press publish about this session?

Huysmans read out the text of the first communiqué:

The International Socialist Bureau, convened by telegram, met on Wednesday 29 July 1914 at the Maison du Peuple at Brussels. Present were: Executive Committee (Belgium): Vandervelde, Anseele, Bertrand, Huysmans.

France: Jaurès, Vaillant, Sembat, Guesde, Longuet.
Germany: Haase.
Great Britain: Keir Hardie, Irving, Bruce Glasier.

[16] *Jaurès*: Proposal: agenda as for Vienna, with 'present situation' as the first item. (*Grimm's* version.)

Poland: Rosa Luxemburg, Walecki.
Russia: Rubanovich, Axelrod, Winter, Braun.
Italy: Morgari, Balabanoff.
Holland: Troelstra.
Switzerland: Grimm, Moor.
Denmark: Stauning.
Spain: Fabra Ribas and Corralès.
Austria, Hungary and Bohemia: Victor Adler, Friedrich Adler,
   Nemec, Burian.

The meeting examined the political situation created by
recent events; it listened to and discussed reports by the delegates
from the countries where war rages or threatens to rage. It decided
unanimously not to postpone the congress scheduled for 23 August
at Vienna but on the contrary to advance its date; at the suggestion
of the German delegates, enthusiastically supported by the
French delegates, it was decided that the congress shall meet on
9 August at Paris, that the agenda shall not be changed and that
the first item shall be: 'The war and the proletariat'.

Vandervelde read out a telegram from the Paris *Temps*, indicating
that the situation had become more critical.[17]

Axelrod considered it unnecessary to discuss Russia's position
vis-à-vis Austria or the possibility of a clash. The main task was to
find out whether Russian social democracy was capable of anti-war
action. For about ten years Russia had been in a state of revolution
and he did not think that it was necessary to wait much longer for
the second act of the affair. In his opinion the masses would again
rise to oppose the war. What was the party's position now? A few
days ago they had had strikes of a revolutionary character.[18] On
the one hand the party was weakened. The organization had
suffered big losses because of the present strike. But the prestige of
the socialist idea had risen enormously. They could say with
certainty that revolution would break out if there was a war.

He read out the following statement by the Russian socialists:[19]

[17] *Temps* telegram: Austria has notified Russia that no Serb territory will be
touched, nor Belgrade occupied. Customary phrase. (*Grimm's* version.)
[18] Strikes of an economic nature began in Russia on 17 July 1914. The movement spread rapidly and on 21 and 22 July 200,000 workers stopped work in
St. Petersburg. The Western socialist press began to speak of a revolutionary
situation in Russia. The general strike ended in 27 July.
[19] There must be an error in the report of the meeting. The statement came
from the Polish socialist party (PPS) of the Polish territories which formed part of
Russia.

The attempts that are made outside Russia, namely in Austria, to create the impression that in case of war between Russia and Austria there would be a pro-Austrian revolt in Russian Poland, are completely misleading.

About Galicia we know nothing. But all our information, particularly that provided by our comrades from Russian Poland, is unanimous: any popular movement that emerges in Russian Poland as the result of a war will form part of the Russian empire's revolutionary movement whose aim is autonomy for Russian Poland and a democratic Russia.

Rubanovich: The Russian situation is different from that in Austria. We are a secret and unorganized party. Our preoccupations therefore differ. Tsarism is isolated in Europe and seeks diversions. What is its aim? The mobilization shows that its designs are bellicose. A comedy has been enacted in Russia which we shall one day reveal with the help of part of the bourgeoisie. We cannot enter into formal commitments. The Russian proletariat is more revolutionary than the party. There is no doubt that if there is a war the situation will become more revolutionary still. And then, if necessary, the party will have recourse to highly effective means.

Haase: We know the Austrians well enough to understand their attitude. We know their tactics. They have seen the situation from uncomfortably close quarters. Their attitude of passivity and resignation is wrong, firstly because this passivity renders no service to social democracy and secondly because it does nothing to solve the present crisis. If they oppose the war now they will have public opinion on their side after the war. The population will realize that social democracy did not lose its head at the critical moment. I cannot believe that the proletariat's demonstrations strengthen the government's militant attitude. If anything they will, in my opinion, weaken it. I appreciate that great difficulties are involved, but those are my impressions. I hope that the decisions taken at this session and those that will be taken at Paris will not cause further difficulties for the Austrians.

As for Germany the government says that it was not consulted. That may be so. But we knew two weeks before the publication of the Austrian note to Serbia that Austria would in the end present Serbia with an ultimatum. We can be blamed for not having spoken out then. We did not do so because we could not believe that it would happen. The German Government closed its eyes so as to have a free hand when the conflict came. The *Temps* telegram suggests that Germany influenced Austria. We know that Germany wants peace but if Russia intervenes Germany must also intervene. The story about the conversation which I am alleged to have had with the Chancellor is a pure fabrication. The Government has made no attempt to influence the social democrats who were notified by a representative of the Government.[20] Everything that might lead to war is being avoided. Nor have we stopped our activities. Our demonstrations have even benefited by being treated neutrally. Our rallies were tolerated. The most militant element is the liberal bourgeoisie which is anti-Serb and on the side of Austria. But the ruling class and the great industrialists are opposed to the war. The press of the military party declares that Germany has no interest whatsoever in war. But if Russia attacks Germany will intervene. There is no doubt about that. The social democrats are exploiting the present situation. We shall not cease our activities. We shall demonstrate more and make our protests even more anti-militaristic.

Keir Hardie proposed that there should be a meeting the following day. (*Adopted*)

Jaurès wanted to examine the question of what pressure could be exerted. France was unanimous in condemning Austria's action and the hypocritical pretexts used by Austria to reject Serbia's reply which was anyway too accommodating. Austria wanted war and wanted to destroy the small nation. That fact had created universal indignation. The Catholic militarists who, as Catholics, had considerable sympathy for Austria expressed their disapproval. As regards Germany there was not one Frenchman in a hundred thousand who would admit that Germany had not been kept informed. Germany might not have been handed the text of the note but there was no doubt that it was determined to take Austria's side on the occasion of the first incident. Two days before the transmission of the note a German journalist attached to the German embassy in Paris had said: 'I am leaving because there will be a big todo over the Austro-Serb incident.' The view therefore was that Germany knew everything. They therefore knew what the Triple Entente's powers of resistance were. 'If we give way Germany's prestige will have been enhanced without war.' That was how people argued in Germany. Had the governments reached such a nadir of weakness that they failed to see the danger? They were all agreed. The greatest conceivable misfortune awaited them.

[20] *Haase*: It wants to resist the Pan-Slav movements in Russia . . . The bourgeois parties = flag waving patriots and military party support the war . . . German social democracy has stated unequivocally that the secret treaties which came about without the co-operation of parliament are not binding . . . (*Grimm's* version.)

The French Government wanted peace. It would support Britain in its attempts to mediate. It had exerted pressure on Russia so as to avoid a worsening of the situation. All that they could do now was to look out for new and unfavourable influences. Their theme should be: they were not committed to any action nor bound by any treaty. He rejoiced to hear about their German comrades' peace demonstrations and thanked them sincerely for their efforts. In France it was thought that Germany would attack France even if the French did not follow Russia. As far as they were concerned that attitude implied no *arrière-pensée* of war. They wished to prove that to their comrades and asked them to believe the French. If they succeeded in solving their terrible predicament they could be satisfied.[21]

Morgari[22] described the situation in Italy which proved that Italy had not remained loyal to the Triple Entente. The national antipathies were sufficiently well known. It was impossible to predict the attitude of the Italian proletariat to the general strike, etc. Italy understood the difficulties of the Austrians. But it was not those difficulties that counted. The Italian socialists had experience of that during the Tripoli war. They had been insulted and slandered. But after the war their prestige had increased.

The meeting rose at 20.30 hours.

Thursday morning, 30 July

Bruce Glasier regretted the absence of Keir Hardie who together with the other British comrades had been very disappointed by yesterday's debate. Too much preference had been given to the French and the Germans and not enough attention had been paid to the British. The capitalist world regarded Britain as a power but the International Socialist Bureau did not. People in Britain at present were not seriously concerned with the consequences of the Austro-Serbian war. It was true that they felt the economic repercussions of the Balkan war but they did not think that they would be affected by the present war. The British wanted peace. The whole of the Cabinet wanted peace. So did the working class. Militarism and war had been attacked at every trade union congress. Even if

[21] *Jaurès*: The French Government is anxious for peace and has supported Britain's mediation (Sir Edward Grey's initiative) . . . The Alsace question which enters into the general picture will . . . (breaks off) (*Grimm's* version.)

[22] *Morgari*: Italy is not as good [an] ally as thought. [The] parliamentary group met the day before yesterday. [It] demanded that parliament should be called. Demonstrations are being held everywhere and it is thought that if war breaks out there will be a general strike in Italy. (*Grimm's* version.)

part of the population was swept off its feet the trade union and socialist movement would continue to fight that trend.

Vandervelde: The British comrades are wrong in thinking that no attention has been paid to them. There is a misunderstanding here. Whereas in Britain the speaker who stands up has the floor, here it is the chairman who calls upon the speaker who is first on his list. Furthermore it was agreed that delegates should be allowed to speak in order of the importance of their country in the present conflict.

Vandervelde read out the following resolution proposed by Haase:

At its meeting of 29 July, the International Socialist Bureau heard delegates from all the nations threatened by the world war describe the political situation in their respective countries. It unanimously calls upon the proletarians of all the countries concerned not only to continue but to intensify their demonstrations against war and for peace. The German and the French proletarians will make every effort, as they have done in the past, to make their governments exert pressure on their allies, Austria and Russia, so that these two countries cease to threaten world peace.

The congress convened at Paris will be a powerful expression of this pacifist determination of the world proletariat.

Morgari: And the Italians?

Kautsky suggested the addition of: The Italians and the British will support Germany and France in all their efforts.

Vaillant: Those of our socialist comrades who have a seat in the parliaments of the neutral countries can usefully press for a settlement of the conflict by arbitration.

Jaurès asked for that observation to be incorporated into the resolution.

Troelstra regretted Jaurès's proposal. They were now anticipating the work of the congress which would examine the question of the arbitration Court. There were parties which did not share Jaurès's views on that question.

Victor Adler reassured Troelstra. They were doing what the hour demanded. Their comrades in all countries would be happy in spite of their principles if the conflict could be settled in that way. They should vote on the resolution which was restrained and firm.

(*The final text of the resolution was adopted unanimously*)

It read:

At its meeting of 29 July, the International Socialist Bureau heard the delegates from all the nations threatened by the world war describe the political situation in their respective countries.

It unanimously calls upon the proletarians of all countries concerned not merely to continue but to intensify their demonstrations against war and for peace and for a settlement of the Austro-Serb conflict by arbitration.

The German and French proletariats are invited to put more pressure than ever on their governments to ensure that Germany exerts a moderating influence on Austria and that France persuades Russia not to intervene in the conflict. The proletarians of Great Britain and Italy for their part will support these efforts with all their energy.

The congress urgently convened at Paris shall give powerful expression to this pacifist determination of the world proletariat.

Vandervelde: As regards Vaillant's suggestions about the neutral countries I shall personally today see the Belgian *chef de cabinet*. In my opinion this is better done unofficially.

Vaillant: We leave the choice of the road to you provided you reach your goal.

Rosa Luxemburg proposed the following resolution which was adopted unanimously:

The International Socialist Bureau warmly welcomes the revolutionary attitude of the Russian proletariat upon whom it calls to persevere in its heroic anti-Tsarist efforts which provide the most effective guarantee against the threat of a world war.

Vandervelde closed the session and convened the International for the Sunday after the next at Paris.

Index